W9-CCL-073

NATURE WALKS IN
NEW JERSEY

ON LINE

2nd Edition

More from AMC Books

Visit the AMC Online Store at **www.outdoors.org**

More books from the *Nature Walks* series:

Nature Walks near Philadelphia

Nature Walks in Northern Vermont

Nature Hikes in the White Mountains

Nature Walks in Southern New Hampshire

Nature Walks in the New Hampshire Lakes Region

Nature Walks in Connecticut

Quiet Water paddling series:

Quiet Water New Jersey: Canoe and Kayak Guide, 2nd edition

Quiet Water Canoe Guide: New York

Quiet Water New Hampshire and Vermont:
    Canoe and Kayak Guide, 2nd edition

Quiet Water Canoe Guide: Maine

Quiet Water Massachusetts/Connecticut/
    Rhode Island: Canoe and Kayak Guide, 2nd edition

Other AMC titles:

Catskill Mountain Guide

Seashells in My Pocket: A Child's Guide to Exploring the
    Atlantic Coast

A Journey North: One Woman's Story of Hiking the
    Appalachian Trail

Women on High: Pioneers of Mountaineering

NATURE WALKS IN NEW JERSEY

2nd Edition

AMC Guide to the Best Trails from the Highlands to Cape May

Glenn Scherer

APPALACHIAN MOUNTAIN CLUB BOOKS
BOSTON, MASSACHUSETTS

Front Cover Photograph: Leamings Run Gardens, Cape May, NJ
                          © County Department of Tourism
Back Cover Photographs: Raritan River, Lockwood Gorge, NJ © Dwight Hiscano
                          www.dwighthiscano.com
                          Family Hiking, © Jerry and Marcy Monkman
                          www.ecophotography.com
                          Mountain laurel, Appalachian Trail © Dwight Hiscano

All interior photographs by the author unless otherwise noted.
Cover Design: Brandy Polay
Book Design: Amy Winchester
Map Design: Carol Bast Tyler

Distributed by The Globe Pequot Press, Inc., Guilford, CT.

LIBRARY OF CONGRESS CATALOGING-IN-PUBLICATION DATA
Scherer, Glenn.
Nature Walks in New Jersey : AMC guide to the best trails from the Highlands to Cape May / Glenn Scherer.—2nd ed.
p. cm.
Includes bibliographical references.
ISBN 1-929173-40-7 (alk. paper)
1. Hiking—New Jersey—Guidebooks. 2. Nature study—New Jersey—Guidebooks. 3. New Jersey—Guidebooks. I. Appalachian Mountain Club. II. Title.
GV199.42.N5S24 2003
917.4904'44—dc21
2003007793

The paper used in this publication meets the minimum requirements of the American National Standard for Information Sciences—Permanence of Paper for Printed Library Materials, ANSI Z39.48–1984.∞

**Due to changes in conditions,
use of the information in this book
is at the sole risk of the user.**

Printed on recycled paper using soy-based inks. ✪
Printed in the United States of America.

10 9 8 7 6 5 4 3 2 1   03 04 05 06 07 08 09

To my parents, who introduced me to the natural world, and to Marty Fletcher. She and I continue to enjoy New Jersey's wild places together.

Contents

Ridge and Valley Province

Highlands Province

Piedmont Province

Inner and Outer Coastal Plain Provinces

Atlantic Shore Region

List of Nature Essays

Acknowledgments

I would first like to thank my wife, Marty Fletcher, who accompanied me on many of these walks, and who encouraged me to keep writing when the going got tough. I also want to thank Jean LeBlanc, who walked with me often, and who wrote several chapters and sidebars. She is a fine naturalist and patient teacher. Also to thank are fellow walkers Wendy and Jim Elwell, Paul DeCoste, Ron Dupont, Emilie Dupont, George Lightcap, Rick Patterson, Ed Lenik (Sheffield Archaeological Consultants), Marjorie Barrett (Paulinskill Valley Trail Committee), and Jack Epstein (National Park Service). Many others helped in researching the hikes: John Garcia and Celeste Tracy (New Jersey Department of Environmental Protection), Anne Lutkenhouse (New York–New Jersey Trail Conference), Bob Rooke (Morris County Parks), Bob Barth (Canal Society of New Jersey), Karen Carlo Ruhren (The Nature Conservancy), Emile DeVito (New Jersey Conservation Foundation), and Dick Anderson (New Jersey Audubon Society). One of the pleasures in creating this book came from talking with volunteer and park managers and trail builders who love our state's natural and cultural heritage for its own sake. Though too numerous to list here, their heartfelt interest in this project and informed assistance was invaluable.

Introduction

This book is about discovery: the discovery of New Jersey's vast outdoors. It has been an unfolding adventure for me, and I hope it will be a rewarding experience for you.

I was introduced early to New Jersey's natural world: as a child I climbed Mount Tammany in the Delaware Water Gap, wandered the woods behind my house near Merrill Creek, and hiked the Appalachian Trail. But as I gained greater appreciation for my state's wildness, I was appalled to see it slipping away. By the late 1960s I joined with cynical friends in lampooning New Jersey as the "Garden Apartment State," a place where condos sprang up like mushrooms. It seemed that pavement would surely overwhelm the last deer and warbler. In his 1964 book *New Jersey Out-of-Doors*, naturalist Leonard Lee Rue III predicted:

> All living things except people will continue to diminish in numbers in our state. . . . Our birds of prey, the hawks and owls, will be drastically reduced. . . . Wild turkey propagation will fail. . . . The bald eagle will join the ranks of the dodo. . . . The beaver will have no place in New Jersey. . . . [The black bear's] disappearance is inevitable. . . .

Thankfully, these words of doom were heeded as a warning. All wildness did not disappear before an onslaught of neat lawns and minimalls. In 1998 Rue declared, "I live in our state because I've got more wildlife in my backyard than anyone anywhere in the country. Thank God I was wrong!"

Today New Jersey is in the midst of a green renaissance. This spontaneous rebirth began at the grassroots level in the 1960s. Zealous community groups, innocent of politics and policies, organized to kill the Tocks Island Dam on the Upper Delaware, prevent construction of a jetport in the Great Swamp, and stop the building of a "city of the future" in the Pine Barrens.

The act of green transformation has rolled on into the new century as factory sites and dumps were remade into parks at the Great Falls and Meadowlands; as abandoned railroads and canals became greenways along the Paulinskill, Millstone, and Delaware Rivers; as lost towns, ruined iron furnaces, and forgotten farms were preserved at Long Pond, Batsto, Wells Mills, and Holmdel. Priceless Atlantic beachfront that might have been covered in condos stayed the territory of migratory shorebirds.

Volunteers saw to it that trails snaked into the new preserves. Now people come to walk and enjoy the first peepers of spring, the fireflies of summer, the eagles of autumn, and solitude of winter. They come to reconnect with forest, field, and wetland. They come to learn. They come for peace.

The struggle to preserve New Jersey nature continues. Population and economic growth, pollution and habitat loss remain relentless problems. Our flora and fauna will be in danger so long as progress and profit rule. But now ordinary people, in alliance with town, county, state, and federal officials, have decided that the restoration of a natural balance is not only worthwhile but in fact vital.

In researching this book I saw places I've walked since childhood with new eyes and explored fabulous parks that were new to me. I've tried to create a narrative that reads as well from the armchair as it does out on the trail.

I hope this book will serve as a map to some of New Jersey's many green treasures. Let it take you to places near your home and far afield. Put on sturdy walking shoes and pack a lunch, water, insect repellent, and a rain jacket. Take along the flower book, tree book, and bird book.

Don't rush. Hike slowly. Take time to see and your sensitivity will grow. With sensitivity come wonder and a greater appreciation for New Jersey's spectacular natural diversity. With appreciation may come the urge for action, the desire to volunteer with others in the preservation of our green spaces for future generations. Have a good walk!

The Territory

New Jersey is a small state—the fifth smallest in the United States, at just 7,509 square miles. It is, however, the most densely populated. Its 7.7 million people are spread over the land at an average density of 1,029 persons per square mile. We're packed in more tightly here than in India or Japan. The state evokes stereotypical images of superhighways lined with oil refineries and housing developments. But there is another New Jersey. More than 2 million acres of the state are forested today, with some counties possessing more woodland now than they did a century ago.

This little state encompasses some of the most diverse natural landscape and habitats concentrated within a small area to be found anywhere in America. This book divides the state into five unique regions:

- **The Ridge and Valley Province** covers 625 square miles in New Jersey's northwest corner, about 8 percent of the state. The region's mountain ridges are topped by remote crags and blanketed by mixed oak forest. Its fertile limestone valleys are a checkerboard of picturesque farms, sugar maple and mixed hardwood forests, and small villages. Geographically, the Ridge and Valley Province is part of the larger Appalachian Geologic Province running from Canada to the southern United States. In our state, it includes the erosion-resistant sedimentary rock of the 43-mile-long Kittatinny Range (reaching a maximum elevation of 1,803 feet) plus the lowlands of the Delaware River Valley and Great Valley of the Appalachians.

- **The Highlands Province** is a rugged mountainous region, and part of a larger geologic province called the New England Uplands (which includes New York's Hudson Highlands and Vermont's Green Mountains). It encompasses 900 square miles and 12 percent of the state, and runs in a narrowing wedge from the border with New York southwest to the Delaware River. Its billion-year-old banded gneiss bedrock (achieving heights of 1,500 feet) is separated by very narrow limestone and shale valleys. The magnetite iron in these ridges once supported a thriving nineteenth-century iron industry. Today the mixed oak forests of these peaks are home to black bears, coyotes, and white-tailed deer.

- **The Piedmont Province** is a shale-and-sandstone lowland composed of gently rolling hills that display only a 400-foot elevation change between New York Harbor and the Delaware River. A few erosion-resistant igneous ridges, such as the Palisades and Watchung Range (rising to 850 feet), overlook the landscape. The 1,500-square-mile region (about 20 percent of the state) is made up of an urban and suburban corridor connecting New York City and Philadelphia. While this metropolitan landscape holds the largest concentration of the state's population, it also includes a surprising number of natural gems: the Great Swamp, fine urban parks, gardens, and greenways.

- **The Inner and Outer Coastal Plains** are the largest of New Jersey's geographic regions. The two provinces combined cover 4,475 square miles and nearly 60 percent of the state, and stretch east from the Delaware Bay to the Atlantic Ocean. This vast sandy lowland gently slopes to the sea. A series of small gravel hills (just 373 feet high) divide the Inner Coastal Plain from the Outer. At the heart of the Outer Coastal Plain are the Pinelands, resembling the Pine Barrens of Long Island and Cape Cod but covering many more remote acres. While the flat topography seems less than exciting, the flora is fascinating, with many ancient plant species now recognized as living fossils.

- **The Atlantic Coastal Region,** a narrow band of tidal wetlands, stream mouths, back bays, barrier islands, sand dunes, and ocean beaches, is not truly a geographic province. But its unique ecosystems demanded a separate section in this book. This habitat, shaped by the sea, supports some of the most unusual flora and best birding on the East Coast. Highlights include Cape May, a focal point in the ancient annual songbird, raptor, and butterfly migration; plus the Edwin Forsythe National Wildlife Refuge, where bald eagles, ospreys, and snow geese roost within a few miles of Atlantic City gaming tables.

The Trails

Natural New Jersey is accessed by a vast network of public and private trails. There are more than 1,000 miles of federal, state, county, and township trails already in existence, with many more miles being built each year.

Private organizations including the Appalachian Mountain Club, New York–New Jersey Trail Conference, The Nature Conservancy, New Jersey Conservation Foundation, New Jersey Audubon Society, Canal Society of New Jersey, and Sierra Clubs are all active in building new trailways and in maintaining and upgrading existing ones. Obviously, with so many hike possibilities, it was hard to narrow down the walks for this book.

The walks selected were chosen to profile the many faces of natural New Jersey. They are equally distributed over the state's five distinct geographic areas. Each hike focuses on one or more aspects of New Jersey's unique natural history, such as the Great Eastern Forest, Atlantic white cedar swamps, beaver colonies, or barrier island ecology. In some cases a historical resource—such as a nineteenth-century canal, iron mine, or farming community—is explored, along with its intimate connection to the land. A few hikes highlight annual natural events: cherry blossom time in Branch Brook Park, the raptor migration over Kittatinny Ridge, and the songbird migration at Cape May.

The book's hikes vary in length from 1 to 8 miles, with the average length being about 4 miles. Eight miles may seem like a great distance, but the longest hikes are (with a few exceptions) the easiest, passing over level terrain, such as an old railroad bed, a canal, or a beach. The walks traverse federal, state, county, municipal, and private (conservation group) lands.

Most walks are easy or moderate (crossing level or hilly terrain), while some are challenging, especially climbs to the state's major summits, such as Mount Tammany in the Delaware Water Gap or Pinwheel's Vista on the Wawayanda escarpment. Steep ascents have been minimized wherever possible to allow children, seniors, and even the disabled to enjoy the walks. But of course this is the woods, and hikers should come prepared for a workout on all kinds of terrain and in all kinds of weather.

Directions are given to each trailhead from interstate, state, and county roads. Parking and park facilities are listed with phone numbers, as are adjoining nature and environmental centers or related museums.

Getting Started

It is beyond the scope of this book to teach you how to hike, but I have included some tips to get started.

- *What to Bring:* Walkers must be prepared for the unexpected when venturing into the natural world. To quote an old Russian proverb: "There is no bad weather, only bad clothing." Sturdy waterproof footgear is a must, as is rain gear. Dress in layers so you can add or remove clothing depending on temperature. Carry a small pack containing a lunch, snacks, and at least 2 quarts of water. Carry insect repellent, sunscreen, hat, watch, toilet paper, flashlight, extra clothing (such as a sweater, gloves, and dry socks), compass, whistle, small first-aid kit, and trash bag. Remember that whether hiking in the mountains or on the beach you will be exposed to sun, wind, and precipitation.

- *On the Trail:* Read the hike description in this book before setting out. Check weather reports shortly before your trip. Always try to take a walking companion with you. On arriving at a trailhead, check bulletin boards and visitor centers for present trail conditions and changes in trail routes and blazing. Align the maps in this book with those shown at the trailhead.

- *Leave No Trace:* New Jersey's trails receive heavy use. Every walker has a responsibility to protect our parks. Never litter.

Carry out what you carry in. Don't pick flowers or remove wildlife. Stay on trails and avoid trampling plants. Respect animals and other hikers by traveling quietly. Take only photographs. Leave the lightest of footprints.

Trail Safety

Hiking is an exhilarating and enjoyable pastime. With a little extra effort, it can also be a very safe activity. The following list of common hiking hazards is not meant to scare you, only to make you aware of outdoor safety.

- *Getting Lost:* If you lose your way, don't panic. Stay in one spot and carefully look for trail blazes. Study the map. Discuss your position with fellow walkers. Do not leave the trail. Do not push on without ascertaining your location. If you can't figure out where you are, retrace your steps to determine where you went wrong. Never divide up your group or hurry when lost. Three blasts on a whistle is a distress signal in the woods.

- *Insect Pests:* Mosquitoes and ticks are everywhere in the outdoors. Tiny deer ticks (smaller than a sesame seed), sometimes infected with Lyme disease, are common in New Jersey. Lyme disease is usually (but not always) indicated by a red bull's-eye rash at the tick-bite site, followed in days or weeks by aching joints and muscles, fever, flu-like symptoms, and headaches. If untreated, chronic arthritis and neurological problems can result. Use insect repellent and wear a long-sleeved shirt and long pants tucked into socks. Light-colored clothing makes tick spotting easier. Check your body after a hike and take a shower on returning home. If a tick has embedded itself under the skin or if you experience unexplained symptoms, see a doctor.

- *Poisonous Plants:* Poison ivy is common in our area. Learn to identify poisonous plants. The old adage "Leaves of three, let it be" is a good maxim. Wash skin immediately when it is exposed to a poisonous plant. If a poisonous-plant rash becomes serious, see a doctor.

- *Drinking Water:* Stop regularly to sip water. The hotter the day, the more water you need. Drink only the water you bring with you. No matter how pure streams and ponds look, they may contain invisible bacteria that can cause serious intestinal illness.

- *Hypothermia:* One of the greatest hazards in the outdoors is hypothermia, in which the body is drained of heat. It can occur well above freezing temperatures. Wet clothing, wind, sudden temperature drops, and precipitation can all bring on the condition. Shivering, lethargy, mental slowing, and confusion are symptoms. If you suspect hypothermia, remove wet garments, replace with warm clothes, and seek shelter immediately.

- *Heat Emergencies:* Sunburn, heat weakness, heat cramps, heat exhaustion, and heatstroke can all result from over-exertion in high temperatures, high humidity, and sun exposure. Drink plenty of water on the trail. If someone shows the first symptoms of being overheated (heavy sweating, high pulse rate, fatigue and general weakness, headache, and mental and physical inefficiencies), rest in a cool, shaded place and apply cold wet compresses. Use sunscreen to protect against sunburn.

Staying safe in the outdoors is ultimately a matter of being prepared, of staying calm in an emergency, and of using common sense. Take proper precautions and stay aware so that every hike can be a safe hike.

Highlights Chart

Region	Walk	Page	Distance (Miles)	Difficulty
Ridge and Valley Province	1. Mount Tammany	1	3.5	Challenging
	2. Raccoon Ridge	9	5.8	Challenging
	3. Millbrook Village	17	5.1	Moderate
	4. Merrill Creek Reservoir	24	4.1	Easy
	5. Paulinskill Valley Trail	32	6.4	Easy
	6. Sussex Branch Trail	40	3.7	Easy
	7. White Cedar Swamp	48	1.5	Easy
	8. Monument Trail	56	3.5	Moderate
	9. Wallkill River N.W.R.	64	3.5	Easy
Highlands Province	10. Pinwheel's Vista and Pochuck Quagmire	72	2.6 or 8.2	Challenging
	11. Terrace Pond	79	4.0	Challenging
	12. Bearfort Ridge Fire Tower	86	3.6	Moderate
	13. Long Pond Ironworks S.P.	94	3.0	Moderate
	14. NJ Botanical Gardens at Skylands	102	1.0 or 1.7	Easy to Moderate
	15. Wyanokie High Point	109	3.1	Moderate
	16. Four Birds Trail	116	5.6	Challenging

Fee	Visitor Center	Scenic Vista	Wetland/Lake/Pond	River/Brook	Unusual Plants	Birds/Animals
	✔	✔		✔		
	✔	✔	✔			✔
	✔		✔	✔	✔	
	✔	✔	✔	✔		✔
			✔	✔	✔	✔
			✔		✔	✔
			✔		✔	
		✔	✔			✔
			✔		✔	✔
		✔			✔	✔
		✔	✔			
		✔				
			✔	✔		
✔	✔	✔	✔		✔	✔
	✔	✔		✔		
		✔	✔			✔

Fee	Visitor Center	Scenic Vista	Wetland/ Lake/Pond	River/ Brook	Unusual Plants	Birds/ Animals
		✔	✔	✔		✔
	✔	✔	✔	✔	✔	✔
✔	✔		✔	✔	✔	✔
		✔	✔	✔	✔	
	✔	✔		✔		
		✔		✔	✔	
	✔	✔	✔		✔	✔
	✔			✔	✔	✔
	✔		✔		✔	✔
✔	✔		✔	✔	✔	
				✔	✔	✔
			✔	✔	✔	✔
	✔		✔		✔	✔
			✔		✔	✔
	✔		✔		✔	✔

Region	Walk	Page	Distance (Miles)	Difficulty
Inner and Outer Coastal Plain Provinces	32. Dot and Brooks Evert Memorial Nature Trail	241	1.5	Easy
	33. Rancocas Nature Center	250	1.5	Easy
	34. Apple Pie Hill Fire Tower	257	8.0	Challenging
	35. Parvin State Park	265	4.6	Moderate
Atlantic Shore Region	36. Sandy Hook	272	1.0, 2.1 or 9.6	Easy
	37. Cattus Island	280	3.2	Easy
	38. Island Beach State Park	287	4.1	Easy
	39. Holgate	294	5.5	Moderate
	40. Cape May Point State Park	301	2.0	Easy

Fee	Visitor Center	Scenic Vista	Wetland/Lake/Pond	River/Brook	Unusual Plants	Birds/Animals
			✔	✔	✔	✔
	✔			✔	✔	✔
		✔	✔		✔	✔
			✔	✔	✔	✔
	✔	✔	✔		✔	✔
	✔	✔	✔		✔	✔
✔	✔	✔	✔		✔	✔
		✔				✔
	✔	✔	✔		✔	✔

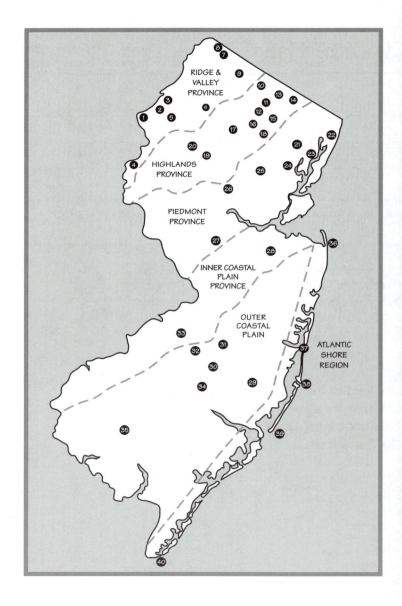

Locator Map

1. Mount Tammany
2. Raccoon Ridge
3. Millbrook Village and Van Campens Glen
4. Merrill Creek Reservoir
5. Paulinskill Valley Trail
6. Sussex Branch Trail
7. White Cedar Swamp Trail
8. Monument Trail
9. Wallkill River N.W.R.
10. Pinwheel's Vista
11. Terrace Pond
12. Bearfort Ridge Firetower
13. Long Pond Ironworks State Park
14. NJ Botanical Gardens at Skylands
15. Wyanokie High Point
16. Four Birds Trail
17. Beaver Brook Trail
18. Tripod Rock and Bear Rock
19. Black River and Kay Environmental Center
20. Schooley's Mountain
21. Great Falls of the Passaic River
22. The Palisades, Bombay Hook
23. Hackensack Meadowlands
24. Branch Brook Park, Newark
25. Great Swamp Outdoor Education Center
26. Leonard J. Buck Garden
27. Delaware & Raritan Canal State Park
28. Holmdel Park and Longstreet Farm
29. Wells Mills
30. Pakim Pond
31. Whitesbog
32. Dot and Brooks Evert Memorial Nature Trail
33. Rancocas Nature Center
34. Apple Pie Hill Firetower
35. Parvin State Park
36. Sandy Hook
37. Cattus Island
38. Island Beach State Park
39. Holgate
40. Cape May Point State Park

Trip 1

Mount Tammany

Delaware Water Gap National Recreation Area

Trail: **Red Dot Trail, Blue Dot Trail, Appalachian Trail (loop)**
Distance: **3.5 miles**
Length: **3 to 4 hours**
Difficulty: **Challenging; 1,200-foot elevation gain**

Breathtaking views of the Delaware River and Mount Minsi

Getting There

Traveling west through the Delaware Water Gap on I-80, follow signs for the rest area exit. Park in the rest area lot on the right. Traveling east on I-80, cross the river and take the first exit in New Jersey. Pass the Kittatinny Point Visitor Center, then turn left, passing under I-80. Turn right at the end of the underpass, then left into the rest area parking lot.

Special Features

- One of the best views in the state
- A very steep climb
- Fascinating geology
- Cascades of Dunnfield Creek

The Kittatinny Ridge (meaning "endless mountain" in the Lenape Native American language) comes to an abrupt, spectacular end at Mount Tammany. The 1,527-foot ridge plunges 1,200 feet into the Delaware Water Gap. This river gorge, one of New Jersey's most acclaimed natural treasures, has attracted painters, hikers, canoeists, and fresh-air lovers since the 1800s.

While the Dutch settled the Upper Delaware River Valley as early as 1700, it was tourism that made the Gap famous. After the Civil War, railroads brought vacationing urbanites to the natural beauty of the Gap. Guests lounged at luxury hotels built in the grand style of the best Adirondack resorts. Refined Victorians sat on hotel verandas, took "the water cure" at the Christian Home Sanitarium, and sought out "the sublime in nature." Filmmaker D. W. Griffith even chose the spot as backdrop for a scene in *Birth of a Nation*.

Today the great resorts are burned or gone bust, but the Gap remains, protected within the Delaware Water Gap National Recreation Area. The gorge serves as gateway to the Upper Delaware River Valley, a tapestry of folded mountains, tumbling waterfalls, and forested bottom land supporting black bears, migrating golden eagles, and spawning shad.

Mount Tammany is one of the most popular hiking destinations in New Jersey. To beat the crowds, set off early on a weekend, on a weekday, or in winter. The climb is strenuous and demands sturdy hiking boots (as do most of the walks in this book). Give yourself plenty of time to enjoy the views.

This 3.5-mile loop hike utilizes the Red Dot Trail, Blue Dot Trail, and Appalachian Trail (AT). It boasts fine vistas from Mount Tammany and ends with a stroll through a shaded ravine along a cascading brook.

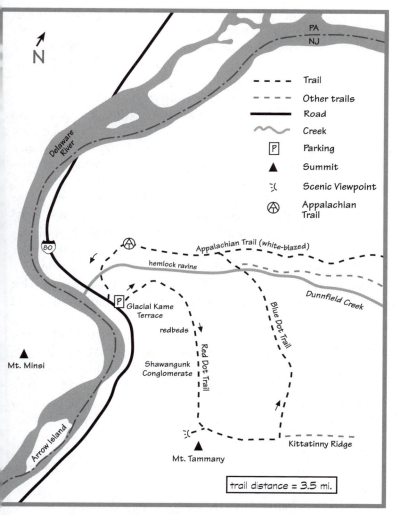

Mount Tammany

Begin at the I-80 rest area parking lot. Follow the Red Dot Trail's red-on-white painted blazes uphill. The trail immediately elevates your heart rate with a brief steep climb, a promise of things to come. The path levels out, and though you're still within earshot of traffic, you're now surrounded by calming forest.

The Red Dot Trail parallels Dunnfield Creek (below to the left) on what geologists call a kame terrace (sorted sand and gravel left behind by outwash from the Wisconsin Glacier, which filled the Gap just 15,000 years ago). In a short distance the path veers sharply right and begins to climb. Tulip trees quickly gives way to sweet birch, red oak, and chestnut oak.

After a 0.5-mile ascent, the hard work pays off with a first look into the gorge. Mount Minsi (named for a Lenape clan) rises on the Pennsylvania side of the Gap. The flank of Mount Tammany (your destination) also looms. The Delaware River snakes gracefully between the peaks. Arrow Island, at midriver, points south to the Great Valley of the Appalachians. This wide valley is part of a much larger geologic feature, a lowland stretching from Alabama to New York.

The trail rises along a spine of Mount Tammany, passing over shale and sandstone sheets called redbeds (named for their color, caused by high iron content). The forest on this exposed slope is an open canopy of chestnut oak, with an understory of lowbush blueberry. Autumn hikers are rewarded when turning blueberry leaves transform the forest floor into a vibrant scarlet blanket.

The most difficult part of the climb comes thirty to forty minutes into the hike with a steep rock scramble up a talus slope (boulders broken loose from above by frost action). This ascent is tricky when wet or icy.

Notice that the redbeds are being replaced by a dark gray rock called Shawangunk conglomerate. This stone explains the

The first view from the Red Dot Trail looks out on the snaking curves of the Delaware River and Arrow Island. Photo credit: George Lightcap

existence of the Kittatinny Ridge. It forms an erosion-resistant backbone, averaging 1,600 feet in elevation, extending from the Water Gap north along the New Jersey border for 43 miles, and continuing into New York as the Shawangunk Ridge. The range also flows southward, rising on the far side of the Gap as Mount Minsi and reaching far into Pennsylvania.

At 1.3 miles into your walk the Red Dot Trail arrives at Mount Tammany's summit, bursting into the open at a boulder-strewn vista. Lichen clings to the rocks, scrub oak grows in low twisted thickets, and a few pitch pines battle for survival. Dry conditions and brutal winter storms prevent the growth of larger trees. Below to the right is the visage of Lenape Chief Tammany, a stony profile imagined by nineteenth-century visitors.

Look west to see the folded strata of Mount Minsi and its jumbled talus slopes; tree clumps tenaciously cling to the mountainside. The Delaware River flows south into the Great Valley. To the northwest is the Pocono Plateau. Autumn visitors may see migrating hawks soaring southward. Humans also take advantage of the ridge's updrafts; this is a popular glider flight path.

Climb back to the top of the rock slope and look to the right for the Blue Dot Trail, leading north along Mount Tammany's narrow crest. Follow the trail for 0.3 mile along the ridge.

Step off-trail and study the bases of the trees; you'll see that they're fire damaged. Heavy use of the Water Gap by inexperienced campers has resulted in wildfires. These fires harm the environment, but have benefits. Fire-resistant pitch pines, for example, thrive in burned-over areas. Fire also converts leaf litter into fertilizer, causing a fast release of minerals to plants.

At 1.6 miles the Blue Dot Trail turns left, steeply descending from the ridge, at first on a narrow trail, then on a fire road. The flora quickly changes from a hardy ridge-top chestnut oak forest to a sheltered woods dominated by maples and a mountain laurel understory.

At 3.1 miles the Blue Dot Trail descends into Dunnfield Hollow, crosses Dunnfield Creek on a bridge, then turns left and intersects with the Appalachian Trail. The last 0.4 mile of the walk is along this white-blazed, 2,100-mile Maine-to-Georgia trail. The AT follows a gently descending woods road beside the stream, which cascades over falls and tumbles through chutes into pools. It is shaded by hemlock, yellow birch, and rhododendron. The hemlocks are dying, their branches stripped of needles. They've fallen victim to hemlock woolly adelgid, an insect accidentally imported to the United States from Asia on ornamental trees. In 1998 New Jersey introduced a tiny ladybug that, it is hoped, will control the adelgid and save the hemlocks.

Dunnfield Creek is popular with anglers, and you're likely to share this peaceful grotto with them. At 3.5 miles cross a small bridge, reaching the Dunnfield Natural Area parking lot. The rest area parking lot is a few hundred yards to the left and reached via a small unmarked trail.

For More Information

Trails are open daily, year-round. Call the Delaware Water Gap National Recreation Area for Kittatinny Point Visitor Center seasonal hours.

Delaware Water Gap National Recreation Area Headquarters, Bushkill, PA 18324; 570-588-2451

Kittatinny Point Visitor Center: 908-496-4458; www.nps.gov/dewa/

Water Gap Geology

The view from Mount Tammany inspires visitors to wonder how this great gorge was formed. Many imagine the mountains came first, with the Delaware River backing up behind the ridge in a vast lake before eventually cutting a gap through from north to south.

Geologists doubt this story. They think the erosion-resistant sandstone strata of Kittatinny Ridge began as muddy sediment layers at the bottom of an ancient shallow sea. These layers were compressed into rock, were uplifted and folded into the ancestral Appalachian Range, mountains that 230 million years ago rivaled the present-day Rockies. Over time these old peaks eroded away. Then, in another episode of mountain building, Kittatinny Ridge was raised about 80 million years ago.

The Delaware River probably started as a fast-moving mountain stream on the south (Atlantic Ocean–facing) slope of Kittatinny Ridge. It found weaknesses and fissures in the Shawangunk conglomerate and redbeds, cutting downward at a point that would eventually become the Water Gap (this cutting action is what geologists call stream headward migration). Once the gap was formed, the stream linked up with others on the north side of the ridge, forming the Upper and Lower Delaware River Valley as we know it.

Today the twin sentinels of Mount Tammany and Mount Minsi tower above the landscape, while the river grinds its course deeper into the bedrock.

Raccoon Ridge and Appalachian Trail

AMC Mohican Outdoor Center

Trip 2

Trail: **Appalachian Trail (out-and-back)**
Distance: **5.8 miles**
Length: **4 hours**
Difficulty: **Challenging; 500-foot elevation gain**

Hawks migrate south by the thousands

Getting There

From I-80 east or west, take NJ 94 north for 8.0 miles to Jacksonburg. Turn left onto Mohican Road and follow it for 3.5 miles (bearing right at forks along the way). Turn left onto Gaisler Road, go 0.5 mile, and turn right onto Camp Road. Follow this for 1.0 mile. Park at either the Mohican Outdoor Center gate or the main lodge.

Special Features

- Autumn raptor migration
- 360-degree view
- Rocky, 1.4-mile climb
- Classic ridgetop oak-hickory forest

Every autumn New Jersey plays host to the raptor migration, one of nature's most mysterious and magnificent events. Starting in late August, peaking in September and October, and fading into November, birds of prey sweep down from northern skies, riding thermals and updrafts on outstretched wings. For some, like the osprey, this is a journey of 6,000 miles, beginning in Canada and concluding in Argentina.

Autumn hawk watching is akin to meteor-shower watching. Annual observers gather on Appalachian mountain crags in crisp winds or during the last sultry days of Indian summer to stare attentively up at empty skies. Then the birds come, often in clusters, like sudden shooting stars, growing from specks into shining, silvery silhouettes. They surge briefly past the lookouts, swiftly dipping and climbing on air currents, then disappear southward.

More than fifteen raptor species regularly glide through the region: soaring buteos (red-tailed, red-shouldered, broad-winged, and rough-legged hawks); bullet-shaped falcons (kestrels, merlins, and peregrines); swiftly maneuvering accipiters (goshawks, sharp-shinned, and Cooper's hawks); northern harriers (also called marsh hawks); majestic ospreys, golden eagles, and bald eagles; and the unjustly maligned carrion eaters (turkey vultures and black vultures). All these raptors also fly our skies in spring, during northern migration, but weather conditions cause them to be more dispersed then.

One of the best places to view the great autumn migration is atop Raccoon Ridge, a peak in the Kittatinny Mountain Range. In fact, raptor counts here are only 10 to 15 percent below those at Hawk Mountain, Pennsylvania, a world-renowned raptor-watching spot. But while Raccoon Ridge boasts many hawks (more than 15,000 in a typical migration),

Raccoon Ridge and Appalachian Trail

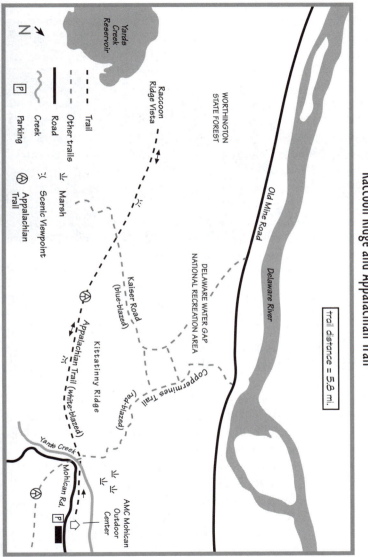

trail distance = 5.8 mi.

Birders are alert to the swift flight of "sharpies" (sharp-shinned hawks).

human crowds are smaller. You'll rarely run into the binocular-wielding mobs encountered in Pennsylvania.

This 5.8-mile out-and-back hike along the Appalachian Trail (AT) to Raccoon Ridge is not just a climb to a birder's paradise. It also rewards walkers year-round with a sweeping 360-degree view of the Delaware River Valley and the broad, fertile farmlands of the Great Valley of the Appalachians.

Start at the AMC's Mohican Outdoor Center lodge. Face the lodge and turn left, walking 0.2 mile down Mohican Road. This edge environment supports light-loving plants including sassafras with its mitten-shaped leaves. Note the red maple swamp to the right. This is a good place to watch for deer at twilight.

Leave the road, turning right onto the white-blazed Appalachian Trail. (This 2,100-mile footpath runs from Maine to Georgia. There are 73 miles of AT in New Jersey.)

Immediately cross Yards Creek on a footbridge. A single red maple stands on the opposite streambank. This tree's leaves are smaller than those of the sugar maple; reaching 4 inches across, they are differentiated by coarse, irregular teeth on leaf margins. Red maples are common to wet bottom lands.

In 0.1 mile the AT intersects the Coppermines Trail. Its wooden sign is affixed to a sweet birch (also called black birch), one of the most numerous trees of New Jersey uplands. Its twigs and leaves give off a distinct and refreshing odor of wintergreen. Old-fashioned birch beer was brewed by fermenting this tree's sap.

Stay on the AT, following the white blazes. As the path begins its rocky climb to the steep, well-drained ridgetop, the water-loving red maples vanish, replaced by chestnut oaks. These hardy trees, with their deeply furrowed bark, are the masters of northern New Jersey's harsh, bone-dry mountaintops. Beneath the chestnut oaks spreads a carpet of lowbush blueberries. They offer a delicious diversion in late summer and a scarlet leaf show in the fall. Pitch pine and mountain laurel, both of which thrive in thin, acidic hillside soils, now join the forest mix.

At 1.4 miles into the walk, the AT achieves the top of Kittatinny Ridge and reveals a series of stunning views east over the Great Valley of the Appalachians. This wide valley stretches from Alabama to the Hudson River. The New Jersey portion is underlain by the state's second most important freshwater aquifer (the state's largest aquifer is in the Pine Barrens).

Also visible below are the reservoirs of the Yards Creek pumped-storage facility. This public-utility project, when originally planned in the early 1960s, would have destroyed Sunfish Pond, New Jersey's most famous glacial lake. Vocal public protest resulted in the rescue of this National Natural Landmark and in a revamped Yards Creek electrical-power facility.

The hike continues along Kittatinny Ridge through an oak forest where elusive kinglets, red-eyed vireos, white-throated sparrows, and chickadees reveal themselves through their song. These little songbirds provide snacks for hungry raptors.

A stand of mockernut, pignut, and shagbark hickories now closes in around the hiker. Here we saw one of nature's most fearsome-looking insects. The hickory horned devil is the largest native North American caterpillar, a 5-inch-long, spine-covered creature with protruding horns at either end. The horned devil, like many other insects, associates with a particular plant species. It relies largely on hickories for food and camouflage.

The AT weaves over to the west side of the ridge and gives a partial view of the Delaware River Valley and the Pocono Plateau beyond. At 2.7 miles the trail leaves the Delaware Water Gap National Recreation Area and passes a sign welcoming walkers to Worthington State Forest.

At 2.9 miles the trail comes out onto a vista covered with grass and sedge. Windswept Raccoon Ridge is little more than 100 feet wide here. The 1,500-foot peak, topped by a rock cairn, gives 360-degree views south toward the Water Gap, north to Rattlesnake Mountain, northwest to the snaky bends of the Delaware River, and east to the Great Valley of the Appalachians.

Autumn hawk watching is at its best from this vantage point. We climbed here one unseasonably warm, windless October day. Hawks usually sit out such afternoons, preferring to ride strong winds occurring just after the passage of cold fronts. Surprisingly, we were treated to a spurt of migrating raptors. Most numerous were sharp-shinned hawks (birders call them sharpies). With rounded wings and narrow tails, they can deftly pursue small birds through thick woods. Several peregrine falcons, with pointed wings and long streamlined tails, zipped by our lookout. These birds hunt in open country and are among the world's fastest avians. A single northern harrier also swept by. The mature male harrier is called the gray ghost by birders, perhaps for its deathly silent, low-level hunting flights conducted just feet above marshy grasslands.

Under the best conditions, Raccoon Ridge birders spot hundreds of raptors every hour. A single species, the red-tailed hawk, for example, accounted for nearly 1,000 sightings on one remarkable day in 1987. But numbers matter little. Whether you see one raptor or a thousand, these great, graceful birds are a thrill to behold. After enjoying the summit, return the way you came to the Mohican Outdoor Center. For the more adventurous, you can return via a longer loop hike: turn left onto the Kaiser Road Trail (blue-blazed), then right onto the Coppermine Trail (red-blazed), reaching the Appalachian Trail just before Mohican Road (see the map).

For More Information

The Appalachian Trail is open year-round. The AMC's Mohican Outdoor Center is also open all year, renting bunks to club members and nonmembers. The AMC's Camp Mohican, a 1920s-vintage Boy Scout camp, invites outdoor enthusiasts to enjoy ice climbing, canoeing, hiking, wildflower identification, and other workshops. The AMC is also locally active in volunteer trail building.

AMC Mohican Outdoor Center, 50 Camp Road, Blairstown, NJ 07825; 908-362-5670; www.mohicanoutdoorcenter.com

Rapture Over Raptors

Built to hunt, raptors amaze naturalists with their endurance, acute senses, speed, and agility. Look at just one species: the red-tailed hawk. This common bird's 4-foot wingspan makes it an accomplished and powerful glider, vital to the conservation of energy required during long, grueling migrations.

The redtail's telescopic eyesight allows it to spy a scampering mouse from 100 feet in the air. Its vision is specially adapted for rapid change of focus, allowing it to track tiny prey while conducting aerial dives at 120 MPH. A red-tailed hawk, like most hunter-predators, is an opportunist. It often sits atop trees or utility poles and waits. Then it swoops on almost anything that moves. These birds eat insects, rodents, fish, toads, snakes, small birds, skunks, and rabbits.

But even these immense carnivores fall prey to predators. A friend had the once-in-a-lifetime privilege of seeing a golden eagle attack a red-tailed hawk. The immense eagle, with its 6-foot wingspan, dived on the bird, seized it in midair, and killed it instantly with its razor-sharp talons.

Millbrook Village and Van Campens Glen

Delaware Water Gap National Recreation Area

Trail: Orchard, Upper Hamilton Ridge, Van Campens Glen, Millbrook-Watergate Trails (loop)
Distance: 5.1 miles
Length: 4 1/2 hours (not counting village tour)
Difficulty: Moderate; 300-foot elevation gain

Hiking through history on the Old Mine Road

Getting There
From I-80 west, take the last exit in New Jersey. Turn right and travel north for about 12 miles to Millbrook Village.

Special Features
- Farmland returned to forest
- Deer galore
- Waterfalls
- A historic village

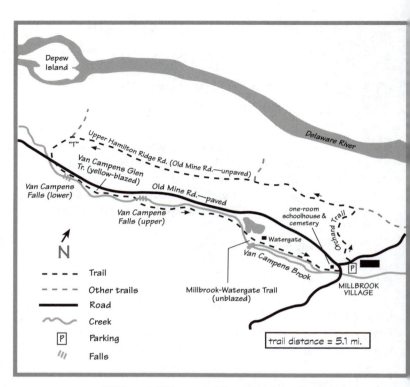

Millbrook Village and Van Campens Glen

The fertile bottomlands of the Upper Delaware River Valley have been shaped by farm life for untold generations. Native Americans cultivated pumpkins, squash, beans, and maize in the soft soils of riverside plots. Dutch farmers settled here in the early 1700s, and the English followed later, planting wheat, rye, flax, and potatoes and raising cows, hogs, and sheep.

These isolated valley farms, cupped between the sheltering hands of the Kittatinny Ridge to the east and Pocono Plateau to the west, measured change more by the seasons than by American history. While tiny communities sent sons to fight in the Revolution, Civil War, and two world wars, dairy cows continued to be milked every day and corn harvested every autumn.

The rhythms of pastoral life were not disrupted until a catastrophic 1955 flood on the Lower Delaware River brought the Army Corps of Engineers to the Upper Delaware in 1962. Their flood-control plan was to build the Tocks Island Dam, which would convert the Upper Valley into a 37-mile-long lake, drowning forest and field. A battle erupted, one of the most significant environmental fights of the 1970s. Locals both won and lost. The dam was never built, but residents were forced from their homes and most of the valley became federal property.

This hike within the Delaware Water Gap National Recreation Area is a walk through history. It begins and ends at Millbrook Village, a re-created nineteenth-century farming community. It explores the Old Mine Road, takes in Van Campens Glen (named for the earliest Dutch settlers), and meanders over Watergate, a manicured twentieth-century estate. Arrive at Millbrook Village early and save a town tour until hike's end. From the north end of the parking lot, cross the paved road and enter the woods on the Orchard Trail. This path leads 0.5 mile uphill through abandoned farmlands that are slowly returning to forest, a classic example of field succession.

Fruit trees and open pasture are gone, replaced by light-loving red cedar, sassafras, and gray birch. But reminders of farm days linger: ornamental lilac bushes, Japanese barberry, and buckthorn (planted as hedges) grow along old stone walls and near the ruins of a springhouse. They compete with native hay-scented fern, milkweed, and winterberry. Shade-tolerant trees—beech, dogwood, and sugar maple—are also taking hold. They'll eventually push out most of the light-loving vegetation. In autumn and winter, views east to the Kittatinny Ridge are exceptional.

At the hill's crest the Orchard Trail intersects with Upper Hamilton Ridge Road, an abandoned section of the original Old Mine Road. Turn left here.

The Old Mine Road was once touted as the first commercial highway in America. Myth had it that the 104-mile byway was built around 1650 by Dutch miners hauling Delaware Valley copper to the Hudson River. But ore found south of Millbrook is of such low grade that historians doubt if any sane prospector would ever have gone to the trouble. The Old Mine Road was probably constructed by farmers in the 1700s. It was once dotted by blockhouses as protection from Indian raids. Washington moved his Continental army along the road to shield his troops from prying British eyes.

Follow Upper Hamilton Ridge Road gently downhill for about 2 miles. This walk over crumbling, moss-covered pavement is easy. It passes through former pastures, now a crazy quilt of native and introduced plant species. Oaks, white ash, and mockernut and pignut hickories coexist with privet (a garden escapee with tubular white flowers), Japanese barberry (with showy red berries in autumn), and buckthorn. White-tailed deer don't seem to mind the mix. They freely browse along overgrown stone fences and near a farmhouse foundation.

When Upper Hamilton Ridge Road reaches a T roughly 2.5 miles into the walk, turn left. At 2.7 miles turn left again on a paved section of the Old Mine Road. In a few hundred feet turn right into the Van Campens Glen parking lot. At the end of the lot, follow the yellow-blazed Van Campens Glen Trail into the woods.

The glen, the almost exclusive domain of native species, is a shaded grotto. Eastern hemlocks predominate. These trees create their own microclimate, with temperatures several degrees cooler than in the surrounding forest. They also cast dense "blue" shade because, like other conifers, they filter out light across the complete spectrum. Tulip trees and beeches grow in the gorge too, and reach high to gather sunlight. Rhododendron and spicebush (identified by its acrid scent) fill out the understory, while wood, polypody, and Christmas ferns add lacy decoration to steep rock slopes. Hepatica also grows in deep shade, a delicate lavender flower blooming in early spring. In days past, plant shape often indicated medicinal use to herbalists (a doctrine called signatures). Hepatica's three-lobed, rounded leaves once suggested it as a liver cure, a bogus assumption.

The trail climbs steeply on stone and log steps along the left side of the brook, rising above the lower Van Campens Falls and passing through clefts in the redbeds (Bloomsburg Formation sandstones stained by iron deposits). The path then descends steeply through sweet birch, reaching a small level plain beside the stream. This area is covered in a mature stand of sycamore, tulip tree, and yellow birch. Resist the temptation to leave the trail. Where people have trampled, nothing grows; where they have not, native ferns abound.

As you head upstream (about 0.5 mile into the gorge and 3.3 miles into the hike), watch for a place where the yellow blazes indicate a sharp turn to the right as the path crosses the brook on steppingstones (this crossing can be dangerous in high water).

Just ahead is the highlight of the walk, upper Van Campens Falls, plunging over violet-hued sandstone. Fly fishermen stand waist deep and cast the wide pool at the falls' base for native trout (no bait fishing is allowed).

A quick rock scramble to the top of the falls is the most challenging part of the hike. Watch closely for the yellow blazes following along the top right edge of the glen. The stream pinballs below through the narrow slotted gorge, bouncing off eroded walls and plunging in white sheets of foam into pools.

A human-made stone wall on the brook's left bank, probably the remains of a dam, marks the head of the glen. Follow the yellow blazes north as the ravine widens into a little valley and passes through a forest of sugar and red maple, beech, and oak. The path parallels the stream, crosses two roads, then dips down into the brook's shrubby floodplain, where it passes beneath power lines.

At 4.2 miles into the hike, the yellow-blazed trail ends as it crosses Van Campens Brook on a wooden bridge. Continue straight ahead, curving to the right along the gravel roads of Watergate, the 1950s estate of George Busch (there is no political affiliation!). You are now on the unblazed Millbrook-Watergate Trail.

All that remains of Busch's retreat are a stone dam capped by a Victorian turret and the grave of his beloved dog Bozo (look for the marker under a tall Norway spruce). Canada goose droppings and rabbit pellets dot the mowed grass, now a National Recreation Area picnic ground.

Follow the gravel road closest to Van Campens Brook, passing a number of small ponds where there may be evidence of beaver activity. Gnawed river birch and speckled alder logs (favorite beaver food), a ruined lodge, and beaver mudslides proved the recent presence of the animals when we were there, as did a beaver skeleton we uncovered in the brush.

The road continues straight ahead, reaching the outskirts of Millbrook Village at about 5.0 miles. Just past the one-room schoolhouse, make a short detour left to the town cemetery. The tilted nineteenth-century stones of Permella Sutton, Uriah Hill, Abram Garis, and others stand beneath mature oaks and a 70-foot-tall paper birch.

The road leads on into Millbrook Village and to the parking lot. This rural community once was home to seventy-five people. Today summertime volunteers demonstrate weaving, blacksmithing, woodworking, and milling to visitors. The sugar shack (for boiling down maple syrup), cider mill, smokehouse, gristmill, general store, and Methodist church met the physical and spiritual needs of surrounding nineteenth-century farms. Now the sleepy village is home only to wild animals. We've watched wintering juncos here and, in spring, have seen a mother groundhog carry her young by mouth to a streamside burrow just opposite the gristmill.

For More Information

Delaware Water Gap National Recreation Area trails and Millbrook Village grounds are open dawn to dusk year-round. Millbrook Village buildings are open from late April until the end of October, Wednesday through Sunday. Craft demonstrations are on weekends only. No admission fee.

Millbrook Village: 908-841-9531

Delaware Water Gap National Recreation Area Headquarters, Bushkill, PA, 18324; 570-588-2451

Kittatinny Point Visitor Center: 908-496-4458; www.nps.gov/dewa/

Merrill Creek Reservoir
Merrill Creek Environmental Preserve

Trail: Shoreline Trail, Creek Trail, Orchard Trail (loop)
Distance: 4.1 miles
Length: 2½ hours
Difficulty: Easy

*A changing ridgetop habitat supports
bird and wildflower diversity*

Getting There

From I-80, take Exit 12, Hope/Blairstown. Follow County Route 521 south for 1.0 mile to Hope town center. Continue straight on County Route 519 south for about 16 miles. Bear left on 519 south at a Y-intersection with County Route 646. In 1.3 miles look for a small Merrill Creek sign and turn left onto Fox Farm Road. In 4.5 miles turn right at a stop sign onto Richline Road. In 0.6 mile make a right onto Merrill Creek Road. Follow signs right to the visitor center.

Special Features

- Merrill Creek Reservoir
- Diverse forest and swamp
- Farmstead ruins
- Streamside areas are wet

A contemporary visitor to Merrill Creek views the placid, sun-dappled surface of a 16-billion-gallon lake encircled by forest and field atop Scotts Mountain. But this is my home ground, where I wandered as a child and where I witnessed the swift remaking of the natural landscape by human beings.

In the 1960s I played explorer here with boyhood friends, puzzling out humankind's past influences. After a spring rain, black chert arrowheads shone against the red clay of plowed farm fields, revealing a 12,000-year Native American legacy. Amid dense second- and third-growth forest, we found incongruous walls and sunken roads, evidence of abandoned eighteenth- and nineteenth-century farms. We explored old homesteads—overgrown, stone-lined cellar holes—with the same romantic zeal as Schliemann uncovered Troy.

In the mid-1970s seven public utilities announced plans to flood the mountaintop with a gargantuan reservoir. My father, a retired public-utility employee, couldn't bear to see this wooded ridge—where he had hunted deer, rabbits, and pheasant—drowned. He was quickly converted from an advocate of progress into an ally of environmentalists.

My dad doggedly fought the project. The utility companies won. Giant earthmovers came; stripped away forest and field; tore a 225-foot-deep, 650-acre hole in the ridge; and erected an ugly 0.5-mile-long earthen dam. A 3.5-mile-long tunnel, blasted through bedrock, connected the top of Scotts Mountain to the Delaware River. Water was pumped from the river into the reservoir and stored for use by downstream power plants during drought times.

The human change carved into Scotts Mountain both impoverishes and enriches the environment, harming some species while favoring others. Where white-tailed deer once ran,

Merrill Creek Reservoir

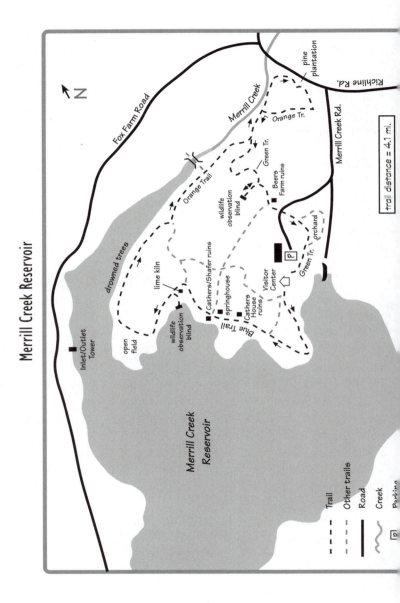

trail distance = 4.1 mi.

Legend:
- Trail
- Other trails
- Road
- Creek
- Parking

Labels on map:
Fox Farm Road, Merrill Creek, pine plantation, Richline Rd., Orange Tr., Green Tr., Merrill Creek Rd., Beers Farm ruins, Orange Trail, drowned trees, wildlife observation blind, lime kiln, Cathers/Shafer ruins, springhouse, Green Tr. orchard, Visitor Center, Cathers House ruins, Blue Trail, open field, wildlife observation blind, Inlet/Outlet Tower, Merrill Creek Reservoir, N

largemouth bass now swim. Where deep forest warblers once thrived, edge and meadow birds such as goldfinches now flourish.

This 4.1-mile loop hike within the 290-acre Merrill Creek Environmental Preserve explores the north shore of the reservoir, passing through a remnant of the deciduous, conifer, streamside, wetland, and field habitats that once covered all of Scotts Mountain.

To begin the walk, face the main entrance of the visitor center and turn right, walking around to the side of the building. Follow the red gravel path toward the reservoir. Straight ahead a sign points to hiking trails. Pass through an open meadow where yellow winter cress blooms in spring and wild bergamot, goldenrod, and bull-thistle flower in fall.

Enter the woods, following the blue-blazed Shoreline Trail to the left. Tulip tree, chestnut oak, and sweet birch rise high overhead, while the understory is filled out by sassafras, red maple, flowering dogwood, witch hazel, and spicebush. Wildflowers dot the leaf litter. Sunny colonies of rue anemone bloom white in late April along with a scattering of blue violets and less common yellow violets. In autumn, wood asters abound in deep shade.

The blue-blazed trail parallels the reservoir and follows a sunken road, its edges stacked high with cobbles by nineteenth-century farmers. Here we found a shrew run, small tunnels ending abruptly on either side of the road and connected by a muddle of tiny footprints. Shrews tunnel through soft forest humus, gaining safe passage from predators. The road, too hard packed for tunneling, must be traversed above ground, exposing the animals to attack.

Another tiny forest creature, the ant, colonizes the roadside. Ants and humans are both considered social animals, though their evolutionary lines diverged about 600 million years ago. Ant species have proven wildly successful, with an estimated million billion ants populating the world today.

Between 0.6 mile and 0.8 mile you'll find evidence of another social species along the blue trail: the ruins of the Cathers farmhouse, a springhouse, the Cathers/Shaffer farm, and a lime kiln. Near these field-stone farm foundations stand old apple trees, planted for fruit, and gnarled sugar and silver maples, planted to provide maple syrup. Their low, spreading branches attest to the open sun in this area when it was farmed. The forest found here today is composed of pillarlike trees that reach high before branching to gather sunlight. Non-native barberry, multiflora rose, and white violets (with purple centers) are also plentiful at the farms. Next to a boardwalk in a small wetland below the springhouse, native blue marsh violets bloom in spring, while great lobelia blossoms in late summer.

A few yards past the lime kiln, detour left and stroll down a short trail to the wildlife observation blind on the reservoir shore. Merrill Creek supports many waterfowl. On an April visit we watched buffleheads, chubby diving ducks aptly called butterballs. Males are easily identified by a large, roundish white head patch. Without the reservoir there would probably be few buffleheads found on Scotts Mountain. Flooded dead trees bordering the shore provide ideal nesting cavities for the birds.

Return to the blue trail. Follow it to the woods edge, where it turns sharply right (1.1 miles). The trail becomes a mowed path climbing a grassy knoll from which you can look west over the reservoir to the Great Valley of the Appalachians and beyond to Kittatinny Ridge. In this meadow, benevolent human efforts attempt to offset naturally destructive human mistakes. Bluebird boxes placed here attract eastern bluebirds, a species made scarce by aggressive European starlings intentionally introduced to America. To the left of the path, Spanish chestnut trees have been planted. They are an exotic replacement for native American chestnut trees destroyed by a fungal blight accidentally introduced to the United States in 1904.

The blue-blazed trail quickly descends to the reservoir edge, reenters the woods, and gets rocky. This reservoir cove, with its drowned trees, offers good birding. In spring, insect-gathering tree swallows swoop above the water, while double-crested cormorants sit on stumps drying their wings. Hysterical laughter, the call of the northern flicker, is heard from birds resting on dead limbs. Pileated woodpeckers, in search of carpenter ants, have blasted huge cavities in rotting trunks.

The blue-blazed Shoreline Trail ends at 1.7 miles. Turn left onto the orange-blazed Creek Trail. At 2.0 miles make a detour 100 feet left onto a footbridge over Merrill Creek. These woods of sweet birch; beech; and red, white, and chestnut oak resemble the forest that once covered the 650 acres submerged by Merrill Creek Reservoir.

The orange trail moves away from the creek briefly, passes a junction with the green Orchard Trail (2.1 miles), then returns to the creek for the most secluded part of the walk. Sleek tulip trees and peeling yellow birches rise above gracefully spreading spruce limbs. In late April a blaze of golden marsh marigolds, trout lilies with yellow drooping blossoms, white dwarf ginseng, and false rue anemone bloom amid greening skunk cabbage and false hellebore.

The orange Creek Trail forks at a wooden bench (2.4 miles). Take the left fork straight ahead as it follows the creek, then

The ruins of a nineteenth-century farmstead.

turns right and away from the stream. The trail climbs through a stand of pine, the remains of a sprawling pine plantation where I once played hide-and-seek with boyhood friends.

At 2.8 miles the orange trail passes through a stone wall, turns sharply right onto a woods road, and loops back to the bench by the stream (3.0 miles). Turn left, retracing your steps along the brook to the junction with the green-blazed Orchard Trail (3.3 miles). Follow the green trail as it climbs through oak and sweet birch. Look for an amazing sight: six 1-foot-diameter tulip trees all rising from a common trunk. Such multiple-trunked trees often sprout from cut stumps.

At 3.6 miles the green trail reaches the gravel, wheelchair-accessible Eagle Trail. Detour briefly right and stroll through a black cherry grove to the wildlife observation blind at a field edge. Walk silently and you may see a fox, as we did. The fox, hearing our approach, quickly disappeared, using an old woodchuck burrow to make good its escape.

Retrace your steps to the green trail and follow it along the gravel path through the ruins of the Beers Farm, where sweet-scented ornamental white lilacs blossom in springtime. Follow the green blazes straight ahead across a paved road into an old orchard. Take both right forks of the green trail, which returns you to the visitor center at 4.1 miles.

For More Information

The visitor center is open seven days a week, 8:30 A.M. to 4:30 P.M., but is closed Thanksgiving, Christmas Eve, Christmas Day, New Year's Day, and Easter.

Merrill Creek Reservoir, 34 Merrill Creek Road, Washington, NJ 07882; 908-454-1213; www.merrillcreek.net

Paulinskill Valley Trail
Blairstown to Marksboro

Trail: **Paulinskill Valley Trail (out-and-back)**
Distance: **6.4 miles**
Length: **4 hours**
Difficulty: **Easy; flat**

A streamside stroll along a historic railway

Getting There

From I-80, take NJ 94 to Blairstown. At the north edge of town, turn right onto Footbridge Lane at a sign for Footbridge Park. If you reach a right turn for County Route 616, you've gone too far. Park by signs for the Paulinskill Valley Trail. Follow the trail north, back toward the parking lot entrance. For shuttle hikers, place a second car 3 miles north of Blairstown. Follow NJ 94 north just past the Marksboro Country Store and turn left onto County Route 659 west toward Stillwater. In 0.3 mile cross the Paulinskill River and turn left into a parking lot.

Special Features
- Great Valley of the Appalachians
- Limestone outcrops with walking fern
- A quarter of New Jersey's plant species
- Fabulous birding and wildflowers

In 1881 the New York, Susquehanna & Western Railroad (NYS&W) brought progress and the promise of prosperity to the rural Paulinskill River Valley in western New Jersey. Today the trains are gone. What remains is a lush, 26-mile-long greenway and trail where nearly a quarter of New Jersey's plant species, plus numerous bird and animal species, thrive.

At its height in 1916, the railway's iron tracks were polished silver by forty passing trains per day. They brought coal from Pennsylvania to New York City, fueling America's Industrial Revolution. They also carried milk, ice, wood, and farm produce to the urban East while taking manufactured goods, petroleum products, fertilizer, and city-weary vacationers west. Alfred Ringling even shipped his circus elephants via the NYS&W. But by 1962, truck lines had replaced train lines, and the rails turned to rust. Track was torn up, and the abandoned railway became a dumping ground.

A 1985 state plan to turn the railroad into a linear greenway met fierce opposition from adjoining property owners and politicians. That's when local citizens formed the Paulinskill Valley Trail Committee. They garnered overwhelming public support for the new trail corridor. Established as Kittatinny Valley State Park in 1992, the Paulinskill Valley Trail is testimony to the power and promise of grassroots efforts. Today the trail is a boon to hikers, bicyclists, horseback riders, and anglers.

The Paulinskill Valley Trail begins at Columbia on the Delaware River, runs roughly northeast, and ends at Sparta Junction in Sussex County. The section hiked here, between Blairstown and Marksboro, is an easy, perfectly level woods walk paralleling the Paulinskill River. It boasts fine wildflowers, ferns, and birds. The walk can be done as a 6.4-mile out-and-back trip, or a 3.2-mile one-way hike with cars spotted at both ends.

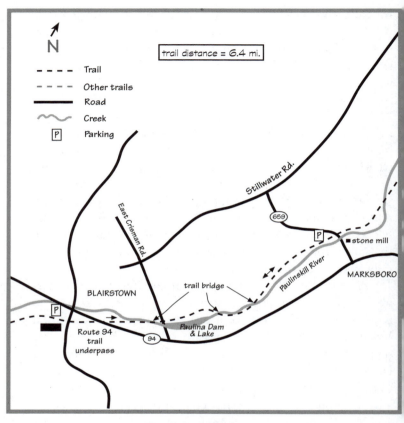

Paulinskill Valley Trail

Begin hiking at the Blairstown parking lot. Pass through
the gate north onto the Paulinskill Valley Trail and notice the
two tall catalpa trees flanking you. With their floppy, foot-long,
heart-shaped leaves, these showy specimens are hard to miss.

Most catalpas are tropical species. Those found in New Jersey are usually planted as shade trees. These two may once have landscaped the Blairstown train station. You won't see another catalpa for the rest of the hike.

The trail quickly passes under NJ 94, shooting straight ahead under a dense canopy of Norway maple, sugar maple, elm, and ailanthus. Whenever you spot ailanthus trees (with eleven to forty-one leaflets along a single stem), you know you're walking in a disturbed forest where humans have left their mark. These exotics were introduced from China. Once planted as speedily growing shelter belts along roadsides and railroads, they now spread out of control, forcing out native trees (a far more valuable source of food for wildlife). The ailanthus, easily confused with sumac, is distinguished by its rank, disagreeable odor.

The Paulinskill River flows as a lazy little stream to the left, lined by water-loving silver maples, sycamores, basswood, and box elders. Spectacular wildflower displays proliferate in these damp woodlands and thickets, peaking in spring but progressing through autumn. Canada mayflower, sweet cicely, mayapple, bloodroot, early saxifrage, wild columbine, Solomon's seal, and aster all blossom at trailside. Bloodroot, a fragile, solitary white flower with a golden-orange center, was especially useful to Native Americans. Its underground stem provided a deep red dye for baskets, clothing, and face paint. It also served as insect repellent.

Soon the trail passes a rock outcrop cut by the railroad. While most of the treadway lies on soft, river valley soils or on grittier glacial tills, such rock cuts reveal the Kittatinny limestone underlying this portion of the Great Valley of the Appalachians. This 3,000-foot-thick blue-gray limestone layer

The view from a scenic footbridge over the Paulinskill River.

consists of compressed organic materials deposited in warm, shallow seas more than 480 million years ago. Today these shady, calcite-rich outcrops support unusual plants. Look for the walking fern. This rare species grows only in limestone. Wherever its long, gracefully pointed leaf tips touch the ground, another plant sprouts. Thus the walking fern strides, step by step across its stony domain (see the sidebar).

The trail briefly escapes the cover of sugar maple, white ash, and hickory at 0.7 mile into the hike. It enters the open, crosses the Paulinskill River on a bridge, intersects sleepy East Crisman Road, and arrives at Paulina Dam. The picturesque little milldam on the right creates a 0.25-mile-long lake where painted turtles, wood ducks, common mergansers, and swans congregate among lily pads. The trail hugs the lakeshore under willows and amid wildflowers. Fragrant white plumes of lizard's tail and erect yellow spikes of common mullein intermingle here from June to September.

At this spot we saw a rare sight: a bat flying in broad daylight. It settled its body awkwardly on a shoreside reed, becoming the perfect imitation of a dried leaf. Little brown bats (only about 3 1/2 inches wide) are nocturnal, and most often seen at twilight, darting above water bodies and feeding on clouds of insects. A bat spotted during the day may be rabid or hurt and is best avoided. Do not touch wildlife you discover on your walks.

The trail passes a small wetland blanketed in pickerelweed and cattails at 1.3 miles. Flocks of goldfinches often perform their bouncing acrobatic flight just above the marsh. This "wild canary" is a New Jersey native and our state bird. An edge-habitat bird, it feeds on the seeds of thistles, dandelions, and wild sunflowers, which thrive at field boundaries and in shrubby wetlands. Goldfinches are among the most visible of the Paulinskill Valley Trail's numerous songbirds.

Crossing a second bridge puts the river back on your left-hand side. The stream now rushes through a series of rapids that challenge canoeists during spring high water and that attract anglers year-round. The trail then passes Mile Marker 81, an artifact of the age of steam. These cement posts gave railroaders the track mileage west from Jersey City.

At 2.0 miles the path crosses the river on a third trestle. The river's edge is lined with black walnut trees and big-tooth aspens. Aspens attest to how recently this area returned to woods; they are pioneer trees that fill in forest clearings.

A concrete pillar etched with the letter W tells walkers they've reached Marksboro. Such markers once warned train engineers of approaching road crossings and cued them to blast their whistles. At 3.2 miles the trail arrives at the Marksboro Paulinskill Trail parking lot. An old stone mill, now a residence, stands on the far side of the stream. Hikers should either return the way they came or use a second car parked here earlier to retrieve their car in Blairstown.

The Paulinskill Valley Trail is an outstanding but tenuous triumph for environmentalists. Just 66 feet wide, this elegant green thread will need the continued support of local residents and hikers to prevent adjoining farmlands from disappearing under suburban development.

For More Information

The Paulinskill Valley Trail is open from dawn to dusk daily.

Kittatinny Valley State Park, P.O. Box 621, Andover, NJ 07821; 973-786-6445; www.state.nj.us/dep/forestry/parks/kittval.htm

Volunteer with the Paulinskill Valley Trail Committee, P.O. Box 175, Andover, NJ 07821; 908-684-4820; http://community.nj.com/cc/pvtc

Fabulous Ferns

The moist, limestone-rich lowlands of the Great Valley of the Appalachians supports luxurious fern growth. Hikers along the Paulinskill find Christmas ferns (an evergreen whose leaflets are shaped like tiny Christmas stockings), maidenhair fern (growing on a graceful circling axis), polypody (found only on rock outcrops), fragile fern, hay-scented fern, walking fern, and the greatest concentration of glade fern in the state.

Ferns are among the most ancient of plants. During Carboniferous times, more than 230 million years ago, they grew to tree size in jungle swamps. These great ferns were compressed to form the coal once transported by the NYS&W Railroad. Today there are 10,000 known fern species in the world, most of diminutive size. Ferns remain extremely successful, with their microscopic spores carried by the jet stream for possibly thousands of miles. There are about a hundred commonly occurring fern species in our region.

"All you need to learn about them is a hand lens and a fern guide," says Marge Barrett, one of the founders of the Paulinskill Valley Trail. "While they may seem bafflingly similar at first, you can identify them by their shape and by the fruit dot patterns appearing on their undersides during late summer and fall."

Sussex Branch Trail
Kittatinny Valley State Park

Trip 6

Trail: **Sussex Branch Trail, gravel road, orange-blazed trail (loop)**
Distance: **3.7 miles**
Length: **3 hours**
Difficulty: **Easy; flat**

A haven for deer and wild turkeys

Getting There
The Sussex Branch Trail parking area is located on NJ 206, 0.2 mile north of Andover on the right, and 3.2 miles south of Newton on the left.

Special Features
- A former iron industry railway
- Wetlands and wildflowers
- Limestone outcrops and columbine
- Lake Aeroflex

For thousands of years the fertile lowlands of the Great Valley of the Appalachians have supported wildlife and attracted human beings. This gently sculpted valley stretches from Alabama to New York and runs in a 45-mile-long, 12-mile-wide diagonal swath across northwest New Jersey.

At the end of the last ice age 12,000 years ago, Paleolithic hunters moved up and down this trough, chasing caribou herds through a frigid New Jersey landscape that was covered in open tundra and spruce forest. A global warming trend melted the ice and caused the rise of a great deciduous forest stretching to the Mississippi River. The vast woodlands became home to wolves and cougars and their prey, elk and deer.

White settlers quickly claimed the prime real estate of the Great Valley. They deforested it, building farms and estates, roads and railroads. Wildlife was hunted to oblivion. Elk and cougars disappeared from New Jersey by 1840, wolves by 1855, and white-tailed deer by 1900. Only in the twentieth century have people felt secure enough in their hold on the Great Valley to allow nature's limited resurgence.

This 3.7-mile loop hike, starting on the Sussex Branch Trail and circling through Kittatinny Valley State Park, offers a chance to see deer, wild turkeys, and songbirds. The flat terrain invites families with children, and cross-country skiers.

The trailhead parking lot on US 206 is bordered by native chinquapin oak, elm, and aspen along with introduced catalpa, apple, and ailanthus. In springtime, walk a few yards left to a limestone outcrop (watch for poison ivy). The drooping fool's-cap-shaped red blossoms of wild columbine thrive upon the calcite-rich rock. These flowers, narrow tubes with pollen hidden deep inside, allow access to just a few pollinators. Hovering

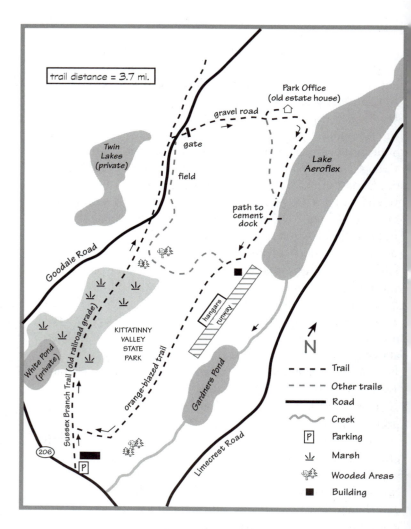

Sussex Branch Trail

ruby-throated hummingbirds, with needlelike bills and an attraction to red, have evolved a specialized pollinating/nectar-gathering partnership with columbine.

Leave the parking lot, following the Sussex Branch Trail through a gate into the woods. This 21-mile-long trail began life in 1849 as the mule-powered Sussex Railroad, hauling ore from the Andover Iron Mine to the Morris Canal at Waterloo Village. The line later became a branch of the Erie-Lackawanna Railroad and was abandoned in the mid-1900s.

Today the rail bed welcomes hikers, bicyclists, and horse riders. The path is lined by tulip tree, ash, maple, and white oak. In autumn, the trailside explodes with color. Yellow spikes of common mullein and goldenrod rise above the white parasols of Queen Anne's lace and ornate blue trumpets of great lobelia. Chicory, wood aster, and the scarlet cones of staghorn sumac fill out the color scheme. The earthy scent of wild bergamot permeates the air.

Songbirds add another accent to these woods. The familiar cardinal resides in this edge habitat year-round. It loves the dense honeysuckle thickets, feeding on wild grapes, dogwood berries, and sumac seeds. You might think that the male cardinal's scarlet feathers would betray it to predators. Not so. Deciduous thickets with their green leaves spread green light while absorbing red and blue portions of the spectrum. The cardinal disappears from sight in its shady habitat. In winter, dense thickets provide protection from hawks.

Within 0.4 mile the raised railroad bed shoots down the middle of a wetland. Quiet, shallow pools support white water lilies, cattails, pickerelweed, and a beautiful display of water marigolds topped by golden-rayed blossoms. Swans and mallards swim amid surfacing turtles. Notice the silvery gray trunks of dead red maples. This area, once a swamp (a tree-filled, seasonal wetland), has gradually become wetter and changed into a marsh (a treeless, year-round wetland).

The path leaves the marsh and enters deep, cool woods. It passes a small limestone outcrop on the left and an isolated pocket of water that in late summer is dusted with a pea-green layer of duckweed, the smallest of flowers.

At 1.0 mile the trail exits the woods, then crosses and parallels Goodale Road. The open meadows and forest of Kittatinny Valley State Park to the right and the cornfields at left make this the ideal spot for wildlife watching. At dusk, deer congregate at treeline, waiting for darkness before making their cautious way into the corn for a late-night snack. We've seen bold turkeys, in groups of twenty or more, commute from forest to corn in full morning sunlight. Both the white-tailed deer and turkey were wiped out by early settlers and had to be reintroduced into New Jersey wilds. The immense deer herds of today are descended from the few animals kept in pens on the Worthington and Rutherford estates. Wild turkeys returned on their own in 1958, when eleven birds flew across the Delaware River from Pennsylvania and began taking back their old haunts.

As the meadow ends to the right (about 1.3 miles into the walk), leave the Sussex Branch Trail, turn right and cross Goodale Road, and enter Kittatinny Valley State Park through a gate. Follow a gravel road along an impressive stone wall lined by stately white ash.

The ash tree's hard wood was once shaped into canoe paddles by Native Americans, and later into furniture and Louisville Slugger baseball bats. This stand, with its tall, straight trunks, may explain why the ancient Norse imagined ash as a tree that could support the weight of the world. In the

The 1823 stone farmhouse, expanded to become an estate house in 1906, landscaped with pin oak, white oak, silver maple, and black walnut trees.

woods to the left look for devil's walking-stick, also known as prickly ash. This spiny shrub was planted on Victorian estates as a grotesque ornamental.

Reaching the far corner of the meadow, avoid forks to the left and right. Walk straight ahead on the gravel road. At 1.8 miles the road glides into the open, passing the Kittatinny Valley State Park office. This stone farmhouse, built in 1823, was expanded in 1906 as an estate house. It is landscaped with pin oak, white oak, silver maple, and black walnut trees. Follow the gravel road as it swings right, sweeping alongside hemlock-lined Aeroflex Lake.

At 2.3 miles an obvious but unmarked path leads left to the lake and a cement dock, a fine lunch spot. Sunfish rise to snap up crumbs on this, the deepest glacial lake in New Jersey.

Continue to the end of Aeroflex Lake and follow the gravel road as it sweeps to the right (before the white fence) past the building overlooking the runway of the Aeroflex-Andover Airport. Once you enter the woods, look for an orange-blazed trail leading left. Along this trail you'll pass vernal kettle ponds, habitat for the spotted salamander. In less than a mile the orange-blazed trail swings right and returns to the Sussex Branch Trail near where the hike began. A left turn quickly leads back to the parking lot.

For More Information

Trails are open from dawn to dusk year-round. The park office is open daily.

Kittatinny Valley State Park, P.O. Box 621, Andover, NJ 07821; 973-786-6445; www.state.nj.us/dep/forestry/parks/kittval.htm

Flights of Wonder

A dragonfly zigzags across the sun-drenched marsh; a seagull sweeps over the lake; a single-engine plane arcs toward the runway. Kittatinny Valley State Park is a study in flight, a place to let your imagination soar.

A flight-friendly wing is the secret to flying. An effective wing is convex above and flattened below, rounded in front with a rear edge tapered to a point. This elegant design moves air faster across the upper wing surface than below. This reduces air pressure above the wing, resulting in lift.

Unlike airplanes, birds have flexible airfoils to control air speed and direction. Bird flight is actually a combination of wing movement alternating with swooping glides. Flight is a high-energy enterprise for birds; wing feathers wear out quickly and must be replaced.

A pilot must guard against losing too much airspeed and stalling a plane. Birds land by gliding to a stall precisely over the spot on ground, water, or limb where they wish to "fall." Such efficient avian gliders as turkey vultures and seagulls actually lose altitude at the same rate that warm air rises. Thus these feathered gliders fall without falling.

The cellophanelike, intricately veined wings of an adult dragonfly allow this hunter to fly at 25 MPH and catch mosquitoes in flight. The scale-covered, leaflike wings of a monarch butterfly carry this insect at top speeds of only 6 MPH, but the seemingly fragile butterfly can flap itself hundreds of miles to Mexico during autumn migration.

—Jean LeBlanc

White Cedar Swamp Trail

Dryden Kuser Natural Area, High Point State Park

Trail: White Cedar Swamp Trail (loop)
Distance: 1.5 miles
Length: 2 hours
Difficulty: Easy; with gentle climbing

The wonders of an Atlantic white cedar swamp

Getting There

Take I-80 west to NJ 23 north through the town of Sussex. Eight miles north of Sussex, climb Kittatinny Ridge and turn right into High Point State Park (the park headquarters building is on the left side of NJ 23). Within 1.0 mile reach Lake Marcia; follow signs to the Cedar Swamp Picnic Area. Follow the road to a dead end at the picnic area parking lot.

Special Features

- A mountaintop sphagnum moss bog
- Look for insectivorous sundews
- Easily accessible
- Rhododendrons blossom in late spring

Not so long ago swamps evoked primal fear and disgust. Their slime-covered pools, muck, mosquitoes, and dismal forests thwarted America's drive toward wilderness conquest. For the past century people could find no better use for these trackless wastelands than to drain, bulldoze, and plop subdivisions down where they had been, attaching prettified names like *Willow-brook* or *Pleasant Valley* to the once swampy locales. And good riddance, too . . .

Luckily hydrologists, botanists, and biologists have set us straight. Today we recognize wetlands as vital to our own survival and to planetary biodiversity. These self-cleaning organic sponges are recognized as natural waste treatment plants. They capture polluted runoff and purify it, while recharging groundwater. Hikers have also recognized these once forbidding places as magical—they are the habitat for large mammals such as the black bear, and haven to strange flora such as insectivorous sundews or magnificent Atlantic white cedars. The National Wildlife Federation estimates that 43 percent of threatened and endangered species rely on wetlands at some stage in their life cycles.

The 850-acre Dryden Kuser Natural Area in High Point State Park played a role in raising New Jersey's wetland consciousness starting in the 1960s. The preserve's highly accessible 1.5-mile Cedar Swamp Trail draws hikers into the mysterious world of an Atlantic white cedar swamp. (You can pick up a numbered "Cedar Swamp Guided Nature Walk" booklet at the High Point State Park office.)

The walk begins at a gate from which a road leads downhill through a deciduous forest of chestnut oak, white oak, pignut hickory, and sweet birch. Notice the 25-foot-tall American chestnut immediately to the left of the gate. It is identified by its long, narrow, oblong leaves with sharp curved teeth. This

White Cedar Swamp Trail

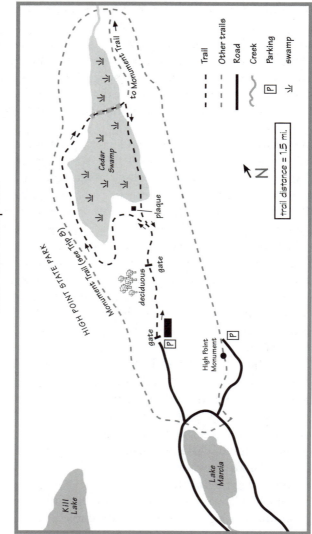

tree dominated upland forests just a century ago, growing to more than 100 feet. Its fruit was food to animals, Native Americans, and pioneers. A fungal blight accidentally introduced to New York City on imported Chinese chestnut trees wiped out these American giants. But hope springs eternal for the chestnut: young sprouts rise from the roots of long-dead trees, grow into spindly saplings, then are blighted. We've seen female chestnuts on this hike in early fall, with ripe spiny fruit. Perhaps an offspring will one day develop blight immunity.

The gradually descending road is lined with large sassafras trees. These can be tricky to identify at first, since mature specimens have very few of the mitten-shaped leaves characteristic of younger trees. Sassafras can be positively identified by its spicy, aromatic scent. Bracken fern and hay-scented fern also grow on this drier ground.

Two stone pillars mark the entrance to the Dryden Kuser Natural Area 0.25 mile into the walk. The preserve is named for a state senator, New Jersey Audubon Society president, and the son of parents who donated their High Point retreat to New Jersey as a park. The wet ground at this spot supports water-tolerant red maples.

At the natural area plaque (0.4 mile), fork left on the Cedar Swamp Trail. The trail encircles the swamp, following the natural boundary between upland and wetland and providing a unique opportunity to see how moisture and soil type dictate plant habitat. In the upland to the left, oaks, sweet birch, and witch hazel dominate. To the right is the swamp, where rhododendron, Atlantic white cedar, and eastern hemlock rise on sphagnum moss (peat moss) hummocks amid pools of rust-brown water. These evergreens are tolerant of the sodden, acidic, nutrient-poor soils, as is skunk cabbage. Graceful,

The spiny fruit and leaf of the American chestnut. These once giant trees were laid low by a fungal blight introduced from Asia.

vaselike displays of cinnamon fern also grow in the wetland.

The swamp, cradled between two Kittatinny Range ridges, is a relic of the last ice age. The retreating Wisconsin Glacier dammed this little depression 15,000 years ago, creating a 30-acre lake. The water body was gradually filled in by a sphagnum moss bog (a permanently flooded, open peatland whose highly acidic waters won't let organic material decay). Conifers then gradually filled in the bog at its margins until no open water remained, turning the area into a swamp (strictly defined as a tree-covered wetland). This northernmost New Jersey Atlantic white cedar swamp is a crossroads for biodiversity. New England plants mingle with southern species.

The trail rises above the swamp (0.6 mile), giving good views over the wetland. Look for a large sour gum tree, also called black tupelo, at the nature guide's number 11 station along the trail. This swamp forest tree is uncommon in northern Jersey, though numerous on the Inner Coastal Plain. It can be identified by its deeply furrowed bark and sharply pointed, shiny leaves, turning scarlet in autumn. The bluish black fall berries are favored by birds.

The trail descends back toward the swamp and cuts through it on a boardwalk (1.0 mile). Notice that shade-tolerant hemlocks dominate the wetland canopy, but wherever an opening has appeared (caused by either a tree-fall or the trail itself), light-loving Atlantic white cedars have seized the opportunity to grow. The white cedar is normally a coastal tree, spreading southward from Maine. Its wood has been variously used in war and music making: it produced charcoal for Revolutionary War gunpowder and served as pipes in the first American church organs. The hemlock has flat, flexible needles, while the cedar has more bristly, scalelike needles.

Great rhododendron forms a thick, impenetrable understory along the boardwalk. This shrub blooms with showy flowers in mid-July, and its long, waxy leaves curl cigarlike at winter's onset. The colder the weather, the tighter the curl. Wild calla, more common to southern Canada than New Jersey, is plentiful at this spot. Its heart-shaped glossy leaves are topped in summer by a pudgy spike of yellow flowers partly enclosed by a white hood. A tight cluster of crimson berries makes this a showy member of the arum family in autumn.

While on the boardwalk, stoop and notice the thick, spongy sphagnum moss blanket covering the shallow water pools on both sides. This unassuming aquatic evergreen actually initiated the bog ecosystem at High Point 15,000 years ago (see the sidebar). Acids and tannins released from dying sphagnum moss inhibit decay-causing bacteria that normally enrich wetland soils. Thus only hardy plants able to survive under nutrient-starved conditions—plants such as the Atlantic white cedar, rhododendron, and calla—can join sphagnum moss in this acid-rich ecosystem.

Just beyond the boardwalk, the trail reaches a major intersection (1.1 miles). The left branch leads to a bridge crossing of a stream on the Monument Trail (see the next trip). The right branch leads back to your starting place at the parking lot in 0.4 mile, where tree-shaded tables provide a fine spot for a picnic.

For More Information

The Cedar Swamp Trail is open from dawn to dusk year-round. Stop at the office for the "Cedar Swamp Guided Nature Walk" booklet.

High Point State Park, 1480 State Route 23, Sussex, NJ 07461; 973-875-4800; www.state.nj.us/dep/forestry/parks/high.htm

Secrets of Sphagnum Moss

This lowly evergreen has one thing in common with North America's beavers: its ability to utterly transform an aquatic environment. Growing in thick green mats, sphagnum moss (commonly called peat moss) is perpetually growing at the water's surface but dying just below the waterline. The dead part of the plant releases acids and tannins that sterilize the water, preventing decay from occurring. Dead layers of vegetation sink to the bottom, creating thick deposits of organic matter sometimes hundreds of feet thick (in the Dryden Kuser Natural Area swamp, sphagnum moss has nearly filled in a glacial lake that was 12 feet deep). Specialized shrubs and trees anchor their roots in the dead material and rise above the floating raft of living moss.

Humans have found many uses for sphagnum moss. Because it is sterile and absorbs up to twenty times its own weight in water, it was used as a wound dressing during World War I. Britons have long cut and burned peat as fuel. Its most frequent use today is by gardeners and farmers as moisture-holding mulch.

According to John Eastman, in *The Book of Swamp and Bog,* one of the least-understood features of sphagnum moss bogs is their ability to moderate climate. Bogs stay cool in spring and summer, possibly reducing temperature extremes in the air around them. With almost half of all U.S. boglands now gone, and with other nations fast depleting this resource, we may unknowingly be destabilizing our weather systems, and possibly inviting environmental imbalance.

Monument Trail
High Point State Park

Trip 8

Trail: **Monument Trail (loop)**
Distance: **3.5 miles**
Length: **3 hours**
Difficulty: **Moderate; 300-foot elevation gain**

A ridgetop walk among forest mammals

Getting There

Take I-80 west to NJ 23 north through the town of Sussex.
Eight miles north of Sussex, climb Kittatinny Ridge and turn
right into High Point State Park (the park headquarters is on
the left side of NJ 23). Follow signs to High Point Monument,
reached within 1.5 miles. Park by the rest rooms.

Special Features

- High Point Monument
- Some rocky footing and climbing
- Ridgetop forest habitat
- Look for evidence of bear and coyote

People sometimes fail to recognize how the accidents of geology shape our daily lives. New York City skyscrapers, for example, can exist only because bedrock underlies shallow soils at the central and southern parts of Manhattan Island. Likewise the rugged, erosion-resistant ridges of the Kittatinny Range at High Point have made New Jersey's northwest corner into a haven for forest mammals, rather than a home to humans.

The tough Shawangunk conglomerate that forms the backbone of the Kittatinny Ridge was born in the deposition of sand and gravel by streams 440 million years ago. These formations compressed, folded, faulted, tilted, and uplifted into mountains once as high as the Rockies. Worn down over millions of years, a new mountain-building period left a several-mile-wide range cresting at 1,803 feet above sea level at High Point.

These ridges are domain to large forest mammals and have attracted hunters for thousands of years. Native Americans tracked mastodons and caribou through boreal spruce forest just 12,000 years ago. More recently white-tailed deer were stalked and beavers trapped by Native Americans and white settlers. By the early 1900s the Kuser family had established a ridgetop estate and game park. Fences enclosed elk and reindeer herds, from which individual animals were loaned to department-store Santas at Christmastime. When the Kusers donated their mountain retreat to the state in 1923, local papers whined that the new park would serve only as "a stamping ground for wild and destructive animals."

Today High Point State Park's Monument Trail, a loop of 3.5 miles, explores the home territory of coyote, bobcat, bear, fox, deer, raccoon, porcupine, skunk, rabbit, and other mammals. Most of these animals are elusive, so you're unlikely to see

Monument Trail

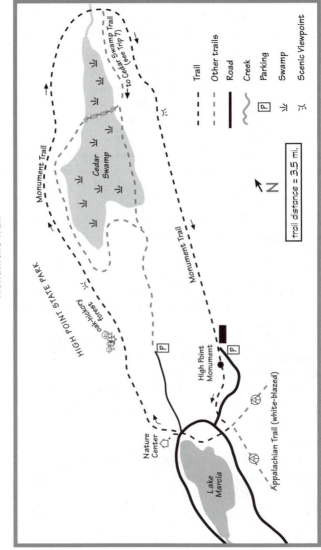

HIGH POINT STATE PARK

Cedar Swamp

to Cedar Swamp Trail (see Trip ?)

Monument Trail

Monument Trail

Monument Trail

oak-hickory forest

High Point Monument

Nature Center

Lake Marcia

Appalachian Trail (white-blazed)

N

trail distance = 3.5 mi.

Trail
Other trails
Road
Creek
Parking
Swamp
Scenic Viewpoint

them; if you know what to look for, however, signs of their presence are everywhere.

Begin hiking at the High Point Monument parking lot (to avoid crowds, go early in the day or off-season). Walk behind the rest rooms and look for the circular, red-on-top, green-on-bottom, metal markers of the Monument Trail. Follow them uphill a few hundred yards to the right of the monument. This 220-foot-tall, trim stone pinnacle resembles the Washington Monument and was built in 1930 to honor New Jersey veterans. The tower was closed for repairs as of 2003, but 360-degree views at the base are great year-round. Look east to the Great Valley of the Appalachians (locally called the Wallkill River Valley) and to the ramparts of the New Jersey Highlands on Wawayanda Mountain. Look north to the town of Port Jervis, New York, and the Catskills, west to Pennsylvania's Poconos, and south along the Kittatinny Ridge toward the Delaware Water Gap.

Blooming next to the monument at summer's end is bristly, bright blue viper's bugloss, or blueweed. At home in limestone (found only in the valleys below), this invading wildflower may have caught a ride to New Jersey's highest summit in the limestone-rich pea gravel that covers the path. More common to these dry, acidic soils are scrub oak, pitch pine, chestnut oak, knapweed, and white snakeroot, which huddle around the monument. Notice how these plants do not grow very tall, in order to withstand exposure to brutal winter winds.

The path descends past the monument (0.1 mile), where black cherry and big-tooth aspen trees grow in more protected areas and reach higher to the sky. The path descends farther past a pump house, crosses a road, goes through a rocky area, interects the white-blazed Appalachian Trail, then crosses a second road, reaching Lake Marcia (0.3 mile). This glacial pond was scraped

High Point Monument marks the highest ridgetop in New Jersey at 1,803 feet.

out by the Wisconsin Glacier more than 15,000 years ago.

The trail circles right, skirting the lake, where a black tupelo (sour gum) tree showed the scars of having been gnawed by beavers when we hiked here. Once populating every New Jersey stream, the beaver was the first fur-bearing animal to be exterminated in the state. By 1820 they were gone from the wild. Preserved on estates, however, escapees reestablished themselves around 1900. The beaver lodge on Lake Marcia was abandoned in the late 1990s, though not before the animals killed so many shade trees that water temperatures rose, causing troublesome algal blooms.

At the end of the lake, the trail ascends on a road to the park's nature center and turns right at a Monument Trail sign (0.5 mile). It enters a classic ridgetop forest where assorted oaks and pignut hickories rise above lowbush blueberry bushes and large boulders, erratics left by the ice age.

A steep descent on stone steps leads into a ravine where a bridge crosses a small stream (0.7 mile). This stonework, like the rest of this trail, was built by the Civilian Conservation Corps. In the 1930s, when Hitler's answer to global depression was to arm unemployed young men with rifles, Franklin Roosevelt's solution was to equip them with shovels. The CCC built roads, lakes, buildings, and trails throughout America's parks.

In this ravine we once tracked two coyotes on winter snow. The graceful animals left a streamlined "posthole" trail, with the track of one hind foot falling directly on top of a front one. In fact the pair perfectly followed each other, matching footsteps for a long distance, only revealing the presence of two animals when they decided to part company. Domestic dogs, with somewhat similarly shaped prints, leave a sloppy trail of overlapping tracks. Coyotes, smart animals that have outwitted relentless hunting and poisoning, leave other sign. Look for piles of hair at kill sites, or 1-inch-diameter scat composed of hair and large bone fragments. (Never touch scat with bare hands; it may contain harmful bacteria.)

The trail climbs back to a ridge dominated by oak and pitch pine (0.9 mile), offering northwest views to the graceful bends of the Delaware River at Port Jervis. Along this stretch look for pitch pines and other trees that have succumbed to driving winter winds. The dead trees are often riddled with ants, beetles, and insect larvae, which provide fine dining for woodpeckers. Flickers and downy and hairy woodpeckers drill small, shallow, roundish holes in bark, while large, prehistoric-looking pileated woodpeckers blast elongated, cavernous trenches. The pileated is often seeking hidden, vertical galleries of black carpenter ants.

The Monument Trail passes a less sweeping view west, topped by a white pine, then descends to the right, off the ridge top at 1.5 miles, into a small valley that cradles the Dryden Kuser Natural Area. This sheltered upland hosts every northern oak: red, white, chestnut, scrub, scarlet, and black oak form a popular animal habitat. Look for frequent deadfalls torn open by skunks, bears, and other mammals rooting for grubs.

At the valley's lowest point the trail crosses a little bridge (2.0 miles). A gravel road to the right leads to the Cedar Swamp Trail (see Trip 7), a fine 1.5-mile addition to this hike if you have an extra hour or two for exploring.

The Monument Trail continues straight ahead and swiftly climbs to a ridge. At the top, the trail turns right, heading south. The oak forest has now been replaced by one almost entirely of hickory. There are several great views east from steep ledges into the Great Valley of the Appalachians, and a single view west into the Cedar Swamp. The path becomes less rocky, then exits the woods at the monument parking lot.

For More Information

The Monument Trail is open from dawn to dusk year-round.

High Point State Park, 1480 State Route 23, Sussex, NJ 07461; 973-875-4800; www.state.nj.us/dep/forestry/parks/high.htm

The Ridgetop Greengrocer

The dry, winter-ravaged forests topping Kittatinny Ridge may seem like a less-than-ideal habitat, but these woods provide a cornucopia for feeding mammals.

The cones of the pitch pine sate red squirrels and chipmunks. Look for middens, heaps of cones stripped of scales right down to the core with seeds removed. Naturalist Paul Rezendes, in his book *Tracking and the Art of Seeing,* reports seeing squirrels strip cones at the remarkable rate of one every nine seconds.

Acorns, hickory nuts, and beechnuts offer a feast to bears, deer, squirrel, shrews, mice, and others. Chewed-open nuts with meat removed are easy to find lying on the ground or in hollow trees. Bears love beechnuts so much they'll climb trees for them. Older beeches sometimes display healed-over scars gouged by the animal's five razor-sharp claws.

If you're lucky, you may spot a porcupine hanging motionless high atop a tree, disguising itself as a burl. They debark hardwoods or gobble down spring maple buds.

White-tailed deer leave plentiful sign. Their beds and heart-shaped tracks are easy to find in winter. They nip and tear at twigs, leaving ragged browse marks on favorite foods such as birch, maple, hemlock, and viburnum.

Wallkill River National Wildlife Refuge and Pochuck Swamp

Trip 9

Trail: Liberty Loop Trail and Appalachian Trail
Distance: 3.5 miles
Length: 3 hours
Difficulty: Easy

Explore the "drowned lands" along the Appalachian Trail

Getting There

Take I-287 to NJ 23 north to the town of Sussex. Turn right onto County Route 284 north to Unionville. In Unionville turn right onto State Line Road (Oil City Road). Follow this for 1.4 miles over the Wallkill River bridge. In another 0.6 mile look for the Wallkill River National Wildlife Refuge Liberty Loop Trail parking lot on the right.

Special Features

- A chance to see muskrats at work
- Waterfowl and wetland plants
- Red maple swamp
- Exposed walking; not recommended on hot, sunny days

The Wallkill River meanders for 37 miles northward to the Hudson, dropping only $7^1/_2$ feet in elevation. Twelve thousand years of floods and vegetative growth along this level floodplain have resulted in deposits of rich black dirt. This walk across the "drowned lands," as early settlers called this flood-prone region, focuses on vital wetland habitats that support flora and fauna of almost overwhelming diversity.

This walk takes you from the edge of the Wallkill River, at the boundary between Sussex County, New Jersey, and Orange County, New York, to the base of Pochuck Mountain, where the Kittatinny limestone floor of the Wallkill Valley meets erosion-resistant Precambrian Highland gneiss. Two distinctive ecosystems—open, marshy floodplain and deeply shaded red maple swamp—impart a split personality to this walk. The juxtaposition offers tantalizing glimpses into the nature of different types of wetlands.

Human intervention is hastening the refuge's transformation from farm to wetland, so change is one of the few constants here. The nature of land in the refuge varies greatly from year to year, as well as season to season. No hunting is allowed in this section of the refuge, so an autumn walk will be just as pleasant and safe as a spring walk. In both seasons you'll marvel at the profusion of wildflowers.

Standing in the refuge parking lot, face Oil City Road and turn left, following the unblazed Liberty Loop Trail along the dike west toward the Wallkill River. In 0.2 mile turn left onto the white-blazed Appalachian Trail (AT). Don't trample the vegetation; poison ivy lurks everywhere. The trail continues straight ahead for the next mile.

This area was an active sod farm until the early 1990s; a network of ditches drained water from the spongelike black dirt.

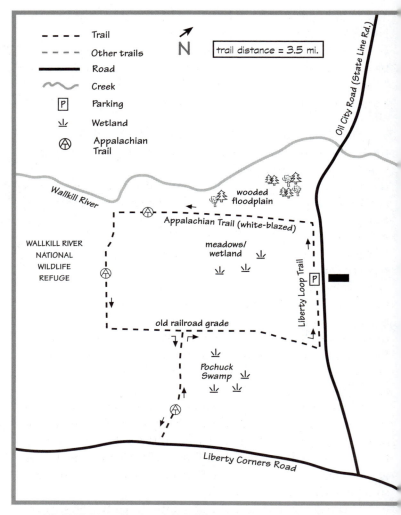

Wallkill River National Wildlife Refuge and Pochuck Swamp

Now lined with aquatic vegetation such as cattails, these water-filled ditches teem with insects and insect larvae, frogs, salamanders, painted turtles, water snakes, small fish, and muskrats. Great blue herons and snowy egrets pursue tasty morsels. Smaller birds flit among the vegetation, feeding on insects. On higher ground short-tailed shrews crisscross the meadow in shallow runways, feasting on worms, insects, and nestling mice.

All this activity attracts two dozen species of raptors. Rare visitors include golden eagles, bald eagles, and peregrine falcons. Red-tailed hawks and American kestrels hunt from on high. A marsh hawk soars just above the vegetation, following the dips and swells like a feathered ship on a sea of flowers and grasses. At dusk in winter, the short-eared owl patrols the refuge.

Prolonged rain or snowmelt floods large areas, summoning flocks of waterfowl. Canada geese, snow geese, black ducks, mallards, wood ducks, mergansers, and green-winged teals are among the twenty-one species of waterfowl that use the refuge as nesting habitat or migratory way station.

In late summer, bright yellow blooms of evening primrose contrast with purple loosestrife, tall blue lettuce, goldenrod, and chicory. Along the drainage ditches, jewelweed attracts ruby-throated hummingbirds; this flower is a significant autumn food for hummingbirds migrating south.

Purple loosestrife looks gorgeous, but this introduced plant decimates North American wetlands. In Europe insects keep it in check, but here purple loosestrife knows no limits. The seeds—hundreds per flower spike—are indigestible to birds; plus, the plant spreads by underground runners. Butterflies obtain nourishment from the nectar, but flowering plants displaced by purple loosestrife would sustain birds, insects, and butterflies.

Experimental release of a European beetle that feeds on purple loosestrife is starting to control this noxious exotic plant.

Sycamores with patchwork bark grace the riverbank. Bigtooth aspen leaves whisper in the slightest breeze; red maples and silver maples join in when the breeze intensifies. Indigo buntings dart from limb to limb. Watch for vivid blue males and woodsy brown, well-camouflaged females.

At 1.0 mile into the hike, the white-blazed AT makes a 90-degree left turn. At least one of the refuge's 125 species of songbirds is sure to provide musical accompaniment to your walk. On this stretch a walker can be overcome by unrelenting sunlight. This may be a wetland, but remember: we're not wetland creatures. Without bottled water, you might well quote Coleridge's ancient mariner: "Water, water everywhere, nor any drop to drink."

Common ragweed and great ragweed flourish here. Both have long green flower heads; each individual flower is small and inconspicuous. These flowers are wind pollinated, so they need not be attractive to animal pollinators. Ragweed's airborne pollen torments hay fever sufferers. While goldenrod is often blamed for inducing allergy attacks, its golden flowers are insect pollinated.

Where the trail parallels a drainage ditch, painted turtles sun themselves. Startled frogs squeal a high-pitched *Eep!* before plunging into the water. White blossoms of arrowhead glisten. Holes in the muddy bank mark the entrances to muskrat burrows (see the sidebar).

At 1.7 miles the trail again turns left onto an old railroad grade. On the right is the densely wooded Pochuck Swamp, while more meadow blooms on the left. Bright yellow goldfinches (the females are more olive in hue) frequent stands of thistles;

Mayapples leaf-out every spring in Pochuck Swamp.

for this bird, thistle seeds are a favorite late-summer delicacy. Virginia creeper festoons trees at the edge of the swamp and creeps out along the ground to trail's edge.

At 2.0 miles a double white turn blaze painted on a post indicates that the Appalachian Trail makes a right turn here off refuge land. Following the AT, bright sun surrenders to deep shade as the trail continues along the boardwalk through Pochuck Swamp.

Red maples block the sky in summer and carpet the swamp with scarlet leaves in autumn. The water level varies, depending upon the beavers that sometimes dam the outflow. Step carefully, because even in low water the swamp floor is soft. Watch where you put your hands as well: poison ivy's hairy-looking air roots embrace many tree trunks.

In summer, jewelweed dots the swamp orange and yellow. It is interesting to note that this plant grows in the shade here, as well as in the sun-drenched drainage ditches of the refuge. Tracks of white-tailed deer and raccoons reveal where these animals trudged through the mud.

In the swamp, sunlight caresses the ground only before the trees leaf out. Spring, therefore, is the swamp's glory. Jack-in-the-pulpits preach to congregations of purple violets, trout lilies, and bloodroot. Royal fern, with its leaflike fronds, thrives in the waterlogged soil. Sweet viburnum offers fragrant white flower clusters. In April, near the center of the swamp, clusters of low-growing marsh marigolds look like a thousand little suns come down to earth.

At 2.5 miles the Appalachian Trail rises a few feet out of the swamp to meet Lake Wallkill Road. Be careful not to tread on nodding trilliums, delicate wildflowers with flower parts in groups of three. Rose-breasted grosbeaks, cardinals, and scarlet tanagers, sometimes seen here, make it seem as if red flowers have taken wing. A lush stand of mayapples, their nodding flowers hidden under umbrella-like leaves, thrives on this moist but well-drained gentle slope.

Make your way back through the swamp the way you came. When you emerge onto open refuge land again turn right, away from the Appalachian Trail, onto the unblazed Liberty Loop Trail and an old railroad bed. In 0.5 mile turn 90 degrees left onto the dike trail that parallels Oil City Road and leads back to the parking lot.

For More Information

The Liberty Loop Trail is open from dawn to dusk year-round (no pets allowed). The AT is open twenty-four hours a day.

Wallkill River National Wildlife Refuge, 1547 County Route 565, Sussex, NJ 07461; 973-702-7266; http://wallkillriver.fws.gov

—*Jean LeBlanc*

The Secret Lives of Muskrats

The musquash (as Native Americans called this animal) can chew through vegetation underwater without drowning, thanks to incisors that protrude even when its mouth is closed. An important member of the wetland ecosystem, this glossy rodent eats cattails, sedges, water lilies, and rushes, clearing water for use by migrating waterfowl. When swimming, a muskrat uses its long naked tail as a rudder, and can even swim backward. It can stay submerged for more than fifteen minutes.

Muskrats have poor eyesight but good senses of smell and hearing. If you see one cavorting in the water, approach slowly from downwind. Though they may build small lodges out of cattails, Wallkill Refuge muskrats prefer to burrow into the black dirt (sometimes undermining a levee, to the consternation of refuge staff). Entrance holes to these extensive burrows pock the drainage ditches; it is not unusual for an entrance to be underwater. Freshly cut reeds and branches may protrude from an entrance. Muskrats also eat freshwater mussels, frogs, crayfish, and fish; their predators include raccoons and mink, which prey on the young.

—*Jean LeBlanc*

Pinwheel's Vista and Pochuck Quagmire

Wawayanda State Park

Trail: **Appalachian Trail (out-and-back)**
Distance: **2.6 miles, Pinwheel's Vista (out-and-back); optional Pochuck Quagmire, 5.6-mile add-on (out-and-back)**
Length: **3 hours to Pinwheel's Vista; 3 hours to Pochuck Quagmire**
Difficulty: **Challenging; 750-foot elevation gain**

Contemplate the mysteries of geologic time

Getting There

Take I-287 to NJ 23 north to County Route 515 north. At the Vernon, New Jersey, stoplight, go straight on NJ 94 north for 2.2 miles to the Appalachian Trail parking area on the right.

Special Features

• Oldest rock on the Appalachian Trail
• Tremendous tree diversity
• 1.3-mile climb up 400 rock steps, great views
• Extraordinary volunteer trailwork

The land we know as the New Jersey Highlands was, a billion years ago, an equatorial Himalaya-high chain of mountains towering over a lifeless landscape. Collisions between our ancestral continent and other continental plates formed these mega-highlands. Ten to 12 miles within these mountains, incredible pressure and heat melted and metamorphosed old sediments into gneiss. Magma found its way up through fissures and cooled into granite. Magnetite—iron-bearing ore—also crystallized out of these molten solutions. A few hundred million years of erosion exposed the roots of these ancient mountains. Then, about 400 million years ago, another continental collision gave birth to the Appalachians, further contorting the Highland gneiss. Subsequent continental collisions and erosion continued to sculpt the landscape.

Recent touches to this topographic sculpture were added during the last ice age. When the most recent glacier melted, about 15,000 years ago, it exposed a New Jersey Highlands scraped of topsoil. Scoured bedrock—the ancient gneiss and granite—glistened beneath a prehistoric sun. Sand, gravel, and other glacial deposits eventually supported tundra plants. Mastodons and giant sloths roamed over Wawayanda Mountain. Present-day Wallkill Valley filled with meltwater. A lobe of this lake reached into Vernon, New Jersey.

This walk begins at the former shoreline of this glacial lake, then winds to the top of the gneiss cliffs, visible from NJ 94 below. The climb of about 600 feet unveils a succession of mountainside plant communities and the animals that today call Wawayanda home.

With NJ 94 behind you, leave the parking lot on the white-blazed Appalachian Trail (AT). Backhoes and dump trucks just beyond the trail corridor denote a gravel quarry. This mountainside

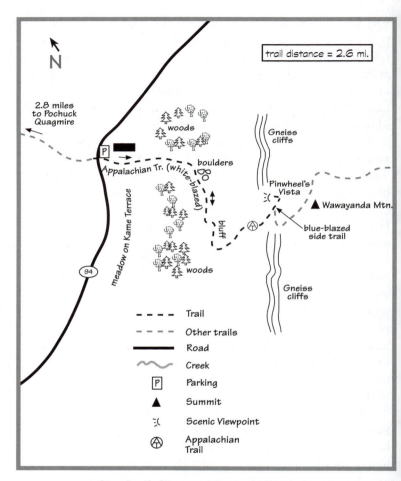

trail distance = 2.6 mi.

N

2.8 miles to Pochuck Quagmire

woods

Gneiss cliffs

P

boulders

Appalachian Tr. (white-blazed)

Pinwheel's Vista

Wawayanda Mtn.

meadow on Kame Terrace

bluff

blue-blazed side trail

94

woods

Gneiss cliffs

- - - - Trail

- - - - Other trails

———— Road

〜〜〜 Creek

P   Parking

▲   Summit

⊰   Scenic Viewpoint

Ⓐ   Appalachian Trail

Pinwheel's Vista and Pochuck Quagmire

strip of sand and gravel is a kame terrace, deposited by outwash from the Wisconsin Glacier as it melted.

In spring, male red-winged blackbirds squawk out territories. A killdeer darts through shorter grass, protecting her nest. Summer produces a show of goldenrod, chicory, aster, and bergamot.

After 0.2 mile the trail enters the woods. To the left, atop a tumbled stone wall, small shrubby trees form a thicket. The American bladdernut sports drooping clusters of white bell-shaped flowers in spring, and puffy, bladderlike fruit in autumn. The leaves, in groups of three leaflets, might be mistaken for poison ivy.

Wawayanda Mountain casts a deep shadow here. Black cherry, red maple, and sweet birch prevail, with a few hickories and oaks mixed in. Witch hazel and sassafras comprise the midstory, while maple-leaf viburnum dominates the understory. Spring wildflowers bloom early to take advantage of light streaming through leafless trees. Look for rue anemone, wild geranium, and white baneberry (better known by its "doll's eyes" autumn fruit). From late summer until the first frost, resilient wood asters thrive in the cool and shady but rich soil.

At 0.3 mile the trail winds through a crop of massive boulders. These are chunks of mountain loosened by thousands of years of frost and root action—normal mountain wear and tear. The roots of a white ash tree snake around and into one of the large boulders on the left. Grapevines form exotic-looking garlands. Moisture-loving jack-in-the-pulpits spring up, and sugar maple and hop hornbeam line the right side of the trail.

The trail begins to climb in earnest now; note the increased amount of light penetrating the forest as you near midslope. Pink-flowered herb Robert decorates the edge of the trail with lacy foliage. After two switchbacks, a small clearing on the right offers a chance to catch your breath. A red oak, its gnarled, twisted, hollow trunk pocked with old pileated woodpecker holes, grows to the left of this bluff. White pines, intolerant of dense shade, now appear on the side of the mountain, as do beech and basswood. Striped maple, a small understory tree with green-and-white bark and large leaves, loves protected but cool conditions. This species will accompany you to the top of the mountain (but not out onto the open vista).

More switchbacks bear you to the upper-slope vegetative zone most noticeably characterized by mountain laurel and chestnut oak. Thanks to the trail-building technique known as sidehilling, you're actually traversing cliffs. Vertical slabs of gneiss rise on the right, covered with leafy-looking lichens. A lichen is two organisms in one: fungus that has captured photosynthetic alga, from which it gleans nourishment even on nutrient-free rock faces. At one turn in the trail, a walker with a good eye for spring flowers might spot pink lady's slippers.

At 1.2 miles, just when you think you can't climb another rock step, the trail levels out. (All of these stone steps were carefully placed by volunteer trail builders between 1989 and 1993.) Watch for a low stone wall on the left; at a gap in the wall a 0.1-mile blue-blazed side trail leads left to the vista.

The immense rock to the right of this blue-blazed trail is not "native" to this mountain. This chunk of dolomitic limestone, light gray and crisscrossed with cracks, is a glacial erratic, dragged here by the mile-thick sheet of ice. A festive sprig of lime-loving wild columbine sprouts from this boulder in spring.

Suddenly the trail emerges onto the top of the cliff at Pinwheel's Vista. On a clear day you can see New York State's Shawangunk Mountains to the right and the Catskills behind them. Just visible on the horizon directly in front of you, High Point Monument marks New Jersey's highest elevation.

Sweet birch, red oak, and bear oak cling to these cliffs, stunted from near-constant wind and a dearth of soil and moisture. Polypody, a rock-loving fern, carpets a few spots where the feet of awestruck walkers seldom trample.

A rustling in the leaves on the sheltered side of the cliff may be a rufous-sided towhee scratching for tidbits. Or it might be a chipmunk. Or a black bear. Sun-drenched cliffs also evoke the possibility of a rattlesnake, though these creatures are rare here.

As warm air rises from the valley, turkey vultures soar. Hawks and eagles also ride the updrafts, as do monarch butterflies on their autumn migration to Mexico.

Wawayanda Mountain was bald up until the middle of this century. Trees were harvested in the 1800s to provide charcoal for iron furnaces; logging continued until the creation of Wawayanda State Park in 1963. Now more than three dozen species of trees flourish on this mountain. As you look out from the vista, try to picture the valley glistening with glacial meltwater, or a mountain rising behind you that could compete with Everest for height. As you make your way back along the blue-blazed trail, imagine meeting a mastodon. Turn right onto the white-blazed Appalachian Trail and step carefully down the gneiss steps, knowing you have participated, if only for a few hours, in the billion-year history of Wawayanda Mountain.

On returning to the parking lot, should you have the time and want to see the largest construction project ever completed by Appalachian Trail volunteers, cross NJ 94 and continue following the AT's white blazes for 2.8 miles of relatively easy, flat walking. This trip (5.6 miles out-and-back) will bring you across 4,000 feet of elevated boardwalk and the 110-foot

Pochuck Quagmire suspension bridge, spanning the former site of an ancient glacial lake. This building project—a joint effort of New York–New Jersey Trail Conference volunteers, the National Park Service, the state Department of Environmental Protection, the Appalachian Trail Conference, and several corporations including Jersey Central Power and Light—took twenty-four years and 9,000 hours of volunteer labor to complete. It was dedicated in autumn 2002.

For More Information

The Appalachian Trail is open year round at all times. For maps of the Pochuck Quagmire and other trails, contact the New York–New Jersey Trail Conference.

Wawayanda State Park, P.O. Box 198, Highland Lakes, NJ 07422; 973-853-4462; www.state.nj.us/dep/forestry/parks/waway.htm

New York–New Jersey Trail Conference, 156 Ramapo Valley Road, Mahwah, NJ 07430-1199; 201-512-9348, www.nynjtc.org

—*Jean LeBlanc*

Terrace Pond

Wawayanda State Park

Trail: **Terrace Pond Trail South, Terrace Pond Red Trail, white-blazed Shoreline Trail, Terrace Pond Trail North (loop)**
Distance: **4.0 miles**
Length: **4 hours**
Difficulty: **Challenging; 400-foot elevation gain**

A Highlands hike to a glacial pond

Getting There

Take I-80 west or I-287 north to NJ 23 north at Wayne. Follow it north of Butler, making a right at the Clinton Road exit. Trailhead parking is 7.5 miles north on Clinton Road on the left.

Special Features

- Glacially carved Terrace Pond
- Mountain laurel thickets
- Puddingstone ledges
- Rocky with some hand-over-hand climbing

About a million years ago the New Jersey Highlands suffered a catastrophe from which the area is still recovering. A world-wide climatic cooling trend caused a devastating ice wall to flow irresistibly south from Canada. The advancing glacier bull-dozed everything in its path, crushing forests, scraping away top-soil, gouging bedrock, and driving animal life before it.

Wave after wave of ice ravaged northern New Jersey. The most recent glacial epoch, called the Wisconsin Glacier, swept south 100,000 years ago, reaching its maximum expansion just 20,000 years ago. An ice mountain embedded with boulders, gravel, and grit dwarfed the state's Highlands, burying and grinding its peaks beneath a mile-thick ice sheet.

Fifteen thousand years ago a global warming trend caused the glacier to retreat, leaving a lifeless, stony wasteland in its wake. Glacial erratics dotted ice-polished ledges. Shallow glacial depressions became bogs, while deeper gouges flooded and became lakes. On Bearfort Mountain one such gouge became Terrace Pond. With the glacial retreat, the frigid, lifeless land awoke.

Twelve thousand years ago a tundra environment of lichen, moss, dwarf birch, and Arctic willow existed around the pond. Browsing mastodons and caribou may have drunk from its waters, while saber-toothed tigers, dire wolves, and Paleo Native Americans may have hunted herbivores from the crags above. The climatic warming trend eventually brought the return of boreal spruce and fir forest, then deciduous forest resembling today's woodlands.

This rugged, 4.0-mile loop takes walkers to Terrace Pond, one of the most pristine of New Jersey's glacial lakes, and provides ample evidence of the Highlands' glacial past. Cross the road from the parking lot and follow the yellow-blazed Terrace

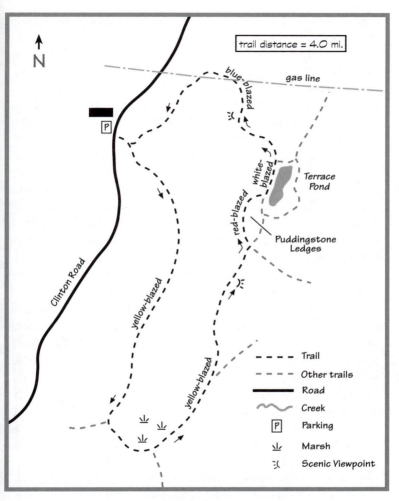

N

trail distance = 4.0 mi.

blue-blazed

gas line

white-blazed

Terrace Pond

red-blazed

Puddingstone Ledges

Clinton Road

yellow-blazed

yellow-blazed

- - - Trail
- - - Other trails
— Road
~~~ Creek
P Parking
⥌ Marsh
⊰ Scenic Viewpoint

Terrace Pond

Pond South Trail into the woods. Ignore the blue-blazed Terrace Pond North Trail as it turns left (this will be your return route).

The yellow-blazed path climbs steadily with rocky footing through a peaceful mixed oak forest. Red and white oak, chestnut oak, pignut and mockernut hickory, and eastern hemlock reach highest to form a leafy canopy. Beneath them witch hazel, shadbush, sassafras, and sweet birch fill in the middle story. The shrub layer alternates between impressive stands of mountain laurel and sweet pepperbush, while cinnamon fern, bracken fern, wintergreen, and mosses rise from leaf litter.

All of this flora testifies to glacial influences. Mountain laurel and eastern hemlock, for example, grow best in acidic, sandy, and rocky soils, an ice age legacy. The Wisconsin Glacier scraped nutrient-rich topsoil from Highlands slopes and left behind glacial till, unsorted rock, gravel, sand, silt, and clay. Over the thousands of years, plants have struggled to enrich the soils, but the process is slow.

At 0.2 mile the trail crosses a small wetland on planks and passes amid yellow birch and hemlocks. Highlands wetlands, like this one, are often glacial in origin, composed of shallow gouged depressions sometimes without inlets or outlets. Look for the large shagbark hickory at swamp's edge.

Mountain laurel dominates this hike. This evergreen, with its wildly twisted branches, shiny leaves, and rounded crown, contributes to forest beauty year-round. But the best time to see the laurel-lined Terrace Pond trail is in June. That's when the plant is covered in white and pink chalice-shaped flowers. Gently finger a single blossom and watch what happens. The stamens are spring loaded and can catapult pollen onto landing bees. Honeybees and bumblebees thrive on mountain laurel nectar and the honey they make from it, but the plant's foliage is poisonous to humans, as is the honey derived from it.

The trail passes through a rhododendron tunnel, with red maple and witch hazel rising above (0.5 mile). In autumn, witch hazel's elliptical, curly-edged leaves burst into yellow flames of color. Like the mountain laurel, this tree relies on an artillerylike mechanism for propagation. When its seedpods contract, they fire seeds up to 20 feet away. Look for small, witch-hat-shaped projections on the leaves. These are galls, tumorous growths, made by parasitic witch hazel leafgall aphids. Each hollow, cone-shaped gall holds several immature aphids. When the young insects leave the galls, they feed and live on birches for the next six generations, before a seventh generation grows wings and returns to a witch hazel to lay eggs.

The trail becomes less rocky as it passes easily along a woods road edged by a farmer's stone wall. Nineteenth-century Highlands farms were belated victims of the glacial epoch. Farmers often harvested more cobble-sized stones from their nutrient-poor fields than they did potatoes. The rocks, dropped by retreating ice, had to be hand-hauled and stacked into walls that crisscross the landscape today. When the railroads allowed access to midwestern produce, most Highlands farms failed. These particular fields have been reclaimed by black cherry, white pine, and tamarack trees. I once tracked a pair of coyotes along this stretch in winter. Terrace Pond's relative remoteness makes it an ideal place to see bear, fox, and coyote sign.

At roughly 1.5 miles and 1.7 miles, two unmarked trails cut to the right as the Terrace Pond South Trail swings sharply left and to the north. Follow the yellow blazes closely as the trail levels out and continues through a diverse forest of oak, hickory, sweet birch, beech, and red maple. Also look for Solomon's seal and the rare Indian cucumber-root blooming here in spring.

After passing over a stream (widened by beavers) on rocks next to a concrete drainpipe, follow the Terrace Pond South Trail left where the Yellow Dot Trail enters from the right. At about 2.2 miles the path gets more rugged as it climbs to a rocky crag. The vista, embossed with scrub oak and blueberry, overlooks a small pocket valley cradled between two ridges, and is an ideal place to enjoy the Highlands' windy silences.

At 2.3 miles the yellow Terrace Pond South Trail crosses the Terrace Pond Red Trail. Go left on the red trail. This is the most strenuous part of the hike, as the trail humps along a series of cliffs. Great gullies, rock faces, glacial erratics, and shattered boulders attest to the power of the ice age. This strikingly beautiful rock is called puddingstone, a coarse, violet-hued sandstone conglomerate speckled with a kaleidoscopic array of white quartz and other pebbles. These redbeds were laid down more than 350 million years ago by fast-flowing streams depositing mud, sand, and abrasion-rounded gravel into an ancient inland sea. Puddingstone is named for a thick concoction made by colonial cooks. The rocky terrain's range of color is broadened by pitch pine, white pine, and blueberry bushes (turning scarlet in autumn). Mosses and rock tripe add still other subtle green hues.

A little hand-over-hand climbing and descending brings a first glimpse of Terrace Pond. A further rocky descent takes you to the shore at 2.6 miles, where the red trail ends. Turn left on a white-blazed trail that follows the shoreline.

The roughly rectangular pond is boxed in by high, elephant-skin-textured cliffs that show evidence of glacial gouging and polishing. Glacial ice excavated this pretty, reflective gem. The water itself is covered in lily pads for most of summer and fall. Sweet pepperbush lines the shore, as do mountain laurel, sassafras, scrub oak, pitch pine, and white pine. There are plenty of places to stop for lunch. Enjoy the views, but don't swim: patrolling rangers will ticket you.

At the pond's far end turn left onto the blue-blazed Terrace Pond North Trail, leaving the white trail. This rugged path repeatedly rises over stony ledges then descends and crosses small wet areas on bog bridging. At 3.2 miles a puddingstone cliff shoots up into the sky like the prow of a sinking ship. From this vantage point, the most far-reaching vista of the day, High Point Monument, the Catskills, and the Shawangunk Mountains are visible to the west and north.

The blue trail crosses a second and third rocky outcrop, providing another workout, this time without good views. It descends through more puddingstone slots and chutes, reaching and briefly following a gas pipeline very steeply downhill. Look for the clearly marked blue trail as it leads left from the pipeline back into the woods. An easy descent through sugar maple, witch hazel, white pine, and hemlock leads back to Clinton Road and the parking lot.

For More Information

The trails to Terrace Pond are open dawn to dusk, year-round. For maps of the NJ Highlands, contact the New York–New Jersey Trail Conference.

Wawayanda State Park, P.O. Box 198, Highland Lakes, NJ 07422; 973-853-4462; www.state.nj.us/dep/forestry/parks/waway.htm

New York–New Jersey Trail Conference, 156 Ramapo Valley Road, Mahwah, NJ 07430-1199; 201-512-9348; www.nynjtc.org

Trip 12

Bearfort Ridge Fire Tower
Newark Watershed

Trail: Highlands Trail (out-and-back)
Distance: 3.6 miles
Length: 4 hours
Difficulty: Moderate; 400-foot elevation gain

A bird's-eye view of Highlands geology

Getting There

Take I-80 west or I-287 north to NJ 23 north. Follow it through Butler. Turn right at the Union Valley Road exit. In 3.3 miles turn right onto Gould Road. The pull-off is 0.3 mile ahead on the left (north) side.

Special Features

- Historic fire tower
- Sweeping Highlands views
- Puddingstone ridges
- A Newark Watershed Conservation and Development Corporation permit is needed to hike here

Billion-year-old stone forms the backbone of most of the New Jersey Highlands. Forged deep within the earth, this rock extends in a series of parallel, erosion-resistant ridges, 800 to 1,400 feet high and running roughly southwest to northeast from the Delaware River to the Hudson River.

Highlands geology displays complex, violent change. The story begins in Precambrian times when coastal sediments were plunged 10 to 20 miles underground and transformed through intense heat and pressure into metamorphic gneisses and igneous granites. Four hundred million years of melting and cooling caused the mingling of these streaked and layered stones.

This durable Precambrian rock eventually resurfaced as it pinballed off landmasses in catastrophic continental collisions. The billion-year-old stone was folded, twisted, broken, and forced up into jagged peaks that may have rivaled the Rockies. Further continental collision, rifts, uplifts, and erosion left only the bare roots of the once great mountains. Finally, a million years of on-again, off-again glaciation gave the Highlands a superficial face-lift, gouging, scraping, and smoothing the area into the low ridges we see today.

These tough ridges also resist human habitation. Only a few mountain passes gave Native Americans and pioneers access to narrow valleys. Today geographic lines have been drawn: people, homes, and roads (such as NJ 23 and Union Valley Road) generally occupy the valleys, while deer, bears, raptors, and songbirds mostly occupy upland forests.

This rugged, 3.6-mile out-and-back hike follows a short section of the Highlands Trail to a state fire tower with sweeping views. The Highlands Trail is a joint project of the New Jersey Conservation Foundation, New York–New Jersey Trail Conference, and state and federal partners. When complete,

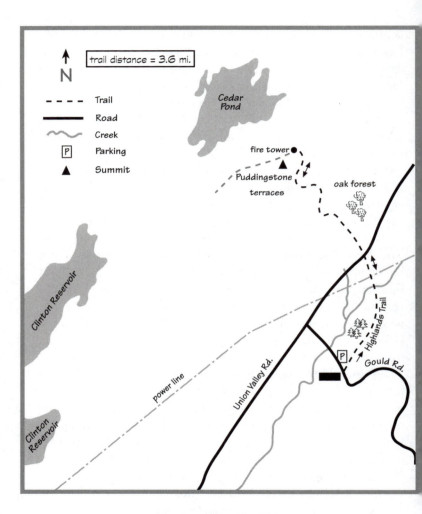

Bearfort Ridge Fire Tower

the 150-mile path will traverse the Highlands from the Delaware River to the Hudson River. The trail section described here is on Newark Watershed land and requires an inexpensive use permit (call 973-697-2850 for information).

Begin at a small pull-off on the north side of Gould Road. Without crossing the road, walk north into a woods of black cherry and eastern hemlock, following the turquoise diamond-shaped blazes of the Highlands Trail.

The first 0.8 mile is an easy valley hike, crossing glacial till (unsorted gravel and sand left behind by melting ice) underlain by softer, erosion-prone Paleozoic sandstone, shale, and limestone. Sugar maple and white pine grow tall in almost pure stands. These are interspersed with beech, red maple, and white oak trees. The pines, all of uniform size, were planted by the Civilian Conservation Corps in the 1930s as part of Franklin Roosevelt's New Deal.

White pine is easily recognized. It's the only eastern pine with five long, soft needles in each bundle. The tree is a mini-ecosystem, supporting eighty species of insects. Its strong, straight limbs are favorite nest sites for sharp-shinned hawks or "sharpies," able to swoop and snatch up finches and other in-flight prey amid the thick forest canopy. Pine grosbeaks and many warblers (common victims of sharpies) also nest in the trees and feed on seeds at the heart of pinecones. Mice, chipmunks, and red squirrels share the pine seed feast. Raccoons often climb white pines for daytime naps (look for territory-marking scat at tree bases).

Not much grows on the forest floor amid the acidic pine needle litter, though sugar maple and sassafras saplings have taken hold, as have partridgeberry and ground pine. Ground pine, a club moss, is a primitive plant originating 300 million

An eastern white pine thrives atop a pudding-stone ledge.

years ago. Ancient club mosses grew into trees, formed jungles, and, along with giant ferns, were compressed into coal deposits. In the 1800s tiny club moss spores were dried, placed in pans, and ignited to make the first flash photography.

As the white pines thin out, they're replaced by maturing sugar maples. Watch blazes closely: at 0.6 mile the Highlands Trail falls into a small dip, cuts sharply right, then climbs out of the dip. The trail also crosses beneath a power line where light-loving black cherry, quaking aspen, and arrowwood grow.

At 0.8 mile the path crosses Union Valley Road. There's parking for five or six cars here, but a watershed permit is needed (call 973-697-2850 for information).

Beyond the road, the trail begins to rise. Note how flora changes as slope increases, while soil thickness and soil moisture decrease. Sugar maple and white pine quickly give way to scarlet and white oak. The white oak, with its easily recognized round-lobed leaves, is another forest smorgasbord. Its acorns are a preferred food of squirrels, bears, chipmunks, and mice. Once sprouted, white oak acorns become hard to digest, so squirrels eat them as they fall, as fast food, rather than storing them up.

All manner of birds feed on acorns, including grouse, woodpecker, and turkey.

The trail heads straight in from the road, jogs right at about 1.0 mile, then climbs sharply. Chestnut oak, red oak, and sweet birch—dominant trees of Highlands ridges—replace white oak as the trail rises. Look for oak-apple galls on red oaks. These inch-round, golf-ball-like growths are made by insects that inject twigs with an irritant, causing the brown, tumorlike gall to grow. The insects lay their eggs inside the galls. Oaks support 800 species of gall-making insects, most of them small wasps.

The path gets considerably rockier and steeper, passing over stony outcrops. Mockernut and pignut hickories join the forest mix. These deep-rooted trees do well on windy ridges. Their nuts are favorites of wood ducks, foxes, and squirrels. Look for large rocks near the bases of hickories, their tops speckled with broken shell husks. The rocks serve as raised dining tables, giving gray squirrels safe, elevated observation platforms from which to savor nutmeats.

The Highlands Trail ascends a series of ledges, zigzagging south and north for brief distances along grassy terraces and sometimes descending into shallow ravines filled with mountain laurel. Each terrace supports scrub oak and blueberry bushes, rock tripe, and the intertwined "antlers" of reindeer lichen. Low-growing scrub oak is also called bear oak, since only black bears find the bitter acorns palatable.

Each ledge offers better views east across Union Valley to Kanouse Mountain. Watch blazes closely; the turquoise diamonds blend in well with forest shadows. Ignore intersections with other trails. Keep climbing.

Each rock terrace is partially composed of a Highlands oddity called puddingstone. This violet-hued sandstone conglomerate (the color is created by the rock's high iron content) is much younger than most of the Precambrian Highlands. Puddingstone, shot through with creamy white quartz, is all that remains of a long, narrow inland sea or sound into which pebbles and sand were deposited by fast-moving rivers more than 350 million years ago.

The trail flows north, cutting diagonally across a final rock shelf, as the Bearfort Ridge Firetower comes into view between the trees. A rock scramble over puddingstone puts you on the ridge's grassy open summit (1.8 miles).

A climb up the tower gives stunning views over the heart of the Highlands and displays the many humps of southwest-to-northeast-running ridges. The tops of New York City skyscrapers gleam above the Ramapo Mountains to the southeast. Cedar Pond lies just to the west, Clinton Reservoir to the south. Also to the south is deeply etched Berkshire Valley. High Point on Kittatinny Ridge is visible to the northwest, and New York's Catskill Mountains rise to the northwest. New York's Bear Mountain–Harriman State Park lies to the east.

As shadows lengthen at day's end, the true ruggedness of this country is revealed. In winter, too, a loss of foliage exposes extreme topography. Only to the southeast do the mountains relent and fade into the flatness of New Jersey's Piedmont. Scanning the lay of the land, it's easy to see how George Washington's Continental army could move freely among the Highlands, safe from attack by the British encamped in the lowlands. Without the natural fortress of the Highlands, the American cause may have been lost.

Picnic tables atop Bearfort Ridge make a perfect lunch spot. When you're through enjoying the view, return the way you came.

For More Information

An inexpensive permit is needed from the Newark Watershed Conservation and Development Corporation to hike the Highlands Trail on Bearfort Mountain. Those without a permit will have illegally parked cars ticketed. To volunteer to help build the Highlands Trail, contact the New York–New Jersey Trail Conference.

Newark Watershed Conservation and Development Corporation, 223 Echo Lake Road, Newfoundland, NJ 07435; 973-697-2850

New York–New Jersey Trail Conference, 156 Ramapo Valley Road, Mahwah, NJ 07430-1199; 201-512-9348; www.nynjtc.org

Long Pond Ironworks State Park

Trip 13

Trail: **Highlands Trail (out-and-back)**
Distance: **3.0 miles**
Length: **3 hours**
Difficulty: **Moderate; 200-foot elevation gain**

Hike back through history to the time of the fiery furnace

Getting There

Take I-287 north or south to Exit 57. Follow signs to Skyline Drive. Take Skyline Drive to its end at a T on the east shore of Wanaque Reservoir. At the T turn right onto County Route 511 north (Greenwood Lake Turnpike), following it for 5.2 miles to a large white Long Pond Ironworks Historical District sign and parking lot on the right.

Special Features

• Ruined iron furnaces and restored waterwheel
• Abandoned villages of Hewitt and Long Pond
• Monksville Reservoir
• Patterson iron mine

Iron transformed colonial America. It provided axes and plows with which pioneers subdued the wilderness. It also provided muskets and shot with which they subjugated the Native population and overthrew the British Crown. Iron transfigured the New Jersey Highlands as well. It made ironmasters wealthy while impoverishing the landscape.

Native Americans had long noted black-streaked Highlands stone, but attributed no significance to it. They freely led whites to exposed black rock. Prospectors, hoping to find gold, had to be satisfied with magnetite. By the 1740s the first New Jersey iron mines and furnace were established at Ringwood. The industry quickly spread across the rugged hills as more speculators joined the game.

By 1776 the Highlands were everywhere blasted and tunneled for ore and stripped of forest to fuel hungry furnaces. Smelting fires burned day and night, spewing plumes of acrid smoke. Wagons hauled ore and charcoal out of the hills and moved pig iron to market. Towns sprang up.

Today casual visitors to the Long Pond Ironworks find an idyllic setting, where nineteenth-century homes and furnace ruins are framed by sycamores and sugar maples. In truth, this was the town of Hewitt, an industrial site that, in its day, was a Little Pittsburgh, a gritty industrial complex that converted Highlands ore into a livelihood for hundreds of people.

This 3.0-mile out-and-back hike takes walkers to the heart of the Long Pond Ironworks Historic District, along a mine road and to a mine. It offers a chance to visualize the once mighty, and now nearly forgotten, industry that helped turn the United States into a world power.

Begin at the Long Pond Ironworks Historical District parking lot. The nineteenth-century general store at the edge of the

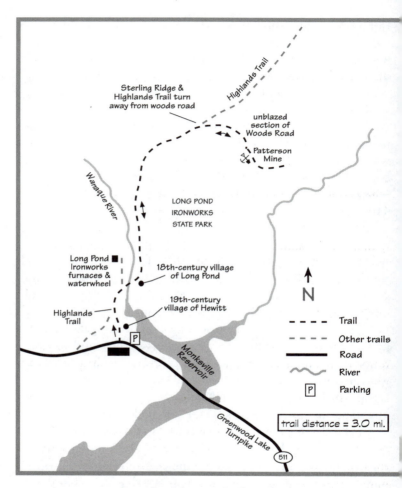

Long Pond Ironworks State Park

parking lot is also the Long Pond Ironworks Museum, open to the public Saturday and Sunday between 1 and 4 P.M., March through November. Face the store/museum and walk around to the left side of the building. Walk parallel to Greenwood Lake Turnpike and away from the store, following a wide grassy path. Pass around a gate and follow a gravel road past the Ward-Ryerson Patterson House (circa 1780), Harty House, and Whritenour House (circa 1800s), not open to the public. Only the Harty House was originally part of the village of Hewitt. The other homes were relocated here in 1986 to save them from the rising waters of the Monksville Reservoir.

The buildings are surrounded by a mix of native and ornamental plants, typical of old town sites. Sugar maples, elms, forsythia, and Asiatic bittersweet thrive. In autumn, the viny tendrils of bittersweet put on a colorful show as capsules burst open to reveal flaming orange berrylike fruit. These fleshy seeds survive into winter, a food for birds that spread the plant.

The road enters the woods. To the left stands the nineteenth-century Double Stone House. A huge sycamore and tamarack grow in the yard. Legend says that sycamores love iron-rich soils. While there's no scientific proof to support the claim, archaeologists often find sycamores topping iron-furnace ruins.

To the right are views of the drowned trees of Monksville Reservoir. In the 1980s, before this valley was flooded, archaeologist Ed Lenik discovered eighteen prehistoric Native American campsites dating from 4000 B.C. to A.D. 1680. He unearthed projectile points, knives, scrapers, and pottery fragments. Today mallard ducks and belted kingfishers scout the reservoir for food.

Five minutes into the walk, the road crosses Longhouse Creek on a bridge then intersects a nexus of roads, once the center of the nineteenth-century village of Hewitt. The blue-dot-on-white Sterling Ridge Trail enters from the left and exits right. This trail is co-aligned with the Highlands Trail (marked by turquoise diamonds). The Highlands Trail will one day stretch 150 miles from the Hudson to the Delaware River. Follow the Sterling Ridge and Highlands Trail to the right.

The trail quickly passes another arm of the reservoir, then crosses the Wanaque River on a bridge. Before crossing the bridge, walk straight ahead a few hundred feet to see the ruins of the Long Pond furnace complex.

The first of three furnaces, a stone jumble surrounded by troughs of water, is the oldest. Built by Peter Hasenclever in 1766, it produced 25 tons of iron per week, some made into equipment for the Continental army. The ruins remained hidden until 1963, when archaeologist Roland Robbins dug beneath a sycamore tree and through a rubble pile to uncover them. Today yellow-flowered jewelweed, purple-berried poke-weed, and the brown nutlets of bur reed lend late-summer color to massive stone blocks.

A second furnace stands just beyond the first. It also profited from warfare. Built in 1862 by Peter Cooper and Abram S. Hewitt, it was a response to the Union army's need for iron during the Civil War. A third, tumble-down furnace stands beyond this one.

The Long Pond furnaces once burned continuously. Wagon-loads of ore, charcoal fuel, and limestone flux (to help molten iron flow) were dumped into the egg-shaped stone chambers from above. Immense bellows, powered by waterwheels, super-heated the fiery mixture. Heat in excess of 2,800 degrees Fahrenheit melted the ore, allowing heavier iron to settle to the bottom where it flowed into sand troughs.

This graceful stone arch is all that remains of the 1862 furnace at Long Pond Ironworks. The iron processed here contributed to the Union victory in the Civil War.

The blast furnaces deafened; they were as loud as a rocket at liftoff. This roar was punctuated by the relentless bang of great hammers at a nearby forge. Columns of fire and smoke rose from the site and could be seen for miles. A film of soot settled on the town and its people. Fatal burns were a hazard, as was lung disease. Long Pond, like most ironworks, was hell on earth.

Walk a few feet farther ahead to a makeshift shed, where two 25-foot-diameter waterwheels are protected. While both wheels were burned by vandals in 1954, painstaking measurements taken by historians Ron Dupont and George Sellmar (members of Friends of Long Pond Ironworks) allowed one of these marvelous structures (made of red and white pine) to be restored.

Retrace your steps to where you left the Highlands Trail and follow it over the Wanaque River on a footbridge. You are now walking a road once used to haul charcoal and ore to the furnaces. It passes through a shaded forest of hickory and maple. The ground, covered in a tangle of bittersweet and grapevines, appears unnaturally lumpy. Beneath leaf litter, humus, and slag lie the buried remains of the eighteenth-century village of Long Pond.

The sunken road rises steadily through a grove of eastern hemlocks. As you climb, look for a small rocky ledge to the left, a sunny lunch spot overlooking the Wanaque River far below.

About a mile into the hike, the hemlocks give way to hardwoods. Beeches, sweet birches, hickories, and oaks overlook a forest floor dotted with Christmas fern. Try to spot a hard-to-see, flat, grassy 30-foot circle to the right. This is the site of a charcoal mound. Charcoal was vital to the iron industry, and its production deforested the nineteenth-century Highlands. A typical furnace burned the charcoal equivalent of an acre of trees each day. Soot-covered, reclusive charcoal makers were often shunned as crazies by polite society. They spent months tending smoldering charcoal mounds in the mountains. Each mound was built of wood lengths stacked in a cone and covered with earth. You'll know you've found the mound site if you see tiny pieces of charcoal still hidden in the grass.

At 1.3 miles the Sterling Ridge and Highlands Trails turn sharply left, leaving the woods road on a narrow path. Continue straight ahead on the unblazed woods road 0.2 mile farther and look for rust-colored ore piles to the right. These fist-sized stones mark the Patterson Mine, dug around 1870 and abandoned in 1903. Explore to the right off the trail for two vertical, water-flooded mine pits. Be careful; stay away from the edge of unstable shafts. Mines were dug with pickax and explosives, and were often several hundred feet deep. Life underground was dangerous. Falling rock, dust-choked air, slippery footing, and premature blasts were daily hazards.

When you've finished exploring, return the way you came. As you go, consider this lost way of life. With the 1890s discovery of the ore fields of Minnesota's Mesabi Range, Highlands mining died. In the past hundred years, the forest has slowly reclaimed the scarred landscape left by the excesses of New Jersey's iron miners.

For More Information

The Sterling Ridge and Highlands Trails are open dawn to dusk year-round. Please leave ore and other artifacts where you found them. For Highlands trail maps, contact the New York–New Jersey Trail Conference.

Ringwood State Park, 1304 Sloatsburg Road, Ringwood, NJ 07456; 973-962-7031; www.state.nj.us/dep/forestry/parks/ringwod.htm

Friends of Long Pond Ironworks, P.O. Box 809, Hewitt, NJ 07421; 973-657-1688; www.LongPondIronworks.org/

New York–New Jersey Trail Conference, 156 Ramapo Valley Road, Mahwah, NJ 07430-1199; 201-512-9348; www.nynjtc.org

New Jersey State Botanical Gardens at Skylands

Trail: Various garden paths (loop), Halifax Trail (out-and-back)
Distance: 1.0 mile; optional 0.7-mile Halifax Trail
Length: 3 hours
Difficulty: Easy, flat gardens; moderate, side trail

A feast for the eyes; a boost for the spirit

Getting There

Take I-287 north or south to Exit 57. Follow signs to Skyline Drive. Take Skyline Drive to its end at a T on the east shore of Wanaque Reservoir. Turn right onto County Route 511 north (Greenwood Lake Turnpike). In 1.6 miles make the second right onto Sloatsburg Road. In 2.1 miles turn right onto Morris Road and follow signs for 1.5 miles to Skylands.

Special Features

- Trees from around the world
- Native wildflower garden
- Opulent manor house
- Short walk to Highlands Vista

Nestled amid the Ramapo Mountains, forested with oak and hickory, stately Skylands Manor was no ordinary summer escape for investment banker Clarence McKenzie Lewis (1877–1959). Beginning with his purchase of the land in 1922, Lewis began to bring a dream to life. As a trustee of the New York Botanical Garden, Lewis's dream was of a garden and arboretum of his own—one that would serve not only as a showplace but also as a living laboratory to research plants from all over the world.

In 1966, after Lewis's death—and the subsequent neglect of the gardens—the state of New Jersey purchased the land and set about restoring Skylands. In 1984 Skylands was designated the New Jersey State Botanical Gardens. Extensive restoration continued, and intensive activity continues to this day to maintain the gardens and grounds. Also maintained is the multifaceted philosophy of a botanical garden's various roles: aesthetics, public education and recreation, botanical research, conservation, and community pride.

Begin in the Winter Garden, across the road from the gatehouse and visitor center, on the front left lawn of the manor house. This collection of trees, mostly evergreens, was created with an eye to form, texture, and color. Many of the trees around the manor house—as well as the house itself—date from Lewis' time. Massive limbs of a European weeping beech sweep majestically over the lawn. Except for this tree, which is fenced off due to human beings' unfortunate inclination to etch smooth beech bark, you can use your sense of touch to further enhance your arboreal admiration. The needles of the Japanese umbrella pine, for instance, look prickly, but feel smooth as silk.

Every imaginable shade of green, and even some subtle blues and golds, can be discovered in the foliage of the Winter Garden. You'll feel you're touring the world as you encounter a

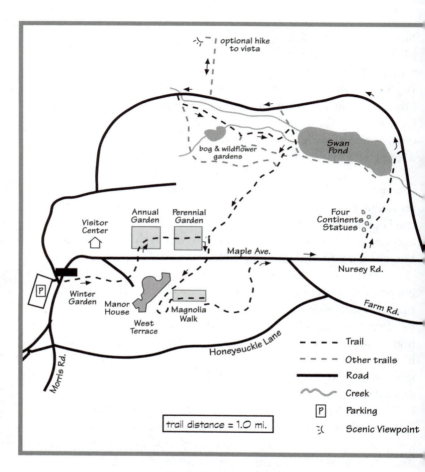

optional hike
to vista

bog & wildflower
gardens

Swan
Pond

Annual
Garden

Perennial
Garden

Four
Continents
Statues

Visitor
Center

Maple Ave.

Nursey Rd.

Winter
Garden

Manor
House

Magnolia
Walk

Farm Rd.

West
Terrace

Honeysuckle Lane

Morris Rd.

- - - - Trail

- - - - Other trails

——— Road

〜〜 Creek

P   Parking

⅄   Scenic Viewpoint

trail distance = 1.0 mi.

New Jersey State Botanical Gardens at Skylands

Japanese cedar, a blue Atlas cedar from the Atlas Mountains of
northern Africa, a Dawyck beech from Scotland, lace-bark pine

and ponderosa dragon spruce from China, and Lawson false cypress and Jeffrey pine from Oregon and California.

After wandering amid the trees of the world, cross Maple Avenue to the right of the visitor center and enter the Annual Garden, where a colorful assortment of unusual and familiar plants bloom from June until the first Highlands frost.

Large white ash trees mark the passage from Annual Garden to Perennial Garden. As if the varieties of floral form and color weren't enough, these flowers also attract ruby-throated hummingbirds, honeybees and bumblebees (see the sidebar), and a rainbow of butterflies. The fruity-lilac-scented butterfly bushes are visited by monarchs, black and tiger swallowtails, and great-spangled fritillaries, to name just a few. A graceful European white birch marks the end of the Perennial Garden. Rows of holes in this and other trees confirm the seasonal presence of yellow-bellied sapsuckers.

Cross Maple Avenue toward the right of the manor house. Interrupted fern, cinnamon fern, royal fern, sensitive fern, maidenhair fern, ostrich fern—these and other shade-loving plants thrive beneath more magnificent trees. Stepping out of this shady area onto the West Terrace provides a sweeping view of the crystalline lakes and verdant hills of the New Jersey Highlands.

From the manor, follow the center walkway through the Magnolia Walk and Azalea Garden. A fountain pool reflects the sky amid cream-, ruby-, and sapphire-hued water lilies. The breathtaking beauty of this area attests not only to the art of landscape gardening, but also to the dedication of volunteers who strive to restore and maintain the grounds of Skylands Manor.

Walk back toward Maple Avenue away from the manor house toward the tree-lined lane. Take a close look at the tall, narrow trees that create this living impressionist landscape.

They are not poplars or cedars, as you might expect, but a columnar form of sugar maple called sentry maples.

Cross the lawn toward the statues known as the *Four Continents*, which are located at the far end of the Crab Apple Vista. Pass through the wooded area behind the statues; here, horse chestnut, black walnut, white pine, tulip tree, and sweet gum intermingle. You can't help but notice that the landscape is becoming less formal. With the *Four Continents* behind you, head left toward Swan Pond. After admiring impressive flowers and trees, it is a challenge to see well-camouflaged turtles sunning themselves on rocks.

From the pond, follow the path out toward Swan Pond Road. Rhododendron, beech, hickory, and sensitive fern grow here, as do sugar maple, white ash, and slippery elm saplings—all the diversity a northeastern mixed forest has to offer. Remember, you are no longer in a well-tended garden; watch out for poison ivy and mountain bikes.

If you feel like venturing into even wilder territory, turn right onto the green-blazed Halifax Trail about 0.25 mile along Swan Pond Road. This switchbacking trail climbs steeply through a deciduous forest of oak, ash, maple, American chestnut saplings, sweet birch, and sassafras. As you ascend, large red oaks and tulip trees shade the way. Farther up the ridge, chestnut oak becomes more abundant. Violets line this walk in spring. In late summer, a patch of woodland sunflowers brightens the trail with yellow blooms. After about 0.25 mile watch for an unmarked left-hand turn; follow this path for about 100 feet to a rocky vista (if your walk on the green-blazed trail brings you to an intersection with a red-blazed trail, you've gone too far). From this vista, you can see the sentry maples on the manor grounds below. Cupsaw Lake gleams like a diamond amid the rolling Ramapos. As you rest under the chestnut oaks, you may catch a glimpse of a pileated woodpecker. Make your way back down to Swan Pond Road, bearing right.

About 0.3 mile from Swan Pond, the path to the Bog Garden turns left off the road. Bear left as the path splits. Wildflowers of all shapes and sizes abound, from sky-blue forget-me-nots to mauve joe-pye weed, which may reach a height of 8 feet. Follow any of the paths to the left to the shady Wildflower Garden. After the formal gardens, cardinal flowers and blue lobelias will seem exotic, though these wildflowers are native to New Jersey.

Make your way back to the visitor center, stopping to explore the meadow, heather garden, or rhododendron garden along the way. Every turn of the path promises a new delight.

For More Information

Skylands is open 8 A.M. to 8 P.M. year-round. It is free on weekdays; a $4-per-vehicle fee is charged on weekends from Memorial Day through Labor Day. New garden volunteers are welcome.

Skylands Association, P.O. Box 302, Ringwood NJ 07456; 973-962-7527; www.njskylandsgarden.org/

—Jean LeBlanc

The Buzz on Bees

The bees you see gathering nectar are all females. Adult worker honeybees live approximately nine weeks, working in the hive first as nursemaids to the larvae, then as hive keepers (secreting wax for the honeycomb) and guards, and finally, for the last five or six weeks of their adult lives, as foragers. Worker bees that locate a rich source of nectar return to the hive and tell the other workers, through a sort of interpretive dance, the location of the nectar source. A worker scouting locations for a new hive performs a similar dance.

Don't be afraid to observe bees. A honeybee stings only as a last resort, when she is under attack (just imagine what flailing arms look like from a bee's point of view). A bee can only sting once; when she does, her stinger is pulled from her abdomen, killing her in the process. Stay calm, even if a bee should land on you. She'll soon realize that your perfume or shampoo scent is not associated with a food source. As social as these insects are, it is not our society that interests them.

The vast numbers of bees you might see amid the flowers at Skylands make it obvious that bees are the most important of pollinating animals. Many species of flowers and bees have co-evolved, each dependent upon the other for finding a successful ecological niche. Without bees, the world would be a lot less colorful.

—Jean LeBlanc

Wyanokie High Point
Norvin Green State Forest

Trail: Mine Trail, Wyanokie Circular Trail, Hewitt-Butler Trail (loop)
Distance: 3.1 miles
Length: 3 hours
Difficulty: Moderate; 500-foot elevation gain

A heritage of trail building and a New York City panorama

Getting There

Take I-287 north or south to Exit 57. Follow signs to Skyline Drive. Take Skyline Drive to its end, then turn left onto County Route 511. Make the first major right on West Brook Road, crossing the Wanaque Reservoir on a viaduct. Bear left at an intersection with Stonetown Road and, in another 0.5 mile, turn left onto Snake Den Road. Follow Snake Den Road signs to the Weis Ecology Center parking lot.

Special Features
- Roomy Mine, Blue Mine
- Wyanokie Falls
- Highlands forest
- View of Manhattan

For those who love hiking, it's easy to imagine that the Garden State's many trails are ancient. Perhaps, we dream, they were old Indian paths or the trails over which the first settlers moved. In fact, their origins are often far more recent.

By 1910 the New Jersey Highlands had attracted a New York City populace grown weary of electric lights, the stench of horse dung, and the roar of the first automobiles. Those far hills beckoned with the romantic illusion of an earlier, simpler, slower time. And so it was that a small rucksack army began fleeing the city on weekends, taking to the mountains in search of adventure.

At first trampers moved west by ferry and train, later by car. But always they struck out on foot into a rural territory only recently returned to woodland. By the early 1900s railroads had bypassed New Jersey's less productive mountain farms and industries. Trampers bushwhacked over newly forested farm fields and hiked to abandoned iron mines and furnaces, to waterfalls and craggy vistas. These wild rambles refreshed tired urban spirits.

Tramping clubs organized and blazed formal trails to favorite spots. In 1912 the New York Chapter of the Appalachian Mountain Club laid claim to the Wyanokie Highlands, a jumble of small peaks 25 miles northwest of Manhattan. Today the Wyanokies boast one of the most concentrated trail systems in the state, protected within Norvin Green State Forest.

This 3.1-mile circuit hike samples three Wyanokie Highlands trails and features a waterfall, two iron mines, and a sweeping view of the Manhattan skyline. As you walk, consider that all these paths (like most in this book) were not built with government labor. They were constructed and are maintained by volunteers.

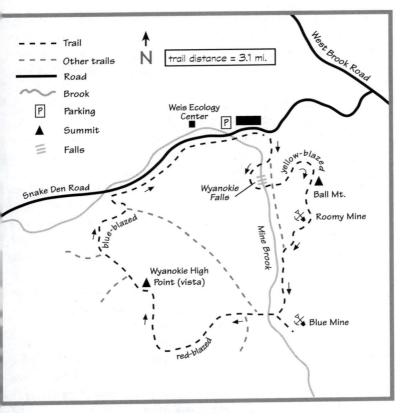

Wyanokie High Point

Standing in the Weis Ecology Center hiker parking area, face Snake Den Road and turn left. Take the road 150 yards, then turn right into the woods, following the yellow blazes of the Mine Trail and red blazes of the Wyanokie Circular Trail. The path skirts several residential backyards, then enters a small spruce and hemlock forest. Low stone walls reveal this area to have been a farmer's field. In the nineteenth century the New Jersey Highlands resembled Scotland, denuded of forest, covered with field and pasture, and broken by stone walls. Only in the past hundred years have forests reclaimed the land.

The trail emerges into a deciduous forest of sugar maple, red oak, and eastern hop hornbeam. The hop hornbeam, with its skinny, vertical strips of scaly bark, is named for fruit clusters resembling hops, a beer ingredient. Also called ironwood, the tree's nearly indestructible wood was once shaped into sled runners and wagon parts. Metal has since replaced hop hornbeam.

At 0.2 mile turn sharply right, following the yellow Mine Trail as it diverges from the red trail. The path swiftly ascends, descends, and crosses Mine Brook. The trail loops back on itself and recrosses the brook at Wyanokie Falls (0.5 mile). This falls sometimes goes dry, but in springtime tumbles in a sparkling cascade over jumbled boulders. It is overhung by an American basswood. This tree's June flowers attract bees that make a minty, gourmet-quality honey from the nectar.

The yellow Mine Trail descends and crosses the red Wyanokie Circular Trail, then steeply climbs Ball Mountain (named for round glacial erratics left behind by the retreating Wisconsin ice sheet). Ascending through sweet birch and chestnut oak, the trail arrives at a vista (0.8 mile) that looks west to Wyanokie High Point. Rock slabs are framed in low-bush blueberry and striped wintergreen. Watch blazes closely: just beyond a second vista the trail turns right and descends, while an unmarked woods road goes straight ahead.

The yellow trail descends steeply to the Roomy Mine (1.1 miles). This abandoned iron mine is dug in solid rock, is stable, and is entered by many hikers (though a hard hat and flashlight are recommended). If you choose to go in, avoid the upper entrance. Crawl in through the lower tunnel. Inside, a 25-foot chamber opens to the sky and to a 50-foot-long shaft. Look for drill marks where black powder charges were set. Dug in 1840, the Roomy Mine produced iron until 1857. Today the cool tunnel is home to bats. Place a compass on the tailings pile outside; they're so iron rich that they skew the needle (a prospecting technique once used to locate ore deposits).

In a short distance the yellow Mine Trail turns left as it rejoins the red Wyanokie Circular Trail on a gently descending woods road. At 1.5 miles the blazed trails both turn sharply right, crossing Mine Brook on a bridge. Before crossing the water, detour 100 yards straight ahead on the old road to the Blue Mine. This flooded mine dives nearly 500 feet underground and once required large waterwheels and pumps to keep it dry. Now it's an ideal home for mosses and mosquitoes.

Retrace your steps and cross the trail bridge, arriving in a short way at the ruins of a stone shelter, built by the New York Chapter of the Green Mountain Club (GMC), which became active in the Wyanokies in 1916 (see the sidebar). Eccentric Will Monroe, a burly bearded Montclair professor and friend to Walt Whitman, organized this club. He blazed some of the Wyanokies' best trails as a rehearsal for his work on Vermont's Long Trail. Monroe was famous for skyline trails that climb and wind through tight rocky passageways to the best vistas.

Just beyond the lean-to, the yellow Mine Trail turns right. Stay on the red-blazed Wyanokie Circular Trail as it climbs very steeply through pillarlike black and white oaks, beeches, and tulip trees, reaching one of Will Monroe's finest New Jersey lookouts (2.1 miles). Slabs of tilted rock, edged by scrub oak, chestnut oak, and pitch pine, look east from the nearly bald top of Wyanokie

High Point out over Wanaque Reservoir to the Manhattan skyline. Near evening, the Empire State Building glows scarlet with reflected sunlight. This is also a perfect spot for lunch.

Just beyond the highest vista, the red Wyanokie Circular Trail continues straight ahead and the blue-blazed Hewitt-Butler Trail enters from the right. Follow the blue blazes sharply right and descend steeply for 0.5 mile through a fascinating series of rock chutes and slots. This trail meanders over ledges and through a boulder-strewn mountain laurel grove. It may again be the work of Will Monroe, whose eye for beauty was second to none.

Stay on the blue Hewitt-Butler Trail, passing an intersection with the white Macopin Trail. Make a left onto the blue trail where it rejoins the yellow Mine Trail. The two paths coincide until they hit paved Snake Den Road at 2.6 miles. Turn right and follow the road 0.5 mile downhill to the Weis Ecology Center parking lot.

The ecology center is another legacy of early trail-building days. It was the camp of the Naturfreunde (Nature Friends), a 1920s group of Austrian Socialist hikers who maintained Wyanokie trails until the 1960s. Today the Weis Ecology Center is run by the New Jersey Audubon Society.

For More Information

Norvin Green State Forest trails are open during daylight hours year-round. To volunteer as a trail builder, contact the New York–New Jersey Trail Conference.

Weis Ecology Center, 150 Snake Den Road, Ringwood, NJ 07456; 973-835-2160; www.njaudubon.org/Centers/Weis/

New York–New Jersey Trail Conference, 156 Ramapo Valley Road, Mahwah, NJ 07430-1199; 201-512-9348; www.nynjtc.org

The 1,500-Mile Miracle

The legacy of trail building born with groups such as the New York Chapters of the AMC, GMC, and Naturfreunde spread quickly throughout the New York metro area. In 1920 these and other tramping groups allied themselves as the New York–New Jersey Trail Conference. Led by Raymond Torrey, a Manhattan journalist and conservationist, volunteers built the first miles of the Appalachian Trail and snaked trail networks across the New Jersey and Hudson Highlands. Their close work with government also led to many new state and county parks.

The New York–New Jersey Trail Conference and its clubs continue as the dominant trail-building organization in the metro area today, managing more than 1,200 trail miles. Volunteers paint blazes, cut brush, place rock steps and stone water bars (for erosion control), and lay down bog bridging. They maintain 73 miles of Appalachian Trail in New Jersey, and are helping build the Highlands Trail, a 150-mile path connecting the Hudson with the Delaware River. The group has been instrumental in preserving parklands, especially Sterling Forest. The New York–New Jersey Trail Conference and its many hiking clubs welcome volunteers eager to give back to the trails the joy they've gained from them.

Four Birds Trail

Splitrock Reservoir and Farny State Park

Trip 16

Trail: Four Birds Trail (out-and-back)
Distance: 5.6 miles
Length: 4 hours
Difficulty: Challenging; 680-foot elevation gain

Explore a secluded mountain and black bear habitat

Getting There

From I-80, take US 23 north to the County Route 513, Green Pond Road, exit. Follow County Route 513 south for 5.3 miles to the town of Marcella, turning left onto Upper Hibernia Road. In 1.1 miles turn left onto Splitrock Road. In 0.6 mile look for a small pull-off parking place on the right. Call the NY–NJ Trail Conference (201-512-9348) to make sure parking area is open and usable. The trailhead is 0.2 mile farther up the road by foot.

Special Features

- Splitrock Reservoir
- Abundant wildlife
- Upland forest
- Native wildflowers

The Farny Highlands is a rugged and wild 35,000-acre watershed that lies only a few miles north of where Interstate 80 pierces the New Jersey Highlands. This jumble of Precambrian gneiss cliffs, scoured by the Wisconsin Glacier, rises above deeply etched, stream-washed valleys. Black bear, river otter, beaver, porcupine, and timber rattlesnake inhabit dense hardwood forests, while native brook trout populate small streams.

The region's rich veins of magnetite were tapped by eighteenth- and nineteenth-century iron miners. In the twentieth century the Farny Highlands' widest valleys were dammed to form the Charlotteburg and Splitrock Reservoirs, which supply drinking water to Jersey City. Overlooking the reservoirs at the heart of this mountainous area is the undeveloped Farny State Park.

In 1996 the 19.5-mile-long Four Birds Trail became the first blazed hiking path to traverse the region. Running from south to north and built by volunteers of the New York–New Jersey Trail Conference, it crosses only one paved road along its entire length. The trail was named in honor of the wild habitats and avian inhabitants hikers may encounter: wild turkeys find shelter in deciduous forest, red-tailed hawks ride thermals above the cliffs, ospreys hunt over the quiet reservoirs, and great blue herons fish secluded marshes.

This challenging 5.6-mile out-and-back hike samples a portion of the Farny Highlands known locally as the Bumps. Here the white-blazed Four Birds Trail repeatedly climbs to stony summits and falls into shaded ravines. The walk rewards with aerial and shoreside views of Splitrock Reservoir, and promises with telltale signs of plentiful wildlife.

From the pull-off spot on Split Rock Road, walk 0.2 mile south and uphill along the road. *Note:* At publication this parking spot was temporarily closed. Call the NY–NJ Trail Conference

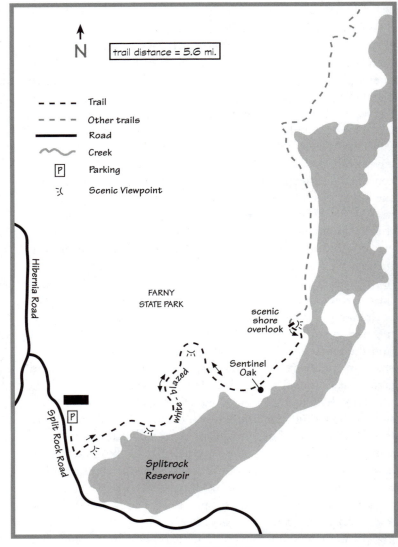

N

trail distance = 5.6 mi.

- - - Trail
- - - Other trails
—— Road
〜 Creek
P Parking
☼ Scenic Viewpoint

Hibernia Road

FARNY
STATE PARK

scenic
shore
overlook

Sentinel
Oak

white - blazed

Split Rock Road

P

Splitrock
Reservoir

Four Birds Trail

(201-512-9348) to assure the pull-off spot is again in use. The Four Birds Trail crosses the road just beyond the hill crest. Turn left, following the white blazes north. The trail immediately demands an energetic scramble to the top of a small stony outcrop (0.3 mile).

The thin soil of this ledge is host to remarkable plant diversity. Lowbush blueberry, maple-leaf viburnum, shadbush, blackhaw, scarlet hawthorn, black cherry, red and chestnut oak, mockernut and pignut hickory all grow here, feeding animals year-round. Shadbush is the first forest tree to bloom in spring. In early April, simultaneous with the Delaware River shad run, its five-petaled white blossoms appear like pearl-white stars amid a gray universe of bare woodland limbs. In early summer, shadbush wears purple, crab-apple-like fruit, a favorite of forty bird and mammal species. Look for shattered shadbush branches, a sign of feeding black bears (see the sidebar). Blackhaw, a shrubby tree, also boasts white flowers (appearing later than shadbush). Its blue-black fruit sustains songbirds, gamebirds, and mammals from autumn into winter.

This first outcrop gives limited views of Splitrock Reservoir's dam and water-pumping station. The trail immediately descends and crosses a woods road at 0.4 mile, passing beneath a dense canopy of chestnut oak, sweet birch, beech, and sugar maple. American chestnut saplings and dogwood fill in the understory, while green fronds of Christmas fern, hay-scented fern, and cinnamon fern crisscross the forest floor. Just beyond the woods road, at the ravine's bottom, a brook crosses the trail. It is surrounded by water-loving tulip trees and yellow birches with silvery, peeling bark and exposed snaky roots.

Now the trail starts a challenging climb, amid boulders topped by leathery olive-drab rock tripe and the delicate forest green fronds of polypody fern. The ledges form a small rock shelter that could serve as a hiker haven in a rainstorm. This climb leads to a cliff-top view of Splitrock Reservoir at 0.7 mile. From here we watched a kettle of turkey buzzards as they rode the boiling thermals above the reservoir.

As the trail descends from the vista over billion-year-old banded gneiss, notice that 350-million-year-old chunks of purple-hued puddingstone erratics have been dropped here like so many scattered marbles, left behind by the melting ice of the Wisconsin Glacier 15,000 years ago.

The path reaches a low area at 0.8 mile amid basswood, American chestnut, and yellow birch, then crosses another woods road. Near here we found downy lobelia. This relative of the crimson cardinal flower wears pastel blue blossoms in early autumn. In spring, a scattering of purple violets adorns the leaf litter.

The trail skirts left of a red maple swamp as it begins climbing again at 0.9 mile. Red maple flowers early in spring, creating a scarlet canopy above woodland swamps. Also in spring, walkers may be confused by a ducklike quacking rising from the swamp. This is not the cry of migrating waterfowl, but the massed voices of tree frogs giving their mating call.

Now comes the most athletically demanding climb of the walk, a 200-foot vertical rise over rocks and roots to a nameless, 1,100-foot peak (1.5 miles). Sitting atop this vista, we were perplexed by explosions reverberating over the hills. Later we learned of our proximity to Picatinny Arsenal, where the U.S. Army tests experimental artillery pieces by firing shells into a mountainside. Picatinny Arsenal was established in 1880 on the site of an eighteenth- and nineteenth-century iron forge that produced cannon and shot for Washington's army, the War of 1812, and the Civil War. The arsenal was razed in 1926 when a tree overhanging a powder magazine was struck by lightning. The rebuilt complex played a vital role in World War II and remains the nation's largest arms-research facility. The arsenal offers a mixed blessing to wildlife: much of the army's land is undeveloped and cloaked in forest, but toxic chemicals used in the past may affect water and land quality.

The Four Birds Trail leaves the vista, making a few swift but challenging descents and ascents through rocky terrain as it passes among mountain laurel, chestnut oak, and sweet birch. The path then undulates through an open forest of tulip tree, sugar maple, and hop hornbeam, crossing several low rock ledges.

At 2.0 miles the path winds left around the Sentinel Oak, a 4-foot-diameter red oak. The path continues descending through hickories. Walk quietly and you may see fleeing white-tailed deer, as we did. Why, one wonders, do escaping deer fail to conceal themselves, and instead make a flashy show with their white tails? Some scientists speculate that this gesture is the animal's way of "thumbing its nose" at stalking predators.

Splitrock Reservoir, where diving ducks, geese, and swans flourish.

The defiant tail display informs predators that pursuit is futile once the deer has taken flight. (Fleet-footed deer can hit speeds of 35 MPH and make 30-foot horizontal leaps.)

The trail descends through sassafras and gray birch to the reservoir, then makes its rocky way along the shore to a little island (2.8 mile). Hopping from boulder to boulder, you can easily put yourself out on the island, an ideal spot for lunch and from which to watch for diving osprey and waterfowl. From this point you can continue following the trail north, exploring the reservoir shoreline. When you're ready, retrace your steps to Splitrock Road.

For More Information

The Four Birds Trail is open dawn to dusk year-round. The parking pull off was temporarily closed in 2003. Check with the NY–NJ Trail Conference (201-512-9348) to make sure it has been reopened before hiking and risking a ticket.

New York–New Jersey Trail Conference, 156 Ramapo Valley Road, Mahwah, NJ 07430-1199; 201-512-9348; www.nynjtc.org

The Return of the Black Bear

Native New Jersey black bears were hunted to extinction by the 1800s. But renewed oak and hemlock forests, mountain laurel thickets, rhododendron, and blueberry bogs have brought them back. Migrating east from Pennsylvania's Pocono Plateau, black bears are now breeding in the Kittatinny Range and New Jersey Highlands.

As you walk the Farny Highlands, look for signs of this lumbering omnivore. Overturned logs, branches torn from fruit-covered highbush blueberry and shadbush, clawed beech trees, and excavated anthills or rodent burrows all testify to hungry black bears foraging for twigs, roots, nuts, fruits, insects, and small mammals. The most recognizable signs are heaps of dark-colored scat containing undigested bits of berry in autumn (do not touch!).

Bears are shy and usually run from humans, though they have become more aggressive in recent years. If you meet one, use common sense. Never offer food or interfere with a mother bear and her cubs. If a bear won't run, don't make eye contact; take a nonaggressive stance and speak softly. If the animal still won't flee, whistle, wave arms, speak loudly, or fire your camera flash. Don't run; a black bear will then view you as prey, and it can reach speeds of more than 30 MPH. Warnings aside, these magnificent animals deserve our wonder and respect.

Beaver Brook Trail
Farny Highlands

Trip 17

Trail: Beaver Brook Trail (out-and-back)
Distance: 6.2 miles
Length: 5 hours
Difficulty: Challenging; 700-foot elevation gain

A rugged hike to a beaver colony

Getting There

From I-80, take NJ 15 north for 2.0 miles. Turn right onto Berkshire Valley Road. Trailhead parking is 2.0 miles north on the left just beyond the Rockaway River crossing and the junction with Taylor Road.

Special Features
- Beaver lodges and Lost Pond
- Valley View Vista
- Good hawk watching
- Steep climbing and rocky footing

Many people feel an affinity with the North American beaver, perhaps because of a perceived similarity to human beings. Like us, these industrious animals cooperate to construct elaborate homes and, in the process, transform their environment.

Sixty million beavers controlled precolonial America's waterways, including most New Jersey streams. Unfortunately, the beavers' velvety soft pelts were their undoing. Lenape tribesmen were perplexed at the obsessive interest shown by Dutch traders in the furs. The Dutch offered cloth, iron tools, rum, and brandy in trade for the pelts, which were processed into pricey felt hats for Europe's fashion elite.

By 1656 the New Netherlands was exporting 80,000 pelts a year. At this rate, the animal population quickly declined, as did the value of Native Americans to the Europeans. Colonist Johan Printz, lamenting the failure of the fur trade, cruelly said of the Lenape: "Nothing would be better than that a couple hundred soldiers should be sent here and kept here until we broke the necks of all of them." By 1750 the Lenape were gone, forced west, and by 1820 the last free-roaming New Jersey beavers were exterminated.

Not until 1900, when escapees from the New Jersey Rutherford estate reestablished a wild colony, did anyone give much thought to beavers. The state, encouraged by this success, imported more, until by 1952 limited trapping was again allowed. Today New Jersey's beaver population thrives.

This rugged, 6.2-mile out-and-back hike ascends to a beaver colony. While the animals are nocturnal, daytime visitors will be rewarded with proof of the beavers' engineering feats. The hike also climbs into a classic New Jersey Highlands environment characterized by rocky crags, sweeping vistas, and plentiful signs of shy wildlife, including bear and coyote.

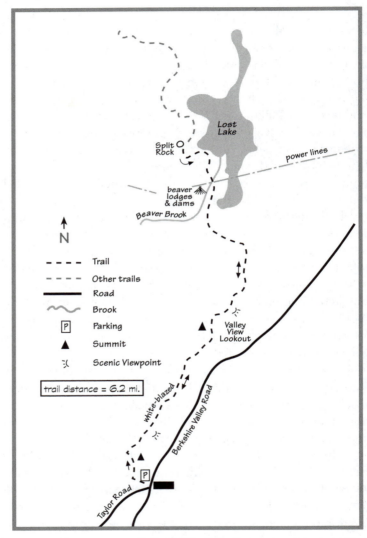

Lost
Lake

Split
Rock

power lines

beaver
lodges
& dams

Beaver Brook

N

- - - - Trail
- - - - Other trails
——— Road
〰〰 Brook
P Parking
▲ Summit
☽ Scenic Viewpoint

trail distance = 6.2 mi.

Valley
View
Lookout

white-blazed

Berkshire Valley Road

Taylor Road

Beaver Brook Trail

The white-blazed Beaver Brook Trail was completed in 1997. It extends for 6.5 miles from Morris County's Mahlon Dickerson Reservation into the state's Rockaway River Wildlife Management Area. This walk uses the southernmost trail section.

The path departs the south corner of the trailhead parking lot, climbing quickly on a woods road through a mixed deciduous forest of sugar maple, oak, hickory, and ash. Steep becomes steeper as the gullied road shoots straight toward the top of the mountain. Watch the blazes. At 0.3 mile the trail makes a sharp right, leaving the woods road and ascending a rock outcrop. Stop to catch your breath, and notice that the Highlands stone beneath your feet is black with iron, a fact that didn't go unnoticed by nineteenth-century entrepreneurs. These hills were heavily mined.

The trail rises less steeply now as it hops from stony outcrop to stony outcrop, with views over Berkshire Valley and to Green Pond Mountain. The best vista comes at about 0.5 mile. You've now climbed 500 vertical feet from your starting point, and are within the territory of Highlands wildlife. Standing here in November, we heard the screams of red-tailed hawks and found bear scat dotted with undigested partridgeberries. Bears put on a good supply of fat in autumn, preparing for a sedentary winter. While they don't truly hibernate, being easily roused from sleep, they won't eat again until spring.

The thin soil at these heights supports black cherry, shagbark hickory, oak, and cedar. Rock slabs are edged in maple-leaf viburnum and lowbush blueberry. Shadbush also grows here. With its nondescript simple-toothed leaf, this little tree blends in with the scenery most of the year. But in April, when the rest of the Highlands forest is still a tangle of naked branches, the shadbush blossoms with downy masses of white-petaled flowers. This

A beaver lodge at Beaver Brook provides year-round safety to these water-loving animals.

blooming coincides with the spawning of shad in the Delaware and Hudson Rivers, explaining the tree's common name.

The Beaver Brook Trail next makes a steep 0.8-mile descent, departing the oaks and open ledges and entering deep forest dominated by sugar maples. The footing is rocky and a little treacherous, especially on slippery autumn leaves or in wet weather. The forest floor is adorned with cinnamon, hay-scented, and Christmas ferns. Birds are plentiful. When we were here, an immense dead hemlock stump had been pulverized by pileated woodpeckers, while tulip trees displayed the neatly drilled horizontal holes made by yellow-bellied sapsuckers.

Falling deeper into a shaded hollow, the trail crosses several major woods roads and passes through a disturbed area where Christmas ferns fill trenches that may have been dug as exploratory mining pits. Partridgeberry, striped pipsissewa, maidenhair fern, and rattlesnake root rise from leaf litter.

At about 1.2 miles the trail steadily climbs through mountain laurel, at first along a woods road and then making its own path. It weaves to the top of the Valley View Vista (1.5 miles), a ledge covered with reindeer lichen. Here we found several trees with hickory nutshells tightly wedged into their bark. This was probably the work of woodpeckers or flying squirrels, which use the trees as a vise for holding the nuts while eating them.

After rising a little farther, the path levels off on a typical Highlands ridge, a rugged, undulating plateau marked by open forest and overlooked by low outcrops. This tableland is mantled in chestnut oak, sweet birch, sugar maple, shadbush, and beech trees. Blueberries and polypody fern hug rocky spots. Rattlesnake plantain, with mottled snakeskinlike leaves, blooms white in summer. At 2.8 miles the trail enters a disturbed area, with clay mounds topped by trees, evidence the area may once have been considered for development.

Just past these mounds, the path descends to Beaver Brook and a sight that never ceases to surprise. The stream runs down the center of a shallow valley crossed by a succession of beaver dams (see the sidebar). Behind each dam, a glimmering pool gathers to protect a dome-shaped beaver lodge. Streambanks are clearcut, with stumps everywhere. Yellow birch logs, a beaver's food of choice, lie on the ground stripped of bark. While this may seem like wanton destruction, beavers actually enrich their habitat. The ponds support insect growth, encouraging fish, which attract raccoons, great blue herons, belted kingfishers, and other animals. Hawks hunt white-throated sparrows and other prey among the newly created forest openings.

The trail follows Beaver Brook upstream, then descends to a rocky place where it passes beneath a power line and crosses the brook on a rickety bridge. It climbs uphill, passing another beaver dam and lodge. Finally, at 3.1 miles, the path reaches Lost Lake, a wide marsh choked at its edge by phragmites. At least two more beaver lodges were visible from shore when we were there. The trail skirts the lake's west edge. We had lunch here and turned back at a lemon squeezer, a large boulder split by frost action through which the trail passes. Those wanting a longer walk may go farther before returning the way they came.

For More Information

The Beaver Brook Trail is open daily, year-round.

New York–New Jersey Trail Conference, 156 Ramapo Valley Road, Mahwah, NJ 07430-1199; 201-512-9348; www.nynjtc.org

Beaver: Born to Build

The beaver, a large rodent, is uniquely suited for its engineering role. Its shovel-shaped, scaly tail serves as a brace when the animal gnaws trees, as a balance when it carries building materials, and as a rudder when it barges heavy logs through open water.

Its incisors, each $1/4$ inch wide, can cut through tree trunks; strip the cambium layer from trees; or nip leaves, buds, and twigs. Beaver can roll branches between their nimble forefeet, chewing away bark as we would corn from a cob. Smaller trees (2 to 6 inches in diameter) are cut for food and building materials (a 5-inch willow can be downed in just three minutes), though sometimes beaver tackle immense trees. Awkward land animals, portly beaver do most onshore work at night, warily sniffing for coyote and river otter, their enemies.

The beaver is built for the water. When the animal submerges, valves close off ears and nostrils, while skin flaps seal the mouth, leaving front incisors exposed for work. Clear membranes, like goggles, protect the eyes. A beaver is a flawless swimmer, with webbed hind feet, a waterproof pelt, and a thick fat layer to withstand icy winter streams.

Human engineers agree that beavers always know the best spot for dams. In fact, strong dam construction of interwoven branches packed with mud frequently foils park officials, who find trails or picnic groves flooded. Beaver foolers, disguised plastic pipes inserted into dams to drain off water, seem to fool no one. The mere sound of water flowing cues the animals to repair their work and plug the "fooler."

Tripod Rock and Bear Rock
Pyramid Mountain, Morris County Park

Trail: Visitor Center Trail, Mennen Trail, white trail (loop)
Distance: 3.0 miles
Length: 3 hours
Difficulty: Moderate; 400-foot elevation gain

A wildflower walk to New Jersey's most celebrated glacial erratics

Getting There
From I-287 north, take the Main Street, Boonton, exit. Proceed to Boonton Avenue (Country Route 511). Turn right (north). The Pyramid Mountain Visitor Center is 3.3 miles ahead, on the left (opposite Mars Court).

Special Features
- Tripod Rock and Bear Rock, glacial erratics
- Manhattan view
- Fine habitat for birds and wildflowers
- One steep ascent and descent

Just north of Morristown's suburban sprawl, a series of low ridges rises to 900 feet above sea level. These Highlands summits, separated by narrow valleys, have remained sparsely settled for centuries. Native Americans once hunted and foraged here. Later, notorious outlaws used the region as a hideout, while nineteenth-century charcoal makers and quarrymen came and went.

This rough country was long recognized for its freakish rock formations, glacial erratics that have since shaped local history. Native Americans may have utilized Tripod Rock (a 200-ton boulder perched atop three round stones) as a celestial calendar. Nineteenth-century surveyors used house-sized Bear Rock as a boundary marker. In the twentieth century, hikers laid out trails and made pilgrimages to both sites. Eventually it was these two unique boulders that inspired conservationists to protect Pyramid Mountain.

By 1980 developers' bulldozers had begun probing lowland hollows, tearing up trees and replacing favorite trails with roads. In 1982 alarmed local resident Lucy Meyer determined that Tripod Rock and Bear Rock were too valuable to lose. She rallied neighbors, government, conservation groups, and corporate interests to save an acre of ground at each site.

The Friends of Pyramid Mountain succeeded beyond their wildest hopes. Lucy's 2 acres grew to 2,000 protected acres of Morris County parkland. Today Pyramid Mountain and adjacent Turkey Mountain are an important stopover on the Atlantic flyway, attracting birds. Bear and bobcat populate rocky hills, as do 200 native plants.

This 3.0-mile loop hike is celebrated for its spring and autumn wildflowers. It takes walkers to both Tripod Rock and Bear Rock, and to a Manhattan skyline vista.

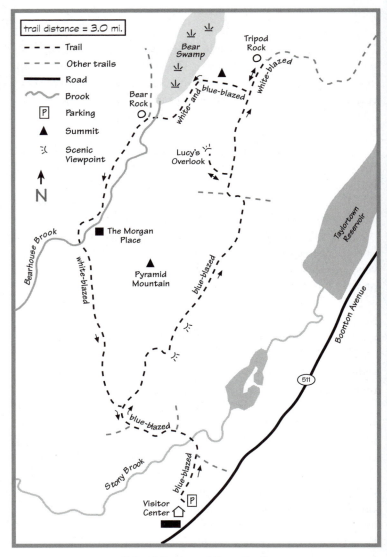

Tripod Rock and Bear Rock

From the Pyramid Mountain Visitor Center, follow the blue trail into a lowland forest dominated by maple, beech, and sweet birch. In late summer, tall blue lettuce grows 10 feet high, while tiny woodland asters, among the most successful of all wildflowers, poke up from leaf litter (see the sidebar).

In about 0.2 mile the blue-blazed visitor center trail ends at a junction with the blue-blazed Mennen Trail. Turn left onto this trail (named for a major Pyramid Mountain corporate sponsor). The blue trail soon crosses Stony Brook on a bridge. Ignore a yellow-blazed trail branching right.

In autumn, woodland sunflower, jewelweed, and joe-pye weed blossom along this wet trail section. Native Americans squeezed juice from the pendant-shaped, yellow-orange jewel-weed flower onto skin to soothe poison ivy rashes, a proven medical treatment. Joe-pye weed, a tall, spindly plant with a curly head of pinkish purple flowers, is named for a legendary Native American herbalist who, it is said, treated typhoid fever outbreaks in colonial times with the herb.

The trail starts an easy climb on stone steps and the first glacial erratics appear, some 10 feet tall and all dropped by the melting ice of the Wisconsin Glacier over 15,000 years ago.

At 0.4 mile the blue trail meets a white trail entering from the left beneath a power line, then makes a steep ascent under red and chestnut oaks to a vista at 0.6 mile. The view, cloaked with scrub oak, looks east over Turkey Mountain to Manhattan's Empire State Building. An unseen quarry on Turkey Mountain once provided local carvers with green serpentine, a soft, waxy mineral that, when shaped and shined, is as beautiful as jade.

The blue trail ascends, then levels off, passing among chestnut oak, sweet birch, and leggy growths of mountain laurel.

This area is beautiful when the laurel blossoms in June with white and pink cup-shaped flowers.

Ignore a yellow-blazed trail entering from the right and exiting to the left. Just a little farther on (at about 1.0 mile), a blue-and-white-blazed side trail leads left over loose rocks to Lucy's Overlook (named for Pyramid Mountain crusader Lucy Meyer). This ledge looks west to Stony Brook Mountain and offers good birding. The hawk migration passes overhead in autumn, and eagles have been spotted. Five types of owls, including the endangered barred owl, live on Pyramid Mountain.

Return along the side trail, continuing left on the blue trail. At about 1.3 miles the blue-blazed trail intersects with a white trail. Continue straight ahead on the white trail along the ridge top for another 0.1 mile to Pyramid Rock. Here the retreating glacier capriciously balanced a mini-van-sized boulder atop three small stones. As precarious as the situation looks, it has remained unchanged for 15,000 years. Whether Native Americans really used this site as an observatory no one knows, but it has lately become a popular solstice celebration spot.

Return 0.1 mile to the junction of the blue-blazed and white-blazed trails. Turn right, following the blue-and-white combined trail as it plummets 150 vertical feet from Pyramid Mountain into the valley. Notice as you drop from the ridge crest how quickly the chestnut oaks disappear, replaced by tall tulip trees, hickories, and red oaks. Virginia creeper and poison ivy wind viny tendrils around bottomland trees. The trail is flat and easy for the rest of the hike.

At 1.8 miles the blue-white trail crosses Bearhouse Brook, where bumblebees crawl headfirst into white-blossoming turtleheads and where cardinal flower blooms in late summer.

Tripod Rock, a 200-ton boulder precariously balanced on three small rocks, has stayed in place since the passing of the last glacier 15,000 years ago.

This wetland flower, named for scarlet clergy robes, is a favorite with hummingbirds.

Just ahead is Bear Rock. This one-story-high boulder, dragged from nearby Stony Brook Mountain, is believed to be the largest glacial erratic in New Jersey. In front of Bear Rock, the blue-blazed Mennen Trail veers right. Go left on the white trail, which follows a woods road edged by a stone wall and shaded by white ash, sugar maple, and hickory. The stone walls and barberry (once forming a natural hedge) testify to ruined nineteenth-century subsistence farms.

At 2.1 miles the trail passes to the right of a tiny foundation, ruins of the Morgan Place. This was not so much homestead as hideout. The Morgans were robbers who made regular raids on Boonton in the late 1800s. The stone cellar hole blooms with violets and wild geraniums in springtime.

The trail crosses a bridge over Bearhouse Brook and enters a wet area with fine autumn wildflower displays. Joe-pye weed grows as high as your head, intermixing its soft purples with the reds of winged sumac. Common New England aster, white snakeroot, and boneset mix with rarer closed gentian and lovely purple gerardia (the two best color pages in *Newcomb's Wildflower Guide!*). There is no deeper blue than that of the closed or bottle gentian as it contrasts with yellowing wetland sedges. Trumpet-shaped gerardia blossoms are dotted with dark spots and yellow ribs on the inside of elegant throats.

Follow the white trail as it swings gently uphill around the south base of Pyramid Mountain back to the power line and the junction with the blue Mennen Trail (2.7 miles). Turn right and return to the visitor center the way you came.

For More Information

Trails are open dawn to dusk, year-round. The visitor center is open Friday and weekends.

Morris County Park Commission, P.O. Box 1295, Morristown, NJ 07962; 973-326-7600; www.parks.morris.newjersey.us

Friends of Pyramid Mountain: www.kinnelon.com/htm/Community/Recreation/Pyramidmt.asp

Late Bloomers: A Riot of Fall Wildflowers

Most of us think of spring as the time for wildflowers. But late summer and early autumn offer displays of purple asters, yellow goldenrods, and blue gentians that are just as dazzling and uplifting as are spring beauties.

This is the time when composites make their showiest appearance. Composites are one of the most recent developments among flowering plants and one of the most successful worldwide. They are flowers within flowers. Look at an aster, sunflower, goldenrod, daisy, thistle, white snakeroot, or joe-pye weed and you'll discover that what appears to be a single central flower head is actually composed of a fused mass of many (sometimes hundreds) of tiny florets. Each floret contributes pollen for propagation.

Autumn wildflowers, along with plentiful berries and nuts, provide a last rich autumn harvest before winter descends. More than fifty varieties of goldenrod, for example, grace our meadows, each providing plentiful seeds for migrating birds as well as nectar and pollen for monarch butterflies, wasps, hornets, beetles, and bees. Goldenrod is often blamed for causing hay fever, a crime it doesn't commit. Its pollen is too heavy to float on the breeze. Other meadow flowers such as red clover, wild bergamot, and bull-thistle attract insect pollinators with colorful displays before the first frosts turn the world golden.

Black River and Kay Environmental Center

Morris County Park

Trip 19

Trail: **Black River Trail, Conifer Pass Trail, Bamboo Brook Trail**
Distance: **4.6 miles out-and-back (optional 8.0-mile hike to hemlock gorge and Bamboo Brook Trail loop)**
Length: **3 hours (or 5 hours)**
Difficulty: **Moderate 4.0 miles; difficult 8.0 miles; approximately 600-foot elevation gain**

A river gorge and bountiful biological diversity

Getting There

Take I-80 east or west to US 206 south, and continue 8.0 miles to Chester. Turn right onto NJ 24 west for 1.2 miles to Cooper Mill on the left.

Special Features

- Cooper Mill
- Black River Gorge
- Tremendous habitat diversity
- Kay Environmental Center

No hike in this book offers a greater diversity of habitats, human history, or beauty, concentrated within so few miles. Black River Park boasts a deeply etched river valley, a deciduous floodplain forest, a hemlock-cloaked ravine, an upland forest with blooming rhododendron, and broad meadows planted in flowering dogwood. Hundreds of migrating bird and butterfly species are attracted to the park, as are diverse mammals, including coyote and black bear.

The Black River Gorge is just as significant historically. Starting in the eighteenth century, the valley was exploited for its resources: trees harvested, iron mines dug, mills and railroads built. In the 1920s the area became the gentrified estate of the remarkable Elizabeth Kay (see sidebar). In the last half of the twentieth century that estate was preserved as crown jewel of the Morris County park system and as headquarters for the New Jersey chapter of the Nature Conservancy.

This walk can be done as a 4.6-mile out-and-back-hike, but can be lengthened to 8.0 miles to include the deepest part of the gorge and to make a long sweeping loop on the Conifer Pass and Bamboo Brook Trails. (A free pass—available at Cooper Mill or Kay Environmental Center—is needed to enter the environmentally sensitive unblazed hemlock ravine area.)

Begin at Cooper Mill. Here the Black River abruptly changes from sluggish stream to roaring river as it begins dropping into the gorge. This was once a prime location for water-powered industry. The first mill was built here in the 1760s. The present one, raised in 1826, is now a living history museum.

Walk behind the mill, past the 16-foot-high waterwheel. This energy-efficient marvel is so well balanced that just 2 cups of water are needed in half the wheel's forty-eight buckets to make it spin. It grinds 400 pounds of flour per hour.

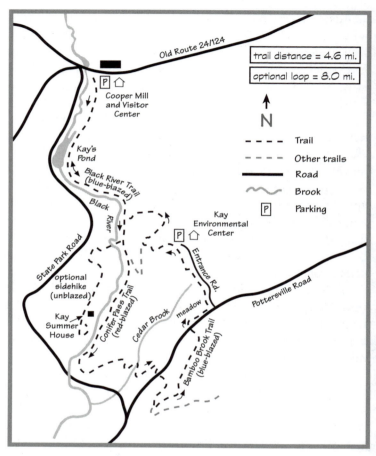

trail distance = 4.6 mi.

optional loop = 8.0 mi.

N

- - - Trail

- - - Other trails

——— Road

∿∿ Brook

P Parking

Old Route 24/124

Cooper Mill and Visitor Center

Kay's Pond

Black River Trail (blue-blazed)

Black River

Kay Environmental Center

State Park Road

optional sidehike (unblazed)

Conifer Pass Trail (red-blazed)

Cedar Brook

Entrance Rd.

meadow

Kay Summer House

Bamboo Brook Trail (blue-blazed)

Pottersville Road

Black River and Kay Environmental Center

Cross over the mill tailrace beneath ornamental catalpa trees. The blue-blazed Black River Trail leads downstream into the forest, entering another world. The river roars between black boulders, while trout rise in shaded, golden pools. Sweet birch, yellow birch, beech, and tulip trees push arrow-straight trunks out of the gorge toward the sky.

The trail traverses a floodplain where spring beauty, rattle-snake plantain, and trout lily bloom in April. Aster, jewelweed, and jack-in-the-pulpit spread across the forest floor in autumn. Jack-in-the-pulpit, with its characteristic green-striped hood (or spathe), has the ability to change sex with size. Bigger plants are female, while smaller ones are male. Easy sex change allows this herb to attune its propagation rate to match lean or plentiful growing seasons.

In a short distance the blue trail along the river becomes easier, seeming to follow an old road. This is really the remains of a nineteenth-century narrow-gauge railroad that served riverside iron mines. As the gorge walls rise around you, look for mine holes and trenches, plus ore tailing piles composed of rust-colored, fist-sized, magnetite-rich stones. (Stay away from mines; they can be dangerous.)

Tulip trees and oaks rise higher now, while smaller American hornbeam and witch hazel trees huddle in the shade. Look for the American basswood, its bark pecked with neat rows of holes. This is the work of yellow-bellied sapsuckers, which tap the trees for their sweet sap. After drilling the trees and eating their inner bark, the birds return later to sip dripping sap and eat insects that have gathered to feast on the sticky flow.

The stream broadens into a lily-covered pond (0.5 mile), backed up behind a stone dam. This nineteenth-century mill site became the electrical-generating plant for Elizabeth Kay's

The open meadows of the Kay Environmental Center attract migrating birds and butterflies.

estate in the 1920s. The pond is overhung with elm, black locust, and sycamore, while escaped hostas dot the ground, attesting to Mrs. Kay's gardening skills.

At 1.5 miles the trail reaches a woods road junction where a sign informs hikers that the Kay Environmental Center lies 0.8 mile ahead on the blue trail. For those who favor a shorter, easier hike on blazed paths, continue on the blue-blazed trail as it leads away from the Black River into upland oak forest to the Kay Center. From there, explore the surrounding meadows, then return the way you came.

For the more adventurous who wish to explore the Black River Gorge hemlock ravine, follow the unmarked but obvious woods road to the right, entering the Environmentally Sensitive Area (free entrance passes available at Cooper Mill or Kay Environmental Center). At a major woods road fork in 0.1 mile, turn right, descending to and crossing the Black River on a bridge. At stream's edge, shade-loving mountain laurel spreads beneath shagbark hickory trees. Follow the road as it climbs uphill on the stream's far side for 0.4 mile, winding into the heart of the gorge under a canopy of eastern hemlock and beech trees. Follow the road until it descends back to the Black River and dead-ends at a turnaround spot.

Return the way you came uphill, looking for a set of concrete steps descending steeply right to the river. At the base of the steps you'll find a cement dam and the ruins of Elizabeth Kay's summer home. This spot was the scene of festive 1930s swimming parties.

Do not cross the dam, but return up the steps to the woods road, following it right, returning over the Black River bridge. After crossing the stream, climb uphill a short distance and turn right onto a major woods road that leads out of the gorge for about 0.1 mile. When this road intersects the red-blazed Conifer Pass Trail, follow the trail to the right. Stay on the Conifer Pass Trail for about 1.6 miles as it follows the Black River Gorge south and swings uphill, then down, to cross Cedar Brook. The trail soon crosses Pottersville Road, then climbs gently uphill to intersect the blue-blazed Bamboo Brook Trail. Turn left, following the Bamboo Brook Trail for about 0.6 mile. Recross Pottersville Road and follow the trail right as it edges the road, then as it turns left to edge the entrance road to the Kay Environmental Center.

The Kay Center meadows, planted with dogwood trees, are a pleasure to the eye in any season. In spring, the trees wear a mantle of white blossoms. In autumn, they glow scarlet, as do Virginia creeper and poison ivy. All three plants exhibit fall foliar flagging: they blaze crimson to advertise ripening berries to birds, which eat the fruit and disperse seeds on southward migrations. Two hundred bird species have been spotted in the

Black River area (with an estimated hundred species nesting here). After exploring the meadows, walk to the Kay Environmental Center, then follow the blue-blazed Black River Trail for 2.3 miles back to Cooper Mill.

For More Information

Trails are open dawn to dusk year-round. The Cooper Mill is open on weekends May to October, and Friday through Tuesday in July and August (fee). The Kay Environmental Center is open daily year-round.

Morris County Park Commission, P.O. Box 1295, Morristown, NJ 07962; 973-326-7600; www.parks.morris.newjersey.us

Cooper Mill, Old Route 24, Chester, NJ 07930; 908-879-5463

Nature Conservancy at Kay Environmental Center, 200 Pottersville Road, Chester, NJ 07930; 908-879-7262; http://nature.org/wherewework/northamerica/states/newjersey/

The Amazing Mrs. Kay

Elizabeth Donnell was born in 1894 to a prominent Philadelphia family, and in 1918 married stockbroker Alfred Kay. The couple, like many wealthy urbanites, sought peace on a gentrified country estate. In the 1920s they moved to rural Chester, New Jersey, establishing their 233-acre Hidden River Farm.

Elizabeth Kay was a far-seeing naturalist and believer in self-sufficiency. She generated her own electricity, raised sheep and dairy cows, and grew organic fruits and vegetables decades before the hazards of chemical fertilizers and pesticides were recognized. Her guests dined on homegrown turkey, squab (pigeon), mutton, peaches, apples, butter, and eggs at tables graced by her own exquisite flower arrangements. Local seniors flocked to Mrs. Kay for rejuvenating herbal cures.

When developers tried to buy the farm, Mrs. Kay declared, "I'll have no part in any bulldozers!" She and her husband bequeathed the entire tract to Morris County as an environmental center so that "each day would bring a new wonder and challenge to learn."

Natural New Jersey has long profited from such benefactors. The Kuser and Worthington families donated extensive tracts in the Kittatinny Mountains, while the Hewitts, Farnys, and Greens offered up their Highlands acreages. Today the New Jersey Chapter of The Nature Conservancy works with landowners large and small who wish to sell or donate ecologically significant lands. The group's 33,000 members have preserved nearly 50,000 wild New Jersey acres.

Schooley's Mountain

Morris County Park

Trail: **Falling Waters Trail, Quarry Stone Path, Grand Loop Trail, Upland Meadow Trail (loop)**
Distance: **2.9 miles**
Length: **3 hours**
Difficulty: **Moderate; 300-foot elevation gain**

Highlands hardwoods and a waterfall

Getting There

From I-80 east or west, take US 206 south for 8.0 miles to Chester. Turn right onto NJ 24 west and continue 5.0 miles to Long Valley. Turn right to stay on NJ 24 and climb Schooley's Mountain. Turn right onto Camp Washington Road, and right again onto East Springtown Road. In 0.3 mile turn right into the park.

Special Features

- Lake George
- Electric Brook Falls
- Views from rocky outcrop
- Oak-hickory forest

Early European map-makers labeled the uncharted emptiness of our continent simply as "The Great Forest of America." And great it was. Stretching from tropics to tundra, from the Atlantic Ocean to midwestern grasslands, it covered a million square miles and a third of what was to become the United States.

The Great Forest was a stately cathedral and treasure house. Old-growth trees grew 10 feet around and rose 150 feet high. Europeans were staggered by forest diversity. Today, even after centuries of ecosystem disruption, parts of the Appalachians still claim 130 species of native trees and 1,300 flowering plants.

The Great Forest provided timber, tools, and fuel to the first immigrants. It offered lumber for homes, shops, and ships; charcoal for iron furnaces; and rich soils in which to plant crops. Woodlands offered fruits and nuts for food, and herbs for medicine. The forest was a primary resource on which the first settlers depended for survival, and on which America built its wealth.

Today the Great Forest of America has been shattered into fragments, cut into national, state, and county parks. Preserved for us are pale reminders of the magnificent whole. And in our time, when plastic and metal often replace wood, it's easy to forget how much we once relied on trees—and still do.

The forests of Schooley's Mountain Park, like most of the Great Forest, have been used and abused since the first settlers. The land, named for the Schooley family who owned it in the 1790s, has been logged, farmed, quarried, and used as a resort and estate. The rejuvenated woods inspired Girl Scouts in the 1920s. Today the park's third- and fourth-growth trees attest to Great Forest resilience and warn of threats to its future.

This 2.9-mile loop hike, on obvious, named, but unblazed trails, starts at the lower, larger parking lot. Walk west toward the boathouse and cross Lake George on a floating dock. Red

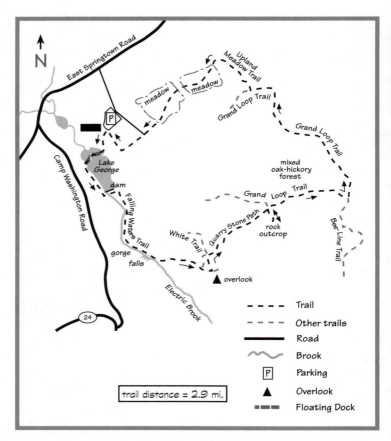

Schooley's Mountain

maple and knapweed line the near shore, while mallard ducks and Canada geese glide the lake. Waterfowl were so plentiful in America's colonial times as to inspire comparisons to Eden. The birds were diminished by unlimited hunting and a loss of wetland habitat. Alarmed hunters lobbied for laws to protect their sport, and waterfowl have seen a comeback. These days 10 million mallards populate North America, while the Canada goose is so numerous it has become a pest in suburban parks.

On the far shore, turn left and walk along the lake where multiflora rose forms a hedge beneath black cherry and red cedar trees. Multiflora rose was introduced by the state of New Jersey to farmers as a "living fence." Unfortunately the prickly bush drives out native plant species. But the news isn't all bad: the fast spread of multiflora rose has helped the northern mockingbird expand its range. It feeds on rose hips and nests amid the plant's thorns.

At the end of the lake (0.3 mile), turn left and take the walkway that passes over the Lake George Dam. On the far side of the dam, turn right onto the Falling Waters Trail and enter the forest. The trail descends into a deepening gorge, paralleling Electric Brook and passing a powerhouse ruin. The power plant once generated electricity for a stone quarry.

Today a rich mix of canopy and understory trees stretch up from the ravine to claim their share of sunlight. Every species was native to the Great Forest and valued by first settlers. White oaks, like those standing beside this brook, were milled into impenetrable hulls for America's navies, including the unsinkable "Old Ironsides"—the USS *Constitution*. Hop hornbeam, or ironwood, was once crafted into sled runners and wagon parts. Witch hazel was endowed with magical powers and used by dowsers to locate water. Sassafras makes an aromatic tea and was useful as a colonial pain reliever.

Many of these trees are still important today. Sugar maples, like those along Electric Brook, are tapped for sugar, a New England cash crop. Beeches provide wood flooring and bentwood furniture. Basswood is a source of gourmet honey, crates, and berry baskets. Tulip tree, made into dugout canoes by Native

Americans, is a valuable commercial hardwood, utilized in furniture making. It also provides pharmaceutical companies with a heart stimulant.

The trail follows the brook's falling cascades, which are edged by Christmas fern. The path becomes more difficult, descending over a sloping rock face to the base of one of the prettiest waterfalls in the Highlands (0.7 mile). The bottom of this 30-foot falls is a fine place to sit, but don't swim. Sadly, this pretty stream has been polluted and supports little life.

As you rest, meditate on the immense diversity of the Great Forest fragment surrounding you. Early immigrants were equally amazed. While Europe claims just dozens of native tree species, North America boasts hundreds. Geography is the reason. European mountain ranges stretch east and west, while American ranges stretch north and south. When the glaciers advanced, European trees were backed against a solid mountain wall and driven into extinction. American trees simply retreated, propagating southward along valleys. When the glaciers melted, the forests again spread north.

The trail continues briefly along the stream, then climbs steeply left through sugar maple, sweet birch, beech, and tulip tree. The tulip tree, its distinct leaves shaped like a child's drawing of a tulip flower, is our tallest eastern tree and one of the most ancient. Fossil specimens 70 million years old have been found, but most of the world's many tulip tree species were wiped out by the ice ages. Only an American and a Chinese variety survive today.

At 0.8 mile the path arrives at a rocky vista framed by black cherry trees. It looks over a ravine through which Electric Brook flows. Black cherry offers another example of forest value: it feeds 200 butterfly species and 70 bird species, plus bear, raccoon, and deer. Native Americans brewed the inner bark as tea. Today its workable wood is made into fine-grained furniture.

From the overlook, climb a little farther on the trail, then turn right onto the Quarry Stone Path. This trail passes through a typical Highlands forest, with chestnut oak, red oak, beech, and pignut and mockernut hickory trees rising overhead. In early spring, the ground is dotted with purple violets. The hickory, so prominent here, has dozens of uses, serving as lumber, furniture, tool handles, and sporting equipment. American hickories are also survivors of the last ice age. All of Europe's hickories were lost in the final glacial advance. Even the common violet has its uncommon uses: it is now being researched for its positive effects on skin cancer.

At 1.3 miles the Quarry Stone Path ends, but a short side trail leads right to a rock outcrop without a view (an interesting detour). On returning from the outcrop, follow the Grand Loop Trail to the right. (Do not take the left fork of the Grand Loop Trail, which leads quickly back to the parking lot.)

Continue on the right fork of the Grand Loop Trail, which descends to a T at 1.6 miles. Turn left, staying on the Grand Loop Trail. At 2.1 miles leave the Grand Loop Trail and swing right onto the Upland Meadow Trail, entering open country. These fields are edged in gray birch (used for barrel hoops and toothpicks) and quaking aspen (a leading pulpwood tree). Native Americans ingested aspen bark as an effective painkiller; it contains salicin, a modern aspirin ingredient. The Great Forest supplies many modern medicines and holds the hope of future cures, should we choose to preserve its fragments.

Walk straight ahead through the meadows back to the parking lot.

For More Information

Schooley's Mountain Park closes at twilight.

Morris County Park Commission, P.O. Box 1295, Morristown, NJ 07962; 973-326-7600; www.parks.morris.newjersey.us

Ode to the Great Forest

In 1680 Mahlon Stacey wrote a letter to his brother in England proclaiming New Jersey as "a country that produceth all things for the support and sustenance of man. . . . It is my judgment, by what I have observed, that fruit trees in this country destroy themselves by the weight of their fruit."

Today we must measure forest health not only by what has been saved, but what has been lost. While we can be proud of our parks, half of the Great Forest's million square miles are gone. The American chestnut and elm have been decimated by imported pests, while eastern hemlocks, beeches, and sugar maples may suffer similar fates. Woodland wildlife may never recover. In 1697 New Jersey offered twenty shillings to any "Christian," and half that sum to "Negroes or Indians," for wolf pelts. Gone today are the state's wolves, panthers, elk, and passenger pigeons (which once darkened our skies).

The future health of our forests is uncertain. While awareness and preservation efforts grow, scientists fear that the Great Forest may be too fragmented and disease threatened to be perpetually preserved.

Great Falls of the Passaic River

Trip 21 Paterson

> Trail: **Various sidewalks and paths**
> Distance: **1.5 miles**
> Length: **2 hours**
> Difficulty: **Easy; minimal elevation gain, some steps**

View the cataract that inspired America's Industrial Revolution

Getting There

From the east, take I-80 west to Exit 57C, Paterson Main Street. Go left two blocks to Grand Street. Turn left and drive four blocks to Spruce Street. From the west, take I-80 east to Exit 57B, downtown Paterson. Pass under I-80 to Grand Street. Turn left and drive one block to Spruce Street.

Turn right onto Spruce and drive three blocks. At the intersection of Spruce Street and McBride Avenue, turn right and immediately left into the Haines Overlook parking lot.

Special Features

- The Great Falls
- Igneous geology
- Urban trees
- Paterson Museum

Two hundred million years ago lava surged out onto the surface of the earth in eastern New Jersey, burying Piedmont sandstone and tropical jungles. That forty-story-high magma wall cooled into erosion-resistant basalt and hardened as the First Watchung Ridge. A weakness in the columnar joints of that basaltic ridge helped shape the future of New Jersey and America.

The powerful Passaic River was the first force to capitalize on the weak basaltic zone. The river cut a gap through the First Watchung Ridge, plunging over igneous cliffs and seeking sea level. Of all eastern U.S. waterfalls, only the Niagara's thundering water volume is greater than the raging torrents of the Passaic River's 280-foot-wide, 77-foot-tall Great Falls.

Alexander Hamilton was the second to exploit the gap in the basalt. A picnic enjoyed with George Washington at the Great Falls in 1778 inspired Hamilton to harness the river's 2,000-horsepower and to declare American industrial independence. In 1792 Hamilton's Society to Establish Useful Manufactures (S.U.M.) hired Pierre L'Enfant (architect of the nation's capital) to design the raceways, waterwheels, and mills of a new industrial-age center.

The planned city of Paterson, which sprang up at the falls, became an epicenter from which technology rippled forth over the world. Paterson mills manufactured clipper ship sails and Holland submarines to master the oceans, Colt revolvers and steam locomotives to win the American West, and the Curtis-Wright airplane engine, with which Charles Lindbergh conquered the air. Finally, however, terrible working conditions at Paterson mills resulted in labor unrest, the flight of industry elsewhere, and the decline of the city along the Passaic.

The first Dutch visitors to the Great Falls in 1680 declared it "a sight to be seen in order to observe the power and wonder

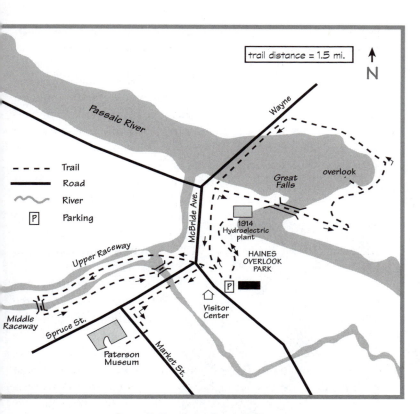

Great Falls of the Passaic River

of God." This 1.5-mile hike shows off that wonder, while demonstrating how people can both wisely use and abuse nature's power.

Exit the Harry S. Haines Overlook parking lot, turning right onto McBride Avenue. The sidewalk immediately passes the Captain Graupe veterans monument, which sits astride a basaltic outcrop. Notice how the black igneous rock has solidified into characteristic five- or six-sided polygonal columns.

Just beyond the Graupe monument, turn right into a cinder parking area and walk straight ahead, crossing a footbridge over a small arm of the Passaic River. Mulberry trees are common here. They were cultivated in a scheme to provide silkworms and raw silk to Paterson's textile industry. While silk manufacturing flourished, the silkworms did not. They succumbed to hard New Jersey weather. Raw silk had to be imported from Asia, then twisted and warped into fabric at Paterson mills. So successful was the business that the town was nicknamed Silk City.

The Great Falls topple over the First Watchung Ridge at Paterson.

Walk straight ahead to a second footbridge spanning the Passaic River. Just before crossing the bridge, look right: a large elm and hackberry tree (identified by its warty bark) cling to a basalt outcrop. Hackberry trees are resistant to air pollution and often planted in cities. Watch for robins, flickers, and squirrels feeding on the tree's autumn seeds.

The gracefully arching footbridge over the Passaic gives spectacular views of the football-field-wide falls and narrow gorge. In wet times, waves of whitewater tumble from above, crashing among broken basalt blocks far below. On sunny afternoons, a rainbow arcs up from the bottom of the gorge through the foam and mist. In dry times, the black basaltic cliffs are divided by multiple sheets, chutes, and trickles of falling water. As beautiful as this scene may be, it seems not to have impressed nineteenth-century urbanites. They often dumped trash from the cliff, using the Passaic River as an open sewer. Today the Passaic is polluted with agricultural runoff and industrial and suburban effluent—though it is getting cleaner.

Beyond the bridge, walk along a wrought-iron fence, descending left on steps to another impressive Great Falls overlook. Mulberry, hickory, and black locust trees (with deeply etched bark) shade the shore. Black locust grows well on depleted soils, such as those of industrial waste places. Like other legumes, its root nodules support nitrogen-fixing bacteria, which enrich nutrient poor soils.

Continue circling left around the Passaic River pool above the falls, passing by neat, nineteenth-century brick industrial buildings. The noise of the powerful falls drowns out city sounds. Huge sycamores, silver maples, and pin oaks overhang a paved bike path that swings up to Wayne Avenue.

Turn left onto Wayne Avenue and follow it back over the river. Mallard ducks and herring gulls find safe haven at the pool above the falls. Both species have adapted to humans. Scavenging herring gulls feed at Mid-Atlantic landfills.

After crossing the stream, swing left back onto McBride Avenue and then cross the street. Just before reaching an intersection with Spruce Street, turn right and enter a path along the upper raceway. Here the Society for Establishing Useful Manufactures harnessed the waters of the Passaic River, channeling the stream's flow into a three-tiered system of raceways used to turn waterwheels and run mill machinery. Today aquatic water marigolds and duckweed bloom in pools overlooked by Norway maple, elm, and hackberry.

In a few hundred feet turn left, cross a bridge over the Middle Raceway, and follow a path back to McBride Avenue. Just before you reach the street, a human-made waterfall topples from the upper raceway into the middle one. In summer, the pool beneath this artificial cascade blooms with white arrowhead.

Cross McBride Avenue and return to the Haines Overlook parking lot. Descend the stairs past the Alexander Hamilton monument to the Passaic River shore at the base of the Great Falls. From this vantage point walkers look along the 280-foot length of the gorge. We once watched a great cormorant resting on a piling here, and viewed English sparrows and starlings flitting over the water.

Pressed against the basalt cliff is the 1914 hydroelectric plant. This churchlike brick building with its gracefully arched windows and steeplelike tower attests to the reverence with which American industry once regarded itself. Today the plant has been renovated to provide electricity to local residents. From here, return to your car or take a side trip to the Paterson Museum (see the sidebar).

Paterson once offered hope to rural America as it sought to grow into a world power. Now the Passaic River, which has suffered years of exploitation, proclaims a new hope. It could become a clean river at the heart of a fine urban park, where the power of the Great Falls could again be viewed in all its glory.

For More Information

The falls are open dawn to dusk year-round, except when mist freezes on the footbridge, making walking hazardous. The Paterson Museum is open Tuesday through Friday 10 A.M. to 4 P.M., Saturday and Sunday 12:30 P.M. to 4:30 P.M., and closed Monday. The suggested donation is $2 for adults; children are free.

Great Falls Visitor Center, 65 McBride Avenue Extension, Paterson, NJ 07501; 973-279-9587

Paterson Museum, Thomas Rogers Building, 2 Market Street, Paterson, NJ 07501; 973-881-3874

A Side Trip to the Paterson Museum

At the Great Falls walkers learn why New Jersey's Piedmont, which covers just 20 percent of the state's land area, supports more than 60 percent of its population. The Piedmont's sudden elevation drops and waterfalls at places such as Paterson and Trenton along the Passaic, Delaware, Black, and other rivers challenged the imagination of Yankee mill builders and attracted settlers.

Walk from Haines Overlook Park across McBride Avenue along Spruce Street. Turn left onto Market Street and enter the Paterson Museum to see products born of the Great Falls and a great city. The redbrick factory housing the museum once manufactured Rogers locomotives. Paterson made 12,000 train engines for America's railroads. The museum also exhibits Colt revolvers and the Holland submarine, which a teacher-turned-inventor modeled after swimming porpoises.

Most beautiful is an exhibit of basaltic minerals found at only two spots on the globe, in Paterson and India. These zeolite minerals resemble fantastic sea coral formations, white and green crystals with showy fanlike and fibrous projections. Pectolite, natrolite, apophyllite, and other mineral crystals formed within gas bubbles of cooling basalt.

An exhibit of nineteenth-century patent medicines, including Doctor Hand's Colic Mixture, Lydia E. Pinkham's Sanitive Wash, and Ayer's Sarsaparilla, is fascinating. Most are herbal remedies containing such locally gathered ingredients as yellow dock root, buckthorn bark, burdock root, and gentian blossom. Some ingredients have medicinal value recognized today; some do not. Other medications packed a real wallop, containing 18 percent alcohol and morphine.

The Palisades, Bombay Hook

Palisades Interstate Park

Trail: **Shore Trail, Forest View Trail, Long Path, Alpine Approach Trail (loop)**
Distance: **5.5 miles**
Length: **4½ hours**
Difficulty: **Challenging; 500-foot elevation gain**

Explore a botanical melting pot

Getting There

From the George Washington Bridge, go north on the Palisades Interstate Parkway and take Exit 2. Continue east past the Palisades Park Commission headquarters, then downhill to the Alpine Boat Basin.

Special Features

- A Hudson River walk
- Spectacular igneous cliffs
- Views of Manhattan
- Eclectic mix of native and exotic species

Visitors to Palisades picnic groves in 1910 could shut their eyes and enjoy a symphony of immigrant voices. Scents of boiled cabbage, sauerbraten, and falafel floated on summer air beside the Hudson. Today trees cloak the shore, though they too represent the world. This exotic "multicultural forest" holds specimens from Europe, Asia, and beyond.

The Palisade cliffs formed about 190 million years ago when a magma wall or sill intruded between beds of Piedmont shale and sandstone. This molten rock cooled and hardened underground into diabase, contrasting with the fast-cooling surface basalts of the nearby Watchung Mountains. Like the basalts, the igneous diabase formed thin polygonal columns. It was these pillars, rising 500 feet above the Hudson River, that caused settlers to name these cliffs the Palisades after their resemblance to wooden stockades.

The Hudson shore "under the mountain" was settled by the Dutch, who farmed its narrow bands of rich soil and sailed round-bottomed river sloops. Later settlers pitched timber from cliff tops, providing fuel for steamships.

Nineteenth-century citizens were environmentally awakened by dynamite as quarrymen blasted Palisades diabase into paving stone. The New Jersey Federation of Women's Clubs led a fight to close those quarries and save the Palisades. In 1900 these women, who still had yet to win the right to vote, triumphed in one of the region's first environmental victories. They preserved 14 miles of cliff, forming the core of Palisades Interstate Park.

The Palisades Shore Path (13.5 miles in length) parallels the cliff base, while the Long Path (which one day will run from the George Washington Bridge to the Adirondacks) follows its

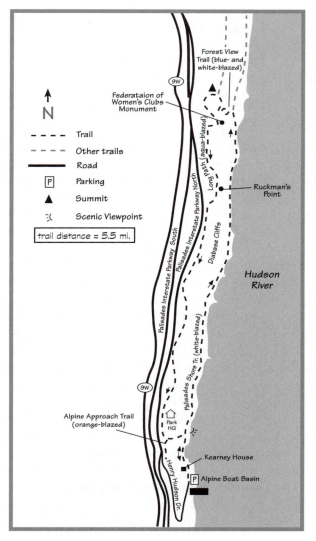

The Palisades, Bombay Hook

top. This 5.5-mile loop hike samples both trails in a strenuous but scenic walk.

An ornamental Norway spruce at the far end of the Alpine Boat Basin parking lot provides a first indication that you're not in a typical American forest. This European native is easily identified by its drooping, or weeping, limbs.

Walk straight ahead past the Kearney House. (0.1 mile). This old building was preserved in 1933 because it was believed then that British general Lord Cornwallis used the tavern as a headquarters before he and 5,000 troops climbed the cliffs in a failed attempt to head off Washington's army in its 1776 retreat to Trenton. Actually Cornwallis and his army came ashore 1.5 miles to the south.

A small concrete-lined stream flows into the Hudson here. Note the change in water level between the start and end of your hike. The Hudson River channel was gouged below sea level by the Wisconsin Glacier. Tidal for the lower 150 miles of its length, it is a fjord. This estuary, where fresh and salt water mix, is rich in life. Ocean shad and striped bass migrate far upriver to spawn. Once a great commercial fishery, the Hudson is currently polluted with carcinogenic industrial PCBs. Pete Seeger and his Hudson River Sloop *Clearwater* group are leading the PCB cleanup effort.

Just past the Kearney House, look for the white blazes of the Palisades Shore Trail as it follows a cobbled road uphill. The path enters what we called a "mixed-up" deciduous forest, where native and exotic tree species rub elbows. Native hackberry, black locust, and oaks mix with Norway maple (a smog-tolerant European shade tree), ailanthus (a fast-growing Chinese species and invasive pest), and Japanese maple (a pretty Asian ornamental).

This castle turret reminds walkers of the Palisades preservation effort won by the New Jersey Federation of Women's Clubs in 1900.

The understory also holds an erratic mix of native plants (poison ivy, joe-pye weed, and jewelweed), plus exotics (Japanese knotweed, garlic mustard, and multiflora rose), which drive out less hardy natives. A naturalist writing in 1959 found that 40 percent of all Palisades plants were European in origin.

At 0.2 mile ignore the orange-blazed Alpine Approach Trail leading steeply left on a cobbled road (this will be your return route). Continue on the white-blazed trail past a usually trickling waterfall, along a picturesque stone wall that offers intermittent but inspiring views of the Hudson.

The bird mix is also eclectic. Tufted titmice, warblers, and European starlings share the trees. "Bird-brained" Eugene Scheifflin deserves blame for the aggressive starling, which drives out native birds. In the 1890s he released a hundred

starlings in New York's Central Park in an attempt to intro-
duce all the bird species mentioned in Shakespeare's plays to
America. That mere hundred launched a starling takeover of
the continent. Coincidentally, the pesty starling helped stem
the spread of Japanese beetles, another destructive exotic. The
starling invasion led to laws curbing the import of exotic
species (see the sidebar).

The white-blazed Shore Path leaves the cobbled road
behind, rising and falling between the cliff base and the river. It
alternates between difficult walking on uneven igneous diabase
and easy walking on an earthen path.

The trail continues through an exotic vegetation mix. A
weird topiary of clinging grape and poison ivy vines lines the
riverbank. Native sweet gum and ash are joined by two odd
immigrants, the royal paulownia tree and Mexican alvaradoa.
The royal paulownia from China blossoms with clusters of purple flowers. The shrubby Mexican alvaradoa (with small,
rounded, pinnately compound ailanthuslike leaves) should only
grow south of the Rio Grande. How it found its way to the Hudson's shore is anybody's guess.

A riverside clearing amid tumbled-down diabase blocks
provides a spectacular view to the cliff tops at Ruckman's Point
(2.2 miles). Here the five- and six-sided columnar jointing of
the stone is plainly visible.

At about 2.5 miles look for the blue-and-white blazes of the
Forest View Trail leading left. This path switchbacks steeply for
500 vertical feet to the top of the cliff. Near the top, the blue-
and-white trail intercepts the aqua-blazed Long Path (2.8 miles).
Follow the combined trails left and south back toward Alpine.

The path rises along a shallow ravine over glacially scratched
diabase slabs. Manhattan lay under the Wisconsin Glacier just

15,000 years ago. You know you've made it to the top when you get to the New Jersey Federation of Women's Clubs monument, a castle turret with views of the Hudson River (3.0 miles).

The cliff has served as a barrier to the invasion of exotics found below. On the flat, even walk south a more traditional forest of beech, red oak, hickory, and maple muffles the sound of nearby Palisades Parkway.

Follow the Long Path's aqua blazes now, ignoring the right turnoff of the blue-and-white-blazed trail (3.1 miles). Short, unmarked paths regularly lead left to cliff views. One of the best paths comes just past a wooden bridge and leads to Grey Crag, a mass of diabase pillars separated from the main cliff by a ravine and reached by a concrete footbridge (cross at your own risk) built by John Ringling, of the circus, as part of his mansion's grounds.

The Long Path exits the woods at the New Jersey Palisades Interstate Park Commission headquarters (5.0 miles). Follow the paved road 0.1 mile past the building and turn left at a sign that reads Path to River. Walk straight ahead on the orange-blazed Alpine Approach Trail as the aqua Long Path turns right through a stone arch. Descend steeply to an intersection with the white-blazed Shore Trail (5.3 miles). Turn right, returning to the Alpine Boat Basin parking lot.

For More Information

Palisades hiking trails are open dawn to dusk. The Palisades Interstate Park Commission's Web site offers hike descriptions.

Palisades Interstate Park Commission; P.O. Box 155, Alpine, NJ 07620; 201-768-1360; www.njpalisades.org

Global Disaster or Global Economy: The Threat of Exotic Species

The largest mass extinction since the dinosaurs is under way in Africa's Lake Victoria, as ravenous Nile perch, stocked for sportfishing, hunt 150 fish species out of existence. Birdsong has ceased on the Pacific island of Guam, where 300,000 native birds have fallen prey to the brown tree snake, unwittingly imported by our military. In 1845 a fungus accidentally imported from the United States doomed Ireland's potato crop and a million people in the Irish potato famine.

Exotic species are plants and animals transported beyond their home ranges, usually by people. Unopposed by predators, exotics can wreak ecological and financial havoc. At least 4,500 exotics have been established in the United States since Columbus landed. Some, like soybeans or the European honeybee, are beneficial to us. But about 15 percent of known U.S. exotics—more than 600 species—cause severe ecological harm.

Who is to blame? Round up the usual suspects: a population that craves imported consumer goods, from rare tropical plants to parrots and pirhanas. Also blame global corporations that maximize profits by manufacturing abroad and shipping in bulk: aliens ride free on planes, boats, and trains. In addition, the globe-trotting U.S. military often transports exotics on equipment.

No study has been done to estimate the number of exotics introduced worldwide. But as the distance between places shrinks and the tide of global commerce swells, the exotic-species problem deepens. A 1993 congressional study declared that, left unchecked, "by the mid–21st Century, biological invasions will become one of the most prominent ecological issues on Earth."

Hackensack Meadowlands
DeKorte State Park

Trail: Kingsland Overlook Trail, Marsh Discovery Trail, and Transco Trail (loop)
Distance: 1.5 miles
Length: 1½ hours
Difficulty: Easy; flat

The revival of an urban estuary within sight of Manhattan skyscrapers

Getting There

From NJ 3 west, take NJ 17 south (Lyndhurst exit). Follow the ramp to a traffic light, make a left onto Polito Avenue, and continue for 0.6 mile to its end. At the stop sign turn left onto Valley Brook Avenue and follow for 1.5 miles to the HMDC Environmental Center.

From NJ 3 east, take NJ 17 south (the Lyndhurst–Service Road exit). At the bottom of the exit ramp is a traffic signal. Go straight through the intersection onto Polito Avenue. Follow the directions above.

Special Features

- Explore the Hudson-Raritan Estuary
- Upland woods
- Tidal wetlands
- Migratory bird haven

The emblem of DeKorte State Park is the egret. It could just as appropriately be the phoenix. This wetland park—today a haven for flocks of migratory birds—arose from the ashes of terrible environmental degradation.

Fifteen thousand years ago New Jersey's Meadowlands lay beneath the chilly waters of glacial Lake Hackensack. As the climate warmed, the ice melted, the lake drained, and the ocean rose to encircle Manhattan. By 1492 the Meadowlands were transformed into a lowland maze of meandering streams and fresh- and saltwater marshes. Vast tracts of Atlantic white cedar with trunks 4 feet in diameter grew to more than 100 feet tall. This part of the Hudson-Raritan Estuary supported a fabulous wealth of waterfowl, mammals, and shellfish, upon which Lenape Native Americans feasted.

Enter the Europeans. Dutch settlers arrived on the banks of the Hackensack River in 1626, driving out the Lenape. Settlers grazed cattle on salt hay and used marsh reeds as roof thatch. White cedars, covering a third of the Meadowlands, were cut for ship timber, fencing, casks, and churns. By the 1800s demand for dry land led to wetland "reclamation" projects. Drainage ditches and dikes were built in endless wars against tides and muskrats. Homes and factories steadily encroached on the marsh.

By 1900 the sunken meadows and tidal creeks had become a dumping ground for raw sewage and industrial pollutants. Wildlife diversity plummeted. In the 1950s flocks of seagulls lurched over mountains of noxious urban garbage. Bulldozers buried tons of filth in landfills. Drainage projects and pesticide spraying temporarily controlled mosquito populations. Railroads, roads, and power lines crisscrossed a dying land.

But in the 1960s efforts to restore and preserve the Hackensack Meadowlands were initiated. From the 1990s on, citizen

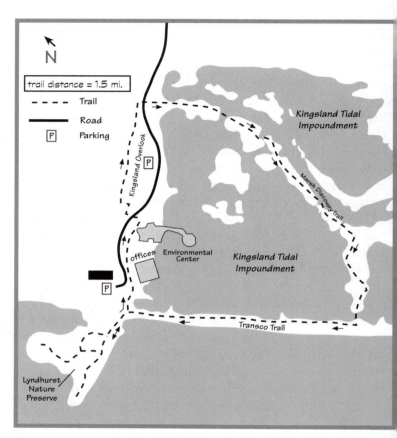

Hackensack Meadowlands

groups such as the New York/New Jersey Baykeeper and Hackensack Riverkeeper successfully fought plans for new development. Hopes are that the remainder of the wetlands, about 8,000 acres, will be protected soon.

Begin this 1.5-mile walk across the parking lot from the environmental center. Follow the trail as it gently climbs a human-made mountain. The 6-acre Kingsland Overlook represents a high-tech solution to the landfill reclamation problem. Tons of household waste were capped by a waterproof fabric made from 400,000 recycled soda bottles. The skin of this artificial hillside was then covered with topsoil, sewage sludge, and decomposed leaves rich in nutrients. Today native and nonnative plants blanket the area. Kingsland Overlook is a miracle of carefully nurtured diversity.

A 0.25-mile stroll along the trail takes you on a tour of natural succession from butterfly meadow through eastern coastal grassland prairie, late woody field, young woodland, and evergreen forest. Wildflowers carpet the knoll. Flower-of-an-hour (pale yellow blossoms with a purple center), rugosa rose, morning glories, daylilies, honeysuckle (with white tubular flowers), and common mugwort (exuding a pleasant kitchen herb smell) offer up a varied palette of rich colors and sweet scents. Sit on a bench and sniff the air while taking in the view of Manhattan.

Monarch butterfly larvae (caterpillars striped yellow, black, and white) browse on milkweed. This plant is toxic and unpalatable to many animals, as is the monarch butterfly. Its bright red-brown color warns would-be predators of a disagreeable meal. The nonpoisonous viceroy butterfly mimics the monarch in color and pattern in an attempt to fool feeding birds.

Kingsland Overlook is also graced by red cedar, shining sumac, gray birch, and big-tooth aspen (representing early successional trees), plus pin oak, ash, and spruce (representing later growth stages). Blue grosbeaks, mourning doves, and mockingbirds flit amid dense foliage.

The Overlook Trail descends gently, crosses a road, passes through a gate, and enters the Kingsland Tidal Impoundment on the Marsh Discovery Trail. This 0.4-mile path connects the mainland with a series of dredge-spoil islands via a wide, floating plastic boardwalk. Handrails, trash cans, and benches are made from recycled material. Explore several short side trails to bird blinds.

This estuary, where Kingsland Creek flows into the brackish Hackensack River, is a tidal wetland. Estuaries provide the lifeblood of the world's oceans. As freshwater streams mix with salt water, nutrients and oxygen are added while pollutants are removed. Estuaries offer food and shelter to two-thirds of all commercially important fish. Of the more than 12,000 square miles of salt marsh that once lined the eastern seaboard, less than 50 percent remains. New Jersey alone has lost a million wetland acres. These facts explain just how valuable the revitalized Hackensack Meadowlands ecosystem is to the world.

More than 260 migrating bird species already know the worth of the marsh. In spring, waterfowl and shorebirds stop off on their flights to northern breeding grounds. In summer, wading birds and songbirds arrive. In autumn, shorebirds stop over on their long migrations to South America. Many raptors, especially red-tailed and rough-legged hawks, and seagulls winter in the Meadowlands.

Listen for the laughing cackle of common moorhens (marsh chickens or gallinules) as they move among the reeds. Endangered pied-billed grebes and ruddy ducks nest in dense cover. Sandpipers gather on the mud flats to feed. Snowy and great egrets stalk fish upon stiltlike legs (see the sidebar). Look for raccoon, muskrat, mouse, and shrew tracks along the shore at low tide.

Bird and beast seem blissfully unaware of overflying jets and the roar of NJ 3 and Pulaski Skyway traffic. There's something very calming about the presence of wild animals here at the very heart of industrial civilization.

Phragmites is a dominant marsh plant here. While some ecologists view this fast-propagating reed as a pesty invasive species, others think it has its place in helping disturbed ecosystems recover. Switchgrass and groundsel trees (with leathery, coarsely toothed leaves and cottonlike fruit in autumn) thrive as well.

Also visible in the estuary are the blackened stumps of Atlantic white cedars. These trees are so rot resistant that submerged stumps have endured in Meadowlands muck hundreds of years after cutting.

About 0.8 mile into your walk, the Marsh Discovery Trail intersects with the Transco Trail, a dike in which a transcontinental gas pipeline is buried. Turn right and follow a wide, flat road for 0.5 mile back to the mainland. Milkweed, phlox, and campion, overshadowed by black locust trees, line the Transco Trail. The showy rose mallow, a hibiscus family member, blooms in late summer.

At the end of the Transco Trail, pass through a gate and turn left into the Lyndhurst Nature Preserve. This $3^1/_2$-acre reclaimed garbage island holds diverse habitats: salt marsh, beach, upland holly woodland, and pine oak forest.

At the end of the trail, backtrack to the parking lot and environmental center. Then check out the kid-friendly Hudson-Raritan Estuary exhibits inside.

For More Information

Trails are open 8:30 A.M. until dusk; closed in inclement weather. Environmental center hours are 9 A.M. to 5 P.M. weekdays, and 10 A.M. to 3 P.M. weekends. To volunteer and help protect the estuary, contact the New York/New Jersey Baykeeper or Hackensack Riverkeeper.

New Jersey Meadowlands Commission Environmental Center, 2 DeKorte Park Plaza, Lyndhurst, NJ 07071; 201-460-8300; www.meadowlands.state.nj.us

New York/New Jersey Baykeeper: www.nynjbaykeeper.org/
Hackensack Riverkeeper: www.hackensackriverkeeper.org/

Among the Great Egrets

A great egret poses statuesque in ankle-deep water. In one smooth motion it unfolds a powerful S-curved neck, dips a sharp-pointed yellow bill beneath the ripples, and snaps up a fish. In an instant it again stands utterly still. Fishing great egrets are among the most public of birds at DeKorte State Park.

These majestic all-white birds are much more private when they breed on barrier islands and in marshes along the Jersey coast in summer. There's a real pecking order to claiming the best nest sites. Great egrets bully their way into the highest trees, bushes, and reeds, pushing smaller herons and ibises into lower places exposed to mammal and snake predators.

Parents take turns sitting on bright blue eggs, protecting them from gulls and crows, while a mate flies off in search of food. In autumn, the birds migrate as far as the Gulf Coast, though some winter in the Garden State.

We're lucky to have these beautiful animals. Like other wading birds, great egrets were hunted nearly to extinction by nineteenth-century plume hunters seeking to beautify ladies' hats.

Cherry Blossom Time
Branch Brook Park, Newark

Trip 24

Trail: **Various walkways and paths (wander out-and-back)**
Distance: **2.0 miles**
Length: **As many hours as you wish!**
Difficulty: **Easy; flat**

Cure wintertime cabin fever with a million spring blossoms

Getting There

From I-280 east, take the First Avenue, Newark, exit. Turn left onto First Avenue, then right at the second traffic light onto Park Avenue. Make an immediate right, following signs into Branch Brook Park. Turn left onto Park Road, passing around a lake, and heading to the north end of the park. Visitor center parking is on the right.

Special Features
• Olmsted-designed urban park
• 2,700 cherry trees—more than Washington, D.C.
• Arriving spring songbirds
• Second River

In Japan winter's passing is celebrated with *hanami*, literally translated as "flower looking"—a few sweet, fleeting days when raucous friends and romantic couples gather to eat, drink, laugh, and sing beneath a white and pink cloud of cherry blossoms. This is a time not only of great joy, but also of spiritual rebirth.

Most Americans imagine cherry blossom time to be celebrated only in Asia or along the Tidal Basin of the Potomac River. In fact, Newark's Branch Brook Park boasts 2,700 cherry trees, outblossoming Washington, D.C., every year. In mid-April, while winter still holds upland New Jersey in its fierce grip, Newark enjoys a profusion of spring color and renewed life.

Branch Brook Park itself is the product of several remarkable rebirths. In 1895 this former Civil War training ground was a tenement-encircled marsh. Old Blue Jay Swamp simultaneously supplied drinking water and sewage disposal to the city's poor. By 1900 the area was transformed into America's first county park, with a new lake and formal gardens. In that same year John Charles Olmsted (stepson of Frederick Law Olmsted, designer of New York's Central Park) redesigned Branch Brook's landscaping along more natural lines.

In 1927 Caroline Bamberger Fuld (heir to a Newark retail fortune) donated 2,000 Japanese cherry tree seedlings to Branch Brook. But as the trees grew to maturity, Newark itself suffered from devastating urban blight. In the 1980s the park enjoyed another rebirth as its waterways, walkways, and playing fields were fully renovated. Today meticulous groundskeepers spend 1,000 annual hours preparing the park's cherry trees for their spring display.

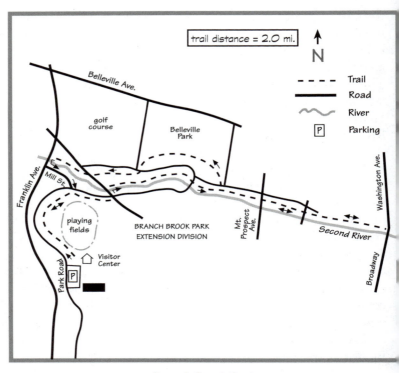

Branch Brook Park

Unlike most of the woodland hikes in this book, this walk requires no sturdy hiking boots or attention to trail blazes. It is best enjoyed as an aimless ramble amid the first bounties of spring.

This seasonal walk does require perfect timing. Arrive too early in April and you'll be greeted by bare limbs. Arrive too late, or after heavy rain or wind, and you'll find only fallen blossoms. The cherry trees usually flower in the second and third weeks of April but make their showiest display for just two or three days. In Japan weather forecasters give daily predictions of progressing cherry blossom peaks. In New Jersey a call to the Essex County Park Commission (973-268-3518) provides the same information.

Most of the ornamental cherry trees are located in the northernmost section of the park, extending between Heller Parkway and Belleville Avenue, called the Extension Division. To begin your walk, face the visitor center and turn left, heading north along a paved pathway paralleling Park Road.

Venerable eastern deciduous trees line the way and contrast dramatically with woodland counterparts. A solitary black oak, for example, seen at a Y in the pathway next to a baseball diamond, has no need to grow tall to compete for light. This stocky tree has a short, thick trunk, above which it spreads outward in a wide, rounded crown. Sycamores (with mottled, light and dark green camouflage-style bark) and beeches (with smooth, bluish gray bark) are two of the easiest trees to spot at Branch Brook before leaves appear.

Fork left at the Y mentioned above. You immediately encounter your first Japanese cherry trees. There are six subspecies of ornamental cherries in the park. While these hybrid trees produce spectacular blossoms, they've had most of their sexual and reproductive traits bred out of them (see the sidebar). Sterile flowers often produce little scent to attract pollinators and no fall fruit. They are, however, a welcome treat for winter-weary eyes.

The absence of foliage makes bird watching easy. Look for juncos (slate-gray snowbirds that winter in New Jersey's urban parks), chickadees, and English sparrows. A trickle of spring warblers sometimes arrives at cherry blossom time. Palm, yellow-rumped, and pine warblers are the first to appear in April, the vanguard of a flood of songbirds arriving in May. The park boasts more than 130 bird species, including 24 types of warblers.

Robins, rooting out earthworms, are prominent on the park's greening lawns starting in March. While these red-breasted thrushes are known as harbingers of spring, global warming may be changing that. Warming trends have resulted in robins wintering not in southern states but deep within northern forests. Experienced birders have seen the birds in New Jersey Highlands woods as late as December.

Many of the earthworms upon which robins feed in spring-time are European imports. The Wisconsin Glacier froze out many New England and Mid-Atlantic species. Nightcrawlers, large and powerful earthworms, arrived in the potting soil of European settlers and quickly colonized our highly compacted glacial soils. Besides serving as a meal for robins, the worms revitalize and aerate topsoil, moving some 18 tons of earth to the surface per acre per year.

About fifteen minutes into the walk, you arrive at Second River. Make a right and wander along the many looping path-ways that play tag with this walled-in urban stream. Now you are truly in what Newark has dubbed "cherry blossom land." At peak times a white-blossom cloud creates the illusion of a bizarre blizzard's aftermath. Tree limbs appear to be blanketed by fresh snow, while tufts of lush green grass waver in the breeze beneath them.

The Higan cherry, or weeping Japanese cherry, with pale pink flowers and gracefully weeping crown, is one of the showiest varieties. The origin of the Yoshino cherry, one of Japan's favorite cultivated trees, is shrouded in mystery. This beautiful tall hybrid was discovered growing in Tokyo in 1872. Kwanzan, Shirofugen, Amanogawa, and Cornelian cherry trees bloom with clusters of pink-and-white flowers. The stone walls of Second River are draped in yellow cascades of forsythia, while clumps of daffodils bloom in scattered beds.

When you reach Mount Prospect Avenue or Broadway, turn back. Cross to the north side of Second River to enjoy cherry trees and beeches on the hillside above the stream in Belleville Park. As you walk, you may encounter the Lenape Trail. This 36-mile, yellow-blazed urban trail connects Essex County parklands between Branch Brook Park and South Mountain.

When you intersect Franklin Avenue on the west side of the park, turn left and meander back to your car at the visitor center parking lot.

For More Information

Branch Brook Park is open dawn to dusk. To avoid crowds during cherry blossom time (usually the second or third week in April), try to walk on a weekday.

Essex County Parks Department, 115 Clifton Avenue, Newark, NJ 07104; 973-268-3518

A National Passion for Flowers

Since ancient times the Japanese have fostered a deep reverence for and sensitivity to nature and the changing seasons. The Shinto religion inspired peaceful gardens, where ornamental bonsai and cherry trees were cultivated for their aesthetic and spiritual value. Flower arranging became a national obsession, with each arrangement seen as a mirror of the soul.

In southern Japan (on the same latitude as Georgia) people stayed attuned to the unfolding seasons with a floral calendar. New Year's Day came in February and coincided with the first appearance of the plum blossoms. March marked the blooming of ornamental peach and cherry trees. The following months saw the appearance of wisteria, iris, lotus, hibiscus, and chrysanthemum blossoms.

Patient Japanese gardeners with a keen eye for selection nurtured many ornamental flowering varieties. Fruit trees, they learned, could be cloned from a single branch, sucker, or cutting of a parent tree. Thousands of years before Gregor Mendel's studies in heredity, the Japanese employed sophisticated grafting techniques. A cutting was fastened to the stem of a tree, resulting in hybrids selected for the very showiest display of blossoms.

Today the sakura cherry blossom is Japan's national flower, and the ephemeral blossoms remain a favorite of Japanese poets:

> What a strange thing!
> to be alive
> beneath cherry blossoms.
>
> —Kobayashi Issa
> (translated by Robert Hass)*

Sit upon the grass beneath a Branch Brook cherry tree and pen your own haiku celebrating the miracle of spring.

*The Essential Haiku: Versions of Basho, Buson, & Issa, edited by Robert Hass. Hopewell, NJ: Ecco Press, 1994, p. 156.

Great Swamp Outdoor Education Center

Morris County Park

> Trail: **Orange Loop, Blue Loop, Pioneer Red Loop, and Green Loop Trails**
> Distance: **1.5 to 3 miles**
> Length: **1 to 3 hours (avoid mosquito season in July and August)**
> Difficulty: **Easy; flat**

Walk the bottom of former glacial Lake Passaic

Getting There

From I-287 south in Morristown, take the Madison Avenue exit, turning left at the end of the ramp onto NJ 124. From I-287 north, take the South Street exit, heading left then immediately right onto NJ 124. Follow NJ 124 east into Madison. Go under a small railroad bridge, and at the second light turn right onto Green Village Road. Continue straight ahead through three lights, then go another mile. The Great Swamp Outdoor Education Center is on the right.

Special Features

- Wetland habitat
- 200-plus bird species
- Diverse wildflowers
- Morris County Outdoor Education Center

Like so many of America's most prized parks, the Great Swamp's 7,500 acres were only preserved due to a close brush with oblivion. Its townless and roadless inaccessibility (so loved by outdoorspeople today) nearly doomed it. This tangle of hardwood swamp, marsh, upland timber, river, and brook just 30 miles from Manhattan was viewed in 1959 as the ideal site for a jetport.

Some 160 million years ago dinosaurs roamed these acres while an impermeable layer of clay and silt was laid down. Twenty thousand to 40,000 years ago the Wisconsin ice sheet covered northern New Jersey. Meltwater trapped between the glacier to the north and the basaltic Watchung Mountains to the south formed glacial Lake Passaic. This 30-mile-long and 10-mile-wide lake was 160 to 240 feet deep near the spot where you'll be hiking.

As the glacier receded 15,000 years ago, the lake drained slowly through the Watchung Mountains via the Passaic River at Paterson (see Trip 21). It is still draining today. Colonists skirted these wet acres, entering only to graze livestock and to harvest trees as fuel and as timber for railroad ties, fruit baskets, shingles, and Morris Canal boats.

To jetport planners, this blank spot on New Jersey maps was appealing. What they failed to see were the Great Swamp's 200-plus bird species (about a quarter of those found in the United States), 600 plant species, 18 amphibian species, 24 fish species, and 33 mammal species, including mink and river otter. A grassroots army of citizens rallied to rescue the swamp. The battle raged until 1964, when the Great Swamp National Wildlife Refuge was dedicated.

The Morris County Outdoor Education Center, with its 3.5 miles of easy trails, provides access to the easternmost section of

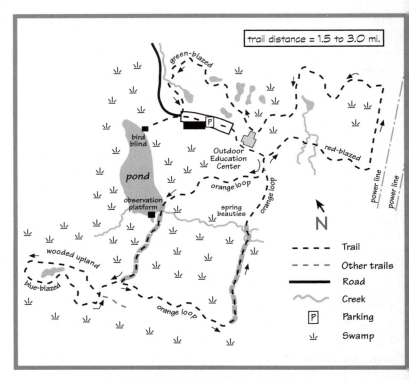

Great Swamp Outdoor Education Center

the national refuge. Begin the hike by leaving the center and following the Orange Loop Trail.

Note immediately how water level determines plant life in the Great Swamp. A variation of a few feet in elevation means the difference among pond, swamp, marsh, and dry woods. The rich former lake-bottom soil here at the swamp's edge supports tall oak, tulip tree, hickory, and beech. Beneath their leafy canopy, mountain laurel and blueberry bushes thrive. Only about 40 percent of the Great Swamp is actual wetland.

To the right is a red maple swamp. Such wetland forests support many species of migrating birds, including Canada warblers, yellow-rumped warblers (identified by the unique golden splash atop their tails), ovenbirds, and catbirds. The slender gray catbird lives in the deep thickets of edge environments, but it is curious and often pops into the open to get a better view. It is identified by its jumbled succession of musical and mechanical-sounding phrases, mixed with a catlike mewing call. It successfully mimics more than thirty other birds. The catbird is valuable to farmers for its voracious consumption of insect pests.

A boardwalk leads to an observation platform that looks out over a pretty pond. In springtime, painted turtles line up on logs to sun themselves (see the sidebar). Beside the boardwalk, poison ivy vines climb maple saplings. In April, tussock sedge, skunk cabbage, unfolding fern fiddleheads, and cattails are renewed.

Cattails are ecologically vital to marsh health. Swamp sparrows, marsh wrens, and red-winged blackbirds nest amid cattail stalks. Goldfinches line their nests with cattail down. Muskrats feed on the plant, as do painted turtles and many birds and insects. The plant had many uses among Native Americans (as bandages, dolls, and pillow stuffing), and has many more among modern people (as a source of flour, ethyl alcohol, burlap, adhesive, and rayon).

At the end of the boardwalk, the trail enters another wooded upland. Turn right onto the Blue Loop Trail, passing through an understory of mountain laurel. Look to the right at the start of this trail for a swamp chestnut oak. This tree, with wavy-edged oblong leaves, was once nicknamed for its particular uses: basket oak (because its fibers were easily woven into baskets) and cow oak (for its sweet edible acorns preferred by cows).

The Blue Loop Trail curls around several open pools of water, which in springtime are filled with flitting pollywogs. The Great Swamp provides New Jersey amphibians with fine breeding habitat. The endangered blue-spotted salamander, for example, is found almost exclusively in the Great Swamp. It spends most of its year underground but emerges to breed in seasonal ponds during the first March thaw.

A tapestry of woodland wildflowers, including starflower, rue anemone, and Canada mayflower, blossom here. The moisture-loving Canada mayflower, with its glossy, heart-shaped leaves and delicate cluster of white flowers, spreads via underground runners (called rhizomes) from which many clones sprout, colonizing the forest floor.

When the Blue Loop Trail returns to the Orange Loop Trail, turn right onto the branch of the Orange Loop Trail that begins closest to the boardwalk. This inner loop skirts the edge of the wetlands. The trail crosses a disturbed area beneath a power line where phragmites plants, topped by seed-covered plumes, are taking over the swamp. Phragmites, a plant with little nutritional value, drives out native cattails and other marsh plants, forming a monoculture.

The path now goes onto another boardwalk over a wet area lined with horsetail rushes, Virginia rose, cinquefoil, skunk cabbage, and sensitive fern. If you are here in May, this is the place to stop and enjoy spring beauties. These tiny, pinkish white flowers speckle the swamp.

The Orange Loop Trail returns to the outdoor center. You've now walked about 1.5 miles. If you want to extend your walk, follow the red-blazed Pioneer Loop to the right just before reaching the center. This trail, named for the group of AT&T corporate volunteers who built it, wanders through a wet woodland where we saw ribbon snakes (resembling garter snakes, but with narrow heads and bodies), a great blue heron taking wing, and blooming mayapple.

As the Pioneer Loop Trail returns to the Outdoor Education Center, follow the Green Loop Trail to the right through a drier upland forest where white-tailed deer have left tracks in soil that once lined the bottom of glacial Lake Passaic. Back at the parking lot, walk out to the bird blind that overlooks the pond. As you sit, try to imagine the irrevocable loss if the flight patterns of migratory songbirds had been sacrificed to those of Boeing 747s.

For More Information

Trails are open dawn to dusk year-round (though insects are fierce in July and August). The center is open daily from September to June and has nature walks and other environmental activities.

Great Swamp Outdoor Education Center, 247 Southern Boulevard, Chatham, NJ 07928; 973-635-6629

Morris County Park Commission, P.O. Box 1295, Morristown, NJ 07962; 973-326-7600; www.parks.morris.newjersey.us

Turtle Talk

A turtle's shell is an ancient structure; turtles witnessed the rise and fall of the dinosaurs. Fused with vertebrae and ribs, the shell can never be shed the way a lobster, for example, molts its exoskeleton. Instead the shell grows outward and thickens as the turtle grows.

The bird blind at the edge of the pond is the perfect place from which to observe turtles. Painted turtles regularly bask in the sun atop logs and rocks. With binoculars, look for red and yellow stripes on the sides of these turtles' heads and necks. These reptiles have good vision; the slightest movement on shore will prompt them to slide into open-water safety.

Snapping turtles also inhabit this pond, though they mostly stay submerged. In early summer, female painted turtles and snappers lay eggs in holes they excavate on dry land. Heat from the sun incubates the eggs. A cool summer (averaging below 88 degrees Fahrenheit) will result in most of the eggs developing into males; warmer temperatures produce mostly female hatches. A late-season clutch of eggs, or even the hatchlings, may spend the winter underground.

Mostly vegetarian, painted turtles occasionally eat decaying animal matter. Snappers are mostly carnivorous, but will occasionally have a salad of aquatic vegetation. In winter, both species burrow into the mud and hibernate. Breathing ceases, and the turtle's heart may beat only once every ten minutes. In spring, when the water becomes warmer than the mud at the pond's bottom, the turtles awaken from their suspended animation.

—Jean LeBlanc

Leonard J. Buck Garden

Somerset County Park

Trail: **Various walkways and paths (loop)**
Distance: **1.5 miles**
Length: **2 hours**
Difficulty: **Easy**

Explore lava flows and an extinct waterfall
landscaped by a fantastic garden

Getting There

From I-287, take Exit 22 (if you're approaching from the north) or Exit 22B (from the south) onto US 202/206 north. Stay right on US 202, following signs for Morristown and Far Hills. At the Far Hills train station, turn right just before reaching the railroad tracks onto Liberty Corner–Far Hills Road. In 0.9 mile turn right onto Layton Road. Buck Garden is on the left.

Special Features

- Remnants of an ancient Passaic River waterfall
- 33-acre pleasure garden
- Rare Franklinia tree and dawn redwood
- Basalt igneous geology

Leonard J. Buck Garden

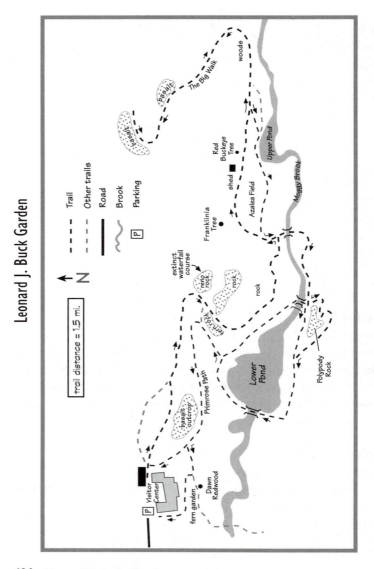

trail distance = 1.5 mi.

N

Legend:
- Trail
- Other trails
- Road
- Brook
- P Parking

The Big Walk

woods

basalt

basalt

Upper Pond

Red Buckeye Tree

shed

Moggy Brook

Azalea Field

Franklinia Tree

extinct waterfall course

fern rock

rock

fern rock

rock

Polypody Rock

Lower Pond

Primrose Path

basalt outcrop

Visitor Center

P

fern garden

Dawn Redwood

Interstate 287 shoots through a gap in the Second Watchung Mountain near Far Hills. The highway pursues the path of least resistance, a low spot in the igneous basalt ridge. During the last ice age a mighty river took advantage of the same gap as it rushed out of glacial Lake Passaic, tumbled over a great waterfall, and surged out to meet the Raritan River on the Piedmont plain.

The mile-high Wisconsin ice sheet melted away 15,000 years ago, no longer damming the 200-foot-deep Lake Passaic. The lake found a new outlet, flowed south into the Passaic River, looped northeast, and passed through the Watchungs at the Great Falls of Paterson (see Trip 21). The 30-mile-long glacial lake eventually drained, becoming the Great Swamp (see Trip 25). The spectacular waterfall at Far Hills faded into prehistory, its dry riverbed a landmark only in the lore of New Jersey geologists. A tiny stream, Moggy Brook, zigzagged among the igneous outcroppings that once marked the falls.

In the 1930s the magic of Moggy Hollow was rediscovered by Leonard J. Buck. This mining engineer purchased the old riverbed as part of his estate. When he discovered the land's fascinating geologic roots, he resolved to turn the spot into one of the Northeast's premier rock gardens. Buck and landscape architect Zenon Schrieber used high-powered hoses to clear away stony debris and dynamite to expose and sculpt the relic waterfall. The unique garden they nurtured among the basalt lava flows offered a sensuous contrast between native plantings and exotics gathered from around the world. In 1976 Buck's widow donated the garden to Somerset County.

Today Buck Garden is a 33-acre pleasure garden where groomed paths meander between rock outcrops, around lily-pad-covered pools, over rainbow bridges, and amid woodland wildflowers, bulbs, azaleas, ferns, and heathers. This is also a fine

The Lower Pond provides a wet microclimate for river birch and cardinal flower.

place to learn trees, since most are labeled.

Begin your walk at the upper parking lot. A deeply furrowed black locust rises in the courtyard of the visitor center (once the Buck family carriage house). This Appalachian native tree was almost wiped out by the Wisconsin Glacier. With human help it has more than reclaimed its range. Black locusts are planted as ornamentals from Maine to California. They were also exported to France in the 1700s and are now one of Europe's most common American trees.

Pass through the visitor center and walk straight ahead into a rhododendron grove where Virginia bluebells and shocking-pink bleeding hearts show off their drooping blossoms in springtime. The path quickly reaches the top of Big Rock. This basalt outcrop forms one wall of Moggy Hollow and is the northern remnant of the extinct waterfall. A small, grassy vista looks over the Lower Pond. To the left of the pond are Reno Rock, New Rock, and Horseshoe Rock, which once formed an island at the center of the great cataract. Opposite the pond is Polypody Rock, the former southern side of the falls.

Continue straight ahead beneath towering hemlocks. Native Christmas fern thrives amid cultivated plum-leaved azalea and Japanese painted fern (with its alternate leaflets).

Turn right just before reaching Reno Rock and walk among Japanese jack-in-the-pulpit, which sports green berries in autumn instead of the red of our American variety. Native

Solomon's seal, hay-scented fern, early saxifrage, and white snakeroot adorn the ground, while witch hazel, chestnut oak, and mockernut hickory fill out the canopy above. Legend has it that Mr. Buck jokingly named Reno Rock for the Nevada "divorce capital" when his wife warned him that she would not tolerate another landscaping dynamite blast.

Pass beneath New Rock and Horseshoe Rock (you're now at the base of the prehistoric falls) and curve left into the Azalea Field, with its many seasonal planting beds. Buck Garden is renowned for its early plantings of spring bulbs, big drifts of purple-spiked salvia, and winter aconite, blooming in late March and early April. The garden is also acclaimed for its display of woodland flowers in May, when trilliums mix with the pinks and whites of native and hybrid azaleas. Summer and fall boast a steady progression of colorful blossoms.

Bordering the left side of this little meadow is a small copse of trees. Look for a shagbark hickory, white ash, Hercules'-club, and rare Franklinia tree. A single grove of Franklinia (named for Benjamin Franklin) was discovered growing wild in 1765 near Georgia's Alatamaha River. Botanists collected seeds before the grove disappeared around 1790. The Franklinia now exists only in cultivation and is valued for its showy white, cup-shaped blossoms, appearing in autumn.

Just past a small shed on the left is a red buckeye tree. This North Carolina native grows this far north only when planted here. Its bright red flowers caused it to be nicknamed the firecracker plant. Its polished bronze-colored seeds are poisonous and were ground up by Native Americans into a powder that, when dumped into still water, stunned fish, making them easy to catch.

At the far end of the Azalea Field a wide path called the Big Walk leads past a tall white oak and into a deciduous forest. The trail parallels Moggy Brook for a short distance, then sweeps uphill in a lazy S-curve. Opposite a bench at the first turn is a large basswood tree. Also called the American linden, the basswood can grow to 100 feet tall and has long served humankind with sweet honey made from its flower nectar, a soothing tea steeped from its dried blossoms, and carvings made from its workable, light-colored wood.

A stone wall beside the Big Walk is covered in Kingsville box, looking like a furry green Chia Pet. Asters and goldenrods spot the open forest floor in autumn. The exposed basalt of the Second Watchung Mountain also lines the path. This material burst from the earth about 200 million years ago as immense waves of molten lava, which then hardened into tough igneous stone. Notice how the basalt fractures into polygonal columnar shapes. Long quarried for paving stone, this igneous rock often forms natural staircases, possibly explaining why it is sometimes called traprock. *Trappen* is Dutch for "step."

After about 0.3 mile the Big Walk reaches a dead end. Return the way you came, cross the Azalea Field, then turn left and pass over Moggy Brook on a wooden bridge. Another left leads up onto Polypody Rock, where bloodroot and rue anemone bloom in spring. Spreading Canadian hemlock (looking like a bonsai-ed eastern hemlock) grows just 2 feet tall.

Circle completely around Lower Pond to enjoy the moist microclimate created by Leonard Buck. River birch (with its acne-like flaking bark) and cardinal flower (with scarlet blooms in late summer) flourish at the edge of the pond, while water shamrock (an aquatic fern that looks like a floating four-leaf clover) rises from the bottom of the pool.

Take the Primrose Path past Fern Rock and beneath Big Rock back toward the visitor center. Enjoy the contrasting textures of the Fern Garden. Japanese toad lilies with star-shaped blooms, ostrich fern with graceful plumelike leaves, and English lady fern are planted here.

Before climbing the wooden stairway back to the visitor center, notice the stately conifer with feathery needles growing beside the path. This tree is Buck Garden's greatest treasure. It is a dawn redwood, or metasequoia. This majestic tree was once the most abundant conifer in western North America, then was devastated by Pleistocene glaciers. Thought to be extinct, only fossil evidence of the dawn redwood was known until the 1944 discovery of a single tree enshrined by the people of the remote Chinese village of Mo-tao-chi. A 1948 expedition to China located one grove of 1,000 metasequoias, the last remnant of the species. Seedlings sent to the Arnold Arboretum in Boston, Massachusetts, were distributed worldwide. Today this living fossil again grows on the North American continent where its ancestors ruled, and at Buck Garden where an extinct river and waterfall once drained the now vanished glacial Lake Passaic. Thus this pleasure garden preserves the treasures of an ancient age.

For More Information

Buck Garden is open from 10 A.M. to 4 P.M. Monday through Friday, 10 A.M. to 5 P.M. on Saturday, and noon to 5 P.M. on Sunday. It is closed on weekends during December, January, and February and on major holidays. A $1 donation is requested.

Buck Garden, Somerset County Park Commission, Horticulture Department, 11 Layton Road, Far Hills, NJ 07931; 908-234-2677; www.park.co.somerset.nj.us/

Delaware & Raritan Canal State Park

Kingston to Rocky Hill

Trail: D&R Canal Towpath, Camden & Amboy Railway trail
Distance: 4.0 miles
Length: 3 hours
Difficulty: Easy; flat

Hike into history along a shady canal towpath

Getting There

From I-287 at Bridgewater, take US 206 south to Princeton, then go left (north) on NJ 27 to Kingston. Parking is on the right, just before the canal crossing.

Special Features
- New Jersey's last intact canal
- Floodplain forest
- Plentiful bird life and wildlife
- Traprock quarry

The red shale, sandstone, and argillite formations of the Piedmont, stretching between Trenton and New Brunswick, rise to a mere 57 feet above sea level. This so-called narrow waist of New Jersey—just 44 miles wide—long tempted entrepreneurs as a potential canal shortcut between Philadelphia and New York City.

While William Penn may have dreamed of a water crossing of the narrow waist, it wasn't until 1830 that the project got launched. By then the Erie Canal had shown the way, and canal building was all the rage in America.

Three thousand Irish immigrants, many brought to the United States by the canal company, were paid a dollar a day to hand-dig the Delaware & Raritan (D&R) Canal. They shoveled from dawn to dusk, cutting through forest and farmland little changed since colonial days. Long hours, inadequate sanitation, and poor food led to an 1832 Asiatic cholera epidemic that killed hundreds of these laborers.

The unsung, unmarked graves of Irish immigrants contrasted sharply with the triumphal canal opening of 1834. Governor Peter Vroom and friends sailed their official barge along the canal, hailed by cheering crowds. Their trip ended with a twenty-four-gun salute at New Brunswick. The D&R Canal boomed. Mule-drawn boats gave way to steam tugs. Civil War gunboats passed through, heading south. In 1871 the canal hauled nearly 3 million tons of freight, surpassing the Erie Canal.

Railroad competition finally killed the D&R in 1932. Today the "big ditch," once the pride of American industrialists, is a 58-mile-long greenway and state park where Piedmont flora and 200 bird species flourish. The park includes a 36-mile stretch beginning near Bordentown and ending at New Brunswick, plus a 22-mile feeder canal on the Delaware River.

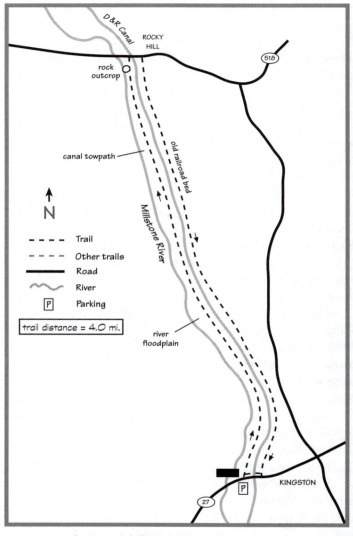

Delaware & Raritan Canal State Park

This 4.0-mile circuit hike passes along both sides of the tree-shaded D&R Canal between the sleepy towns of Kingston and Rocky Hill, and explores the floodplain of the Millstone River.

From the Kingston parking lot, follow the path north through a tunnel beneath NJ 27. A short, unmarked side trail leads left to the Millstone River. Be careful if you decide to venture down the unmarked path. This is a "look but don't touch" forest. Floodplain silver maples and red maples are draped with light-loving poison ivy vines (see the sidebar). Leaves of three, let it be!

Follow the main trail as it swerves right, uphill, onto the wide canal towpath. Here teenage boys and girls in bare feet once led mule teams pulling boats loaded with tons of coal. Each canal boat was guided by a tillerman who blew on a conch shell horn to notify lock and bridge tenders of his approaching boat. Wives typically lived on board in cramped quarters with their families.

The canal and towpath play tag with the Millstone River for the next 1.8 miles. To the left is a classic northern deciduous floodplain forest. Black cherry, black locust, red and silver maple, elm, and ash trees are nourished by the seasonal spill of water and rich silt overflowing the Millstone's banks. Each tree finds its particular niche, depending on how much moisture it can stand. The forest floor is a tangled vine community. Poison ivy, Virginia creeper, Asiatic bittersweet, greenbrier, wild grape, and climbing hemp weed are resilient vines that recover quickly from annual floods.

Black oak, black locust, and sycamore trees hang over the canal, making a grab for sunlight and forming a cool green tunnel. The canal didn't always look like this. In the 1800s trees were cut from banks to allow passage of mules and boats.

A rocky outcrop along the Millstone River.

Canalers endured sun and rain six days a week, sunrise to sunset.

This habitat is a boon for wildlife. In the canal, bluegills, pumpkinseeds, and red-breasted sunfish dodge largemouth bass and chain pickerel. Shad sometimes wander into the D&R from the Delaware River. Mallards, cormorants, and herons patrol quiet waters. Dead floodplain trees provide hollow cavities for raccoons, opossums, kingfishers, and woodpeckers. The dense floodplain undergrowth contrasts drastically with the open farmlands that surround the greenway, offering shelter for mammals and birds in winter.

Just before reaching Rocky Hill, the canal again approaches the Millstone, where open rock slabs overlook the river. This is a fine, sunny lunch spot. Here we found broken freshwater clamshells, the remains of a favorite meal of seagulls and raccoons. In springtime, the Millstone rises and becomes one of New Jersey's most enjoyable canoeing rivers.

At 1.9 miles the towpath passes through a gate into the town of Rocky Hill. Turn right, cross the canal on County Route 518, then turn right again, following a wide path south along the far side of the canal back toward Kingston.

Just to the left of the Rocky Hill canal towpath gate is a large sycamore or buttonwood tree, with its camouflage-style bark. Sycamores grow quickly (70 feet in seventeen years) and display greater girth than other American deciduous trees. A Belvidere, New Jersey, specimen is 8 feet in diameter. The core of older trees sometimes rots out, leaving a deep hollow at the base of the still-living tree. Such cavities can hold several people standing up. Native Americans once made sycamores into huge dugout canoes.

The tranquillity of this portion of the hike is marred by the noise of the nearby Traprock Industries quarry (which provided the trail corridor on this side of the canal). The quarry exploits an underground diabase seam that rises to overlook the Hudson River as the Palisades (see Trip 22). This igneous rock was first dug here in the 1860s, providing crushed paving stone for Jersey City and Newark. If you have time, explore Rocky Hill, a nineteenth-century village that supported farmers with its gristmill, sawmill, taverns, and general stores.

You are now following the abandoned right-of-way of a spur of the Camden & Amboy Railway, built in 1864. Note that the fields and forest to the left are much drier. The canal's embankments have artificially defined the boundary between Millstone River floodplain and surrounding upland ever since its construction in the 1830s.

The trail passes through disturbed quarry lands populated by native plants (black locust, speckled alder, and red cedar saplings) and exotics (ailanthus, catalpa, and royal paulownia trees). This open land is slowly progressing through field succession as it returns to forest.

At 2.5 miles the old railroad bed enters a woods where black willow and locust trees overhang the canal, shading smaller river birches and tickseed sunflowers. To the left an upland forest of mulberry, pignut, and mockernut hickory shades Asiatic dayflower, goldenrod, and evening primrose.

The path reaches the parking lot of the John W. Flemer Preserve in Kingston at 3.9 miles. Turn right and cross the canal on NJ 27, returning to the parking lot and your car on the left (use the tunnel to avoid traffic).

For More Information

The park is open year-round. To volunteer in the restoration of the state's canals, contact The Canal Society of New Jersey.

Delaware and Raritan Canal State Park, 625 Canal Road, Somerset, NJ 08873; 732-873-3050; www.state.nj.us/dep/forestry/parks/drcanal.htm

The Canal Society of New Jersey, P.O. Box 737, Morristown, NJ 07963; 908-722-9556

Poison Ivy: Our Bane and Nature's Boon

While New Jersey long ago eliminated or controlled many woodland "enemies"—wolves, panthers, and rattlesnakes—one perceived pest persists. Poison ivy abounds as creeping groundcover; low leafy shrub; and frayed, ropelike vine. This hardy plant grows in all kinds of soil, and is shade tolerant but comes into its own in bright sun, making it a common trailside companion. Its red rash and persistent itch (caused by people's allergic reaction to the chemical urushiol) have ruined many hiker sojourns.

But as you spread on the calamine lotion or jewelweed juice (a soothing Native American remedy), consider that poison ivy is extremely valuable to the forest community.

More than sixty bird species feast on the plant's autumn white berries. In fact, it is believed that poison ivy leaves turn bright red as a bold announcement of this bounty (called fall foliar flagging by botanists). Feeding grouse, pheasants, warblers, and flickers pass the seeds straight through their digestive systems, spreading poison ivy plants out over the landscape. Insects feed actively on poison ivy foliage and pollinate its flowers. Rabbits browse the plant in winter, a pruning that causes it to branch out ever more luxuriant each spring.

Holmdel Park and Longstreet Farm

Monmouth County Park

> **Trail: Beech Glen Trail, Ridge Walk Trail, High Point Trail, and Marsh Trail (loop)**
> **Distance: 4.1 miles (plus 1.0 mile for farm and arboretum)**
> **Length: 3 hours**
> **Difficulty: Moderate; some hilly terrain**

Enjoy the sights, sounds, and smells of nineteenth-century farm life

Getting There

Take the Garden State Parkway to Exit 114. Head west on Red Hill Road to the first light, then turn right onto Crawfords Corner Road. Turn left onto Roberts Road, then right onto Longstreet Road. Immediately turn left into the Holmdel Park main entrance. Stay right at the **Y** and pull into parking lot 2.

Special Features

- Hilly deciduous woods
- Coastal Plain wetland
- Longstreet Farm
- Arboretum

New Jersey's Coastal Plain was born out of a dance between land and sea. Starting about 135 million years ago, ancient rivers dumped sediments brought from eroding uplands. The ocean then rose, covering the sediments and leaving behind clay, silt, sand, and gravel. This process of sediment deposition and ocean encroachment was repeated many times over millions of years. Today the plains have again risen above sea level.

Dividing the Inner from the Outer Coastal Plain are the cuestas, low, gravel-capped ranges of hills rising a few hundred feet above the otherwise flat landscape and running in a diagonal line from the Atlantic Ocean to Delaware Bay. You can follow the cuestas by tracing town names on a road map southwesterly from Atlantic Highlands, through Hillsdale, Mount Holly, Mount Laurel, and Mullica Hill. These hills, capped by peanut-colored pebbles, are more erosion resistant than surrounding clay and sand lowlands.

Sitting astride a cuesta in Monmouth County is Holmdel Park, the site of Longstreet Farm. Established in 1775 as a subsistence farm growing all its own produce, it had by 1890 shifted to the harvesting of potatoes as a cash crop. In the twentieth century it flourished as a dairy farm. In 1967 Monmouth County purchased and preserved the farm as Holmdel Park.

This 4.1-mile loop walk circles through hilly deciduous woods that once served as the croplands, pastures, and orchards of Longstreet Farm. The hike ends with a tour of the farm complex, where interpreters dressed in period costume demonstrate 1890s agricultural life (see the sidebar).

Begin at parking lot 2, which is lined by sugar maple and Norway maple. It's easy to differentiate these two trees in autumn. The Norway maple, a European shade tree, stays green long after the sugar maple has gone golden.

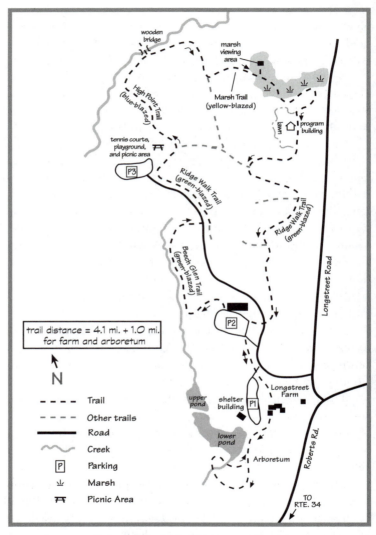

wooden
bridge

marsh
viewing
area

High Point Trail
(blue-blazed)

Marsh Trail
(yellow-blazed)

lawn

program
building

tennis courts,
playground,
and picnic area

P3

Ridge Walk Trail
(green-blazed)

Ridge Walk Trail
(green-blazed)

Beech Glen Trail
(green-blazed)

P2

Longstreet Road

trail distance = 4.1 mi. + 1.0 mi.
for farm and arboretum

N

Trail
Other trails
Road
Creek
Parking
Marsh
Picnic Area

upper
pond

shelter
building

Longstreet
Farm

P1

lower
pond

Arboretum

Roberts Rd.

TO
RTE. 34

Holmdel Park and Longstreet Farm

Leave the parking lot at the corner farthest from where you drove in. Head uphill through a meadow toward treeline. In 0.1 mile you'll pass the Fitness Trail. Continue to the left along a road lined by a split-rail fence and passing a sign that says Trails Straight Ahead. Follow the green-blazed Beech Glen Trail into deep woods.

This beautiful forest trail passes among stately stands of pignut and mockernut hickory, tulip tree, sweet birch, and oak. Dogwood, sassafras, shrubby arrowwood, and sweet pepperbush compose the understory.

The sandy path sinks deep into the glen and parallels a brook (0.3 mile). The highlight of this stroll is a fine stand of American beech, the favorite tree of tufted titmice, Acadian flycatchers, and red-shouldered hawks. Mammals feast on beechnuts, and you'll find plentiful gray squirrels here. Look, too, for the broad beech fern, with wide triangular leaves.

Beech trees, with their smooth tombstone-gray bark, unfortunately have attracted graffiti carvers for centuries (the Anglo-Saxon root of *beech* and *book* is the same word, points out John Eastman in his field guide *The Book of Forest and Thicket*). This vandalism, common at Holmdel, is not only ugly, but also allows the easy introduction of wood-rot fungi into the trees.

Beeches primarily propagate through cloning. Mature trees send underground runners called rhizomes out from their base, from which genetically identical replicas sprout. In winter, young beeches hang on to their leaves, which shrink into rice-paper-thin rolls and rustle eerily in icy winds.

The trail crosses bridges over intermittent streams, then turns right and climbs uphill. At 0.6 mile the Beech Glen Trail ends at a paved road. Walk straight ahead, crossing both the blue-blazed Cross-Country Ski Trail and the road. In a few yards you intersect the green-blazed Ridge Walk Trail. Turn left.

The Ridge Walk Trail follows the crest of a cuesta, a Spanish word for a hill with one gently sloping and one steep side. This cuesta forms the divide between two watersheds and between the Inner and Outer Coastal Plains. The trail parallels the paved road and passes among more beech trees, black tupelo, white oak, and chestnut oak.

At 0.9 mile the Ridge Walk Trail reaches a parking lot and turns right, passing a playground and tennis courts. As the green-blazed Ridge Walk Trail continues straight ahead, turn left onto the blue-blazed High Point Trail (1.1 mile).

The High Point Trail follows a treeline past light-loving shining sumac, sassafras, and big-tooth aspen. Here we saw autumn witch hazel trees in full bloom, with their yellow flowers looking exactly like shredded cheddar cheese.

The trail reenters the beech forest and descends on a sandy path. It levels off and swings right at 1.5 miles to parallel a deeply etched streambed. Take a brief detour left onto a large wooden bridge crossing the stream. This is a nice spot for a snack or water break. The area is blanketed by wood aster, wild rose, partridgeberry, and Indian cucumber-root. In spring, look for pink lady's slippers.

Continue on the blue-blazed High Point Trail as it veers sharply right away from the stream and climbs gently. Watch closely for the yellow-blazed Marsh Trail at about 1.9 miles. Turn left. The Marsh Trail quickly feeds into a boardwalk through a wetland where the spindly trunks of speckled alder rise above jewelweed, joe-pye weed, sensitive fern, and tickseed sunflower. A viewing platform gives birders a chance to study songbirds and waterfowl.

A volunteer demonstrates farm life at Longstreet Farm, circa 1890.

A short dead-end trail leads left, going deeper into the wetland. The Marsh Trail continues on a boardwalk, passes briefly over dry land, then emerges onto another stretch of boardwalk. Spicebush, its leaves giving off a spicy fragrance, surrounds you. Its fall fruit is savored by wood thrushes and veeries.

The Marsh Trail leaves the wetland, climbing on steep steps at 2.6 miles (to the left, a park entrance road passes over a stream). The Marsh Trail ends as it exits the woods onto an open lawn. Walk straight ahead, passing the Holmdel Park Program Building on the right (2.7 miles) and the Activity Area. Follow the green-blazed Ridge Walk Trail leading to the right.

Ignore the first small wooden bridge you come to on the left. Turn left and cross a second bridge at 3.0 miles. You are now following the combined green blazes of the Ridge Walk Trail and blue diamond blazes of the Cross-Country Ski Trail.

Stay left as the trail passes through a beech forest, a spruce grove, and more hardwoods. At 3.8 miles the trail bursts from the woods into open meadows. Walk straight ahead on a well-worn dirt path back to the parking lot (4.1 miles).

From the parking lot continue straight ahead 0.3 mile to the Longstreet Farm, which is within sight. After strolling the farm, enjoy the meditative Holmdel arboretum with its dawn redwood from China.

For More Information

Holmdel Park is open 8 A.M. to dusk. Longstreet Farm is open from 9 A.M. to 5 P.M. Memorial Day through Labor Day, and 10 A.M. to 4 P.M. the rest of the year. The farmhouse is open weekends and holidays, March through December, from noon to 3:30 P.M. or by reservation. Both are free.

Longstreet Farm, Longstreet Road, Holmdel, NJ 07733; 732-946-3758

Monmouth County Park System: 732-842-4000; www.monmouthcountyparks.com

Life Down on the Farm

In the 1890s the Longstreet Farm prospered. This old-style farm relied on horsepower and muscle power to harvest produce at a time when others were mechanizing. Tenant farmers planted potatoes for resale, plus hay to feed draft animals and corn for hogs and chickens. Farm wives used "butter and egg" money to purchase mail-order goods from the Sears and Roebuck catalog.

The choice of potatoes as a cash crop was determined by geography and inexpensive transportation. By the 1890s vast midwestern farms were cheaply meeting most of New York City's produce needs. But spuds were too weighty to haul profitably cross-country by rail. Nearby Longstreet Farm shipped its potatoes to hungry Manhattanites.

While New Jersey's Coastal Plain farmers didn't enjoy the kind of fertile soils found in Kansas, they enriched the earth by both ancient and modern means. They spread locally plentiful marl, or greensand, on their fields. Greensand is made of the mineral glauconite, the fecal pellets of ancient marine filter-feeding organisms. Nineteenth-century South Jersey farmers also imported tons of horse manure from a surprising source: the carriage-covered streets of Manhattan.

Today Longstreet Farm interpreters educate visitors year-round. In spring, they disk, harrow, and plant the fields while caring for newborn lambs and chicks. In autumn, they share their knowledge of harvesting and cider making.

Wells Mills

Ocean County Park

Trail: Penns Hill Trail, Ridge Road/Cook's Mill Road (loop)
Distance: 6.0 miles
Length: 4 hours
Difficulty: Moderate; many steep ups and downs

A hike through a secluded tract of Pine Barrens forest, swamp, and bog

Getting There

From the Garden State Parkway southbound, take Exit 67. Turn right onto County Route 554 (West Bay Avenue) and proceed to NJ 72, then 0.25 mile farther to County Route 532. Turn right and go 3.0 miles to the Wells Mills County Park entrance on the right. From the Garden State Parkway northbound, take Exit 69. Turn left onto County Route 532 west and proceed about 2.0 miles to the park entrance on the left.

Special Features

- Atlantic cedar swamp
- Pitch pine and oak forest
- Good birding
- Hilly terrain

Cloaked in pitch pine and oak, the hills at Wells Mills seem wild and changeless today. But the forest resources of this ancient Pine Barrens ecosystem were heavily exploited by people for 200 years before finally being preserved in the mid-1970s.

These rugged sand hills, cedar swamps, and freshwater bogs were owned first in colonial times by zealous Tory Elishia Lawrence, who backed the wrong side in the Revolutionary War. A vengeful American government confiscated his property. Elishia Lawrence's loss was James Wells's gain.

In the late 1700s James Wells dammed Oyster Creek, creating a 37-acre lake. He built a sawmill and harvested old-growth stands of Atlantic white cedar. Woodcutters and charcoal makers crisscrossed the Wells Mills tract, clearing pine and oak. Some pitch pines were bled for oleoresin, which was distilled into turpentine, while the stumps of cut trees were burned to extract tar and pitch (used to caulk ship hull seams). Quarries provided sand-rich clay for firebrick, terra-cotta ceramics, and redware pottery. Sphagnum moss gatherers prowled swamps collecting the sterile, superabsorbent plant. It served as surgical dressings through World War I and as floral packing material.

By the twentieth century these natural resources, as elsewhere in the Pine Barrens, had either been exhausted or ceased to be of commercial value. In the 1930s the Conrad family built a rustic cabin retreat here and used the tract for hunting. The New Jersey Conservation Foundation, recognizing the land's natural value, bought it in the 1970s. Ocean County purchased its first Wells Mills acreage in 1985, establishing this fine county park.

Today the sugar-sand roads that once guided woodcutters and sphagnum moss gatherers are a well-blazed and meticulously maintained 16-mile trail system. This 6.0-mile loop hike utilizes

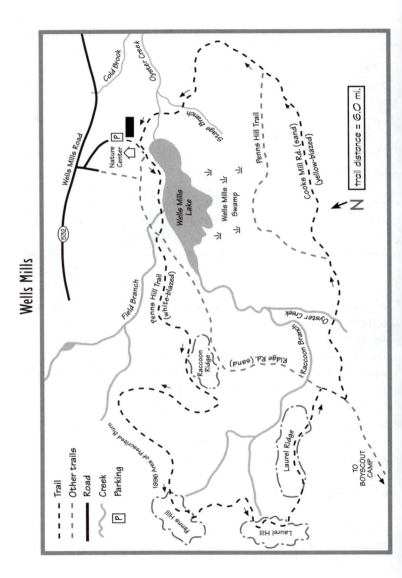

Wells Mills

Legend:
- - - - Trail
- - - - Other trails
—— Road
～～ Creek
[P] Parking

trail distance = 6.0 mi.

N

Wells Mills Road
Nature Center
[P]
532

Cold Brook
Oyster Creek
Strage Branch
Wells Mills Lake
Wells Mills Swamp

Penns Hill Trail
Cooks Mill Rd. (sand)
(yellow-blazed)

Field Branch
Penns Hill Trail (white-blazed)
Raccoon Ridge
Ridge Rd. (sand)
Oyster Creek
Raccoon Branch

1996 Area of Prescribed Burn
Penns Hill
Laurel Ridge
Laurel Hill

TO BOYSCOUT CAMP

both the white-blazed Penns Hill Trail and yellow-blazed Ridge Road/Cooks Mill Road.

Due to the high incidence of Lyme disease in the area, take precautions against ticks before starting your walk. Tuck pants into boots and wear insect repellent. Check yourself thoroughly after the hike. In an effort to curb the tick population, Wells Mills employees tried releasing guinea fowl—what they called the "hunt and peck" method of tick control. Sadly, the birds were curbed themselves, providing easy meals for local foxes.

The first white blaze of the Penns Hill Trail is placed on an extremely tall sassafras tree, the largest I've ever seen. The medicinal power of sassafras tea has been acclaimed for centuries. Sassafras bark was the first forest product exported to the Old World. Aromatic sassafras was once used to flavor and scent root beer, mouthwash, gum, toothpaste, and soap.

The first 0.4 mile of the white-blazed Penns Hill Trail edges the shore of Wells Mills Lake, threading between the pillarlike trunks of Atlantic white cedar. In precolonial times this majestic tree blanketed Pine Barrens swamps, growing to 4 feet in diameter and 100 feet tall. The wood's straight grain, rot resistance, and slowness to burn made it ideal for shingles, barrels, boats, and fences and doomed the great cedar forests. Botanist Peter Kalm, writing in the mid-1700s, noted that all of Philadelphia's homes were roofed with white cedar shingles. He feared the tree would be clearcut into extinction. Conservationists have achieved a limited white cedar comeback in recent years.

At about 0.4 mile the white-blazed trail veers right, leaving water and cedars behind. It climbs gently through a woods of white oak, blackjack oak, pitch pine, sassafras, and blueberry. Blackjack oak, with its three-lobed, thick, leathery leaves, is a

Groundcover enjoys plentiful light and a spurt of growth after a 1996 prescribed burn. The burning of leaf litter reduces the possibility of wildfires.

small, contorted tree that, like pitch pine, flourishes in barren, dry, sandy soils. It is one of the most common oaks of the Coastal Plain.

At 1.0 mile the trail tops Raccoon Ridge. Look for evidence of charring on tree trunks. This area was part of a 20-acre prescribed burn, a fire set intentionally by park foresters in the winter of 1996. Such controlled burns prevent the buildup of duff—the dry pine needles and leaf litter that can lead to wildfire. They also rejuvenate these woodlands (see the sidebar). You'll see evidence of other prescribed burns throughout the park. Descending Raccoon Ridge through the burned area we spied a northern flicker, a ground-feeding woodpecker, as it searched for ants and beetle larvae. The flicker, a cavity-nesting bird, benefits from plentiful dead and hollowed trees left by fire.

The white-blazed trail climbs Penns Hill (2.6 miles), descends and crosses a sand ditch, and leaves the burned area behind. Such ditches, called plow lines, are cut as firebreaks. In the unburned forest we found a luxurious undergrowth of mountain laurel, sweet pepperbush, and wintergreen amid stands of blackjack oak, post oak, chestnut oak, and pitch pine.

The trail next crosses Laurel Hill (2.9 miles) and Laurel Ridge (3.4 miles). These ridges are broken repeatedly by small gullies with streams and trail bridges. While each gully is less than 75 feet deep, the land's ruggedness offers an unexpected workout in the usually flat Pinelands. These gravel-capped hills were created during the million-year-long ice ages. While glaciers never reached South Jersey, raging rivers of meltwater did surge over the Coastal Plain, depositing sand and gravel mounds. Subsequent rising and falling sea levels submerged the area and left behind more sand and silt, plus marine fossils. These hills and surrounding swamps protect the endangered Pine Barrens tree frog, timber rattler, horned snake, rare orchids, swamp pink, Pine Barrens gentian, and bog asphodel.

The trail passes through a small Atlantic white cedar swamp, then turns sharply right onto Ridge Road at 3.7 miles. The path is now blazed both white and yellow. In a few hundred feet follow the combined white and yellow blazes and turn sharply left (don't continue straight on Ridge Road into the Boy Scout reservation).

From here on the walk is easy and flat. The trail, now a wide sandy road, shoots between growths of pitch pine, oak, and sassafras. This old road, eroded about 2 feet below the surrounding forest, was once used by nineteenth-century wagons, woodcutters, and hunters.

The combined white and yellow trails pass over Oyster Creek at 4.1 miles, then reach a trail junction at 4.3 miles. Do not diverge left on the white-blazed Penns Hill Trail, but continue straight ahead, following the yellow-blazed Cooks Mill Road. The road slowly curves left back toward the nature center.

Look for Pine Barrens heather, also called golden-heather, edging the sand road. The trail crosses Stage Branch Creek

(5.7 miles) and Oyster Creek (5.8 miles), offering nice views into a white cedar and red maple swamp. The yellow-blazed Cooks Mill Road crosses the top of the dam forming Wells Mills Lake, and arrives back at the nature center.

For More Information

The park is open dawn to dusk, year-round. Nature center exhibits are open year-round from 7:30 A.M. to 4 P.M.

Wells Mills County Park, 905 Wells Mills Road, Waretown, NJ 08758; 609-971-3085; www.co.ocean.nj.us/parks/wellsmills.html

Fire in the Pines

While people view forest fires as destructive, such infernos have been a part of the natural cycle in South Jersey for thousands of years. Fire fosters unique Pine Barrens plant and animal communities.

Pitch pine and short-leaf pine are well adapted to the cycle. They possess thick bark that resists high temperatures; they also respond automatically to fire by quickly putting out sprouts from scorched trunks. In fact, the specialized cones of pitch pine can only open during intense heat. Pine seeds also need cleared ground and sunlight to germinate. Without regular fires, oaks would replace pines as the dominant Pine Barrens forest tree.

Repeatedly burned areas support rare flora such as Pickering's morning glory and sickle-leaf golden aster, rare moths and butterflies including the Pine Barrens dagger moth and attalus skipper, and rare reptiles like the pine snake and corn snake. Cavity-nesting birds such as the eastern bluebird and great crested flycatcher benefit by finding homes in dead trees.

Pine Barrens wildfires, unlike the small prescribed burns lit by foresters, can be destructive and terrifying. Crown fires burn with white-hot intensity, advancing with frightening speed through the forest canopy. Windborne embers quickly carry the blaze over the heads of firefighters, endangering lives. In 1995 wildfires fanned by 60 MPH winds ravaged thousands of forest acres. The staff at Wells Mills watched the wildfire with fear, praying the wind wouldn't blow their way. Luckily the park was spared.

Pakim Pond

Brendan Byrne State Forest

Trip 30

> **Trail:** **Access Trail, Batona Trail, Cranberry Trail (loop)**
> **Distance:** **6.8 miles**
> **Length:** **4½ hours**
> **Difficulty:** **Moderate; minor elevation change**

Explore the subtle, understated beauty of the Pine Barrens

Getting There

From the NJ 70 and NJ 72 traffic circle, follow NJ 72 east 1.0 mile and turn left at a sign for Brendan Byrne State Forest. The headquarters office is 0.3 mile ahead and to the right on Shinns Road.

Special Features

- Classic Pine Barrens hike
- Oak and pine upland
- Atlantic Cedar swamp lowlands
- Pakim Pond and pitcher plants

The heart of the Outer Coastal Plain has been known as the Pine Barrens since colonial times. In the public imagination the 1.4-million-acre region was viewed as a dreary wasteland of impassable sugar sand, treacherous cedar swamp, and scraggly pitch pine.

In the nineteenth century, urbanites unjustly labeled the region's people "pineys" and painted them in the stereotype of Ozark hillbillies. One 1800s New Jersey state governor smeared the rural folk as a "race of imbeciles, criminals and defectives." In the 1900s the Barrens were viewed by most vacationers as a blank spot on the map through which one sped as quickly as possible to the Jersey Shore.

Starting in the 1960s, however, environmentalists and writers such as John McPhee began to recognize the area's cultural, biological, and botanical richness. Conservationists, attempting to shed past stereotypes, even tried renaming the region the "Pinelands." While the new name sweeps aside old pejoratives, it lacks the air of strange, wild beauty conjured by the old one. No matter what you call this vast forest, it remains the last bastion of the primitive in New Jersey.

A fine Pinelands (or Pine Barrens!) sampler hike is a 6.8-mile loop to Pakim Pond. It begins on the Batona Trail, which weaves through an oak and pine upland to tiny Pakim Pond. It returns via the Cranberry Trail, a series of well-blazed sand roads offering a glimpse into an Atlantic white cedar swamp. To avoid crowds of people and mosquitoes, walk here in spring, fall, or winter.

Begin at the Brendan Byrne State Forest headquarters parking lot. This 34,000-acre park is now named for the New Jersey governor who signed the Pinelands Preservation Act in 1979, though it was originally named for the Lebanon Glassworks

Pakim Pond

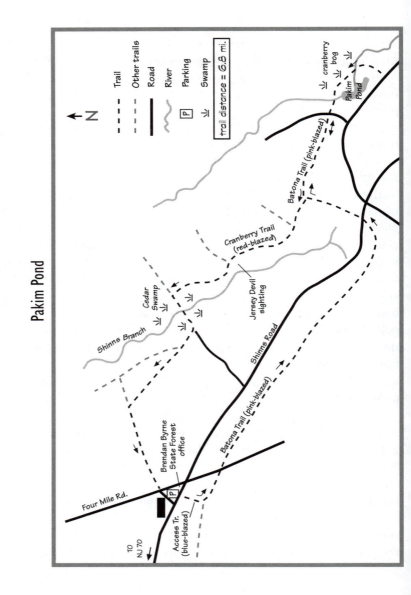

(1851–1866). The glassworks benefited from plentiful sand for silica and charcoal for fuel in the making of windows, fancy bottles, and glass walking canes. All that remains of the enterprise is an earthen mound southeast of Pakim Pond.

Walk from the entrance of the state forest parking lot across paved Shinns Road and past a sign that reads Batona Trail. A blue-blazed access trail leads gently uphill through woods, connecting with the pink-blazed Batona Trail in 0.1 mile. Turn left onto the Batona Trail atop a low sand-and-gravel ridge.

The Batona Trail was built by volunteers of the Batona (ba-to-na—back to nature) Hiking Club of Philadelphia in the 1960s. The 50-mile trail runs from a northern terminus at Ongs Hat south to Bass River State Park. Camping is allowed at designated sites along its length.

This is the hike of many oaks. The path threads between species of the white oak family (chestnut oak, post oak, and white oak with rounded leaf lobes) and red oak family (black oak, scarlet oak, blackjack oak, and scrub oak with pointy bristle tips at each leaf lobe). White pine and pitch pine join the mix. Oaks would dominate the Pine Barrens climax forest if it weren't for the regular fires giving the flame-resistant pitch pine and short-leaf pine their advantage (see Trip 29).

At about 0.7 mile the Batona Trail crosses a sand road. The path now undulates up- and downhill from about 150 feet to 110 feet above sea level as it crosses many unmarked sand ditches and paths. Watch blazes closely!

The Pine Barrens is not known for in-your-face beauty. It boasts no craggy vistas or waterfalls. But the understated splendor can catch you by surprise. On this walk I discovered slender ladder lichen growing beneath a shaggy mountain laurel bush, tiny bluish gray goblets perched one atop another

The veined open lips of the insectivorous pitcher plant beckon to unwary bugs.

like the fantastic multitiered flora of a Dr. Seuss children's book. Gray-green reindeer lichen with jumbled intertwined "antlers" sprawled in clumps amid fallen butterscotch-colored oak leaves and golden pine needles.

At 1.7 miles the forest scenery begins to change. Pitch pine (three stiff needles in a bundle) and short-leaf pine (usually two needles per bundle) become dominant, though blackjack and post oak are still present.

The Batona Trail veers sharply left at 2.0 miles and descends out of the upland, crossing Shinns Road at 2.1 miles. The trail threads its way through a swampy lowland over board-walk, amid sheep laurel, cinnamon fern, red maple, and much pitch pine.

At about 2.5 miles the Batona Trail turns sharply right and intersects with the red-blazed Cranberry Trail entering from the left. Note this turning point, as it marks your return route.

Continue on the pink-blazed Batona Trail for another 0.5 mile along gravel roads that twist their way into a picnic area at the near end of Pakim Pond. This is a fine spot for lunch. The pond's "cedar water," as everywhere in the Pine Barrens, is stained rust brown with iron and tannin (a mild acid derived from tree bark and leaves).

Follow the pink blazes along the left shore of Pakim Pond beneath young Atlantic white cedars. Survey the water for sunning painted turtles and study the shore at your feet for the purple-veined leaves of insectivorous pitcher plants. I found one pitcher plant with a live bee trapped inside (see the sidebar). To the left of the trail is an abandoned cranberry bog. Pakim Pond (the name means "cranberry" in the Lenape language) once served as the bog's reservoir.

At 3.4 miles the trail reaches a small bridge at the far end of the pond. Look in the boggy area to the right for wild American cranberry. This diminutive trailing bog shrub has tiny waxen evergreen leaves and is the forerunner of hybridized cultivated cranberries.

Backtrack along the pond, through the picnic area, and return to the junction with the red-blazed Cranberry Trail (4.3 miles into the hike). Follow the red trail straight ahead on a sand road as the pink-blazed Batona Trail turns left. Watch the red blazes closely, since there are several unmarked turnoffs.

Walking the Cranberry Trail on a rainy day, I heard great wings stir from high atop a pitch pine. An immense dark shadow swept overhead and vanished in the fog before I could even look up. My first thought was an eagle, then maybe a turkey vulture. But as eerie silence reasserted, a new sinister thought took hold: *Jersey Devil*. This spawn of Satan with leathery wings, horse's head, razor-sharp teeth, talons, and serpent's tail feeds on sheep and small children. It has held a profane place in the pantheon of Pine Barrens mythological fauna since the early 1700s. The beast personifies all the irrational fears that race through a lone walker's mind while traveling these weird woods. Fortunately the more common winged creatures sighted along the Cranberry Trail are brown thrashers and great crested flycatchers.

At 5.5 miles turn left, following red blazes onto a major sand road that passes over Shinns Brook and through a magnificent and mysterious Atlantic white cedar swamp. At 5.7 miles the Cranberry Trail turns right onto another sand road. The trail turns sharply left onto still another red-blazed road at 6.3 miles.

At 6.7 miles the path exits the woods and crosses a paved road. Follow the trail into the state forest headquarters parking lot (6.8 miles).

For More Information

Brendan Byrne State Forest trails are open dawn to dusk. The headquarters office has maps and rest rooms and is open 8 A.M. to 4:30 P.M. seven days a week.

Brendan Byrne State Forest, P.O. Box 215, New Lisbon, NJ 08064; 609-726-1191; www.state.nj.us/dep/forestry/ parks/lebanon.htm

Batona Trail Club: 215-657-1058; http://members.aol. com/batona

Pitcher Plants

In nutrient-poor acidic bogs, plants must find a way to obtain nitrogen, potassium, and phosphorus other than through their roots. Insects are an abundant source of nutrients, and pitcher plants (such as sundews and Venus flytraps) have evolved into passive hunters. Within a pitcher plant's pale green, red-veined tubular leaves lurks a strange brew. An insect, trapped by the leaf's downward-pointing bristles and slick walls, will drown and be digested in this mix of rainwater, bacteria, and enzymes.

Ah, but co-evolution works in mysterious ways. Some insects have adapted to life within pitcher plant leaves. Several types of flies and mosquitoes lay their eggs in the leaves, and the larvae thrive in this wetland within a wetland. A veritable zoo of microorganisms also inhabits this mini-ecosystem, and the waste products of these protozoans may be another nutrient source for the plant. The flowers of the pitcher plant—tall, deep purple nodding spheres that look like life-forms from another planet— are pollinated by bees. The complex relationships between pitcher plants and insects chronicle the workings of evolution and the many special adaptations to life in the bog.

—Jean LeBlanc

Whitesbog
Brendan Byrne State Forest

Trip 31

Trail: **Nature Trail and various sand roads (loop, out-and-back)**
Distance: **2.5 miles**
Length: **2 hours**
Difficulty: **Easy; flat**

Explore cranberry bogs and the birthplace of the commercial blueberry industry

Getting There

From the NJ 70 and NJ 72 traffic circle, follow NJ 70 east for 7.0 miles and turn left onto County Route 530. In 1.2 miles turn right at a sign for Whitesbog. In 0.4 mile park in the large lot in front of the general store.

Special Features

- Insectivorous plants
- Fine birding
- Working cranberry bog
- Origin of the world's domestic blueberries

Wild cranberries and blueberries have thrived in sodden, acidic Pine Barren bogs since the end of the last ice age. The tasty fruits of both these hardy heath family plants were savored by Lenape Indians and early settlers. Native Americans made a staple winter food called pemmican by pounding nourishing dried blueberries and cranberries onto venison strips. Colonial sailors stowed cranberries (loaded with vitamin C) aboard ship as protection against scurvy.

But it wasn't until 1816 that New Englanders grew the first commercial cranberries in the bogs of Cape Cod, Massachusetts. Colonel James Fenwick followed their lead, harvesting the nutritious red berries at Skunk's Misery in the New Jersey Pine Barrens in 1854. Fenwick's daughter Mary married J. J. White, a cranberry entrepreneur. The couple launched a venture scoffed at as "White's Folly," an attempt to dig bogs and cultivate cranberries where they didn't already grow. The couple succeeded beyond their wildest hopes. By 1900 Whitesbog was a thriving agricultural community with 600 workers.

In 1911 the Whites' daughter Elizabeth allied with Dr. Frederick Colville to develop the first commercial blueberry. Elizabeth rode horseback throughout the Pine Barrens, meeting with locals and collecting bushes with the plumpest berries. Hybridization experiments led to the world's first commercial crop in 1916.

Modern agricultural techniques utilizing immense tractor-driven harvesters eventually made small, irregularly shaped bogs obsolete. Today Whitesbog (part of Brendan Byrne State Forest) offers a 3,000-acre window through which walkers can look back to the year 1900 and view bog agriculture as it was practiced in the Pine Barrens. Abandoned bogs also abound with wildlife. Where cranberries were once harvested, tundra

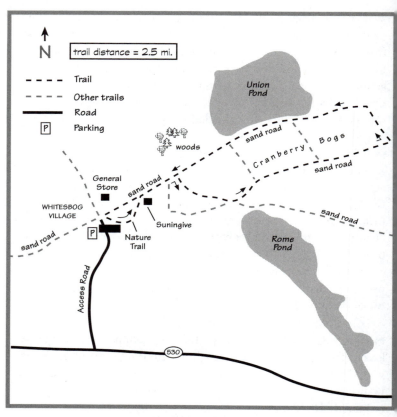

Whitesbog

swans, gull-billed terns, whip-poor-wills, white-tailed deer, and foxes flourish amid wetland and woodland flora.

This 2.5-mile walk explores the Whitesbog company town, traverses a forested nature trail, then loops through the bogs. A word of caution: there is little shade. Wear a hat, carry plenty of water, and avoid this hike on humid summer days when mosquitoes rule.

Tour the town first. Worth a look are the 1900s-vintage cranberry packing and storage buildings, water tower, a boardinghouse for unmarried workers, and entomologist's home (insect control was crucial to the bog!). The general store and post office from which Elizabeth White mailed blueberry bushes to farmers worldwide is now the Whitesbog Preservation Trust office. Begin the trail walk by following the numbered posts of the Old Bog Nature Trail. From the front of the general store, walk straight ahead across the street and circle right around to the back of what in 1910 was a lily-covered pond. Walk left along the edge of this former pond, now a seasonal wetland overgrown with marsh plants. Near the far end of the pond (at Nature Trail post 4), sphagnum moss grows in a thick mat while cinnamon fern rises to the right.

At post 7 on the Nature Trail (about 0.2 mile into the walk), park officials have fenced off several pitcher plants. Stoop down and peek within their cupped leaves. You may see a bug struggling to escape. These native Pine Barrens plants, along with insectivorous sundews, grow in nutrient-poor soils and supplement their diets with nitrogen-rich insects.

The Nature Trail now twists through a pitch pine lowland where this dominant tree is joined by red maple and black tupelo. The black tupelo, also called black gum, is among the first South Jersey trees to turn color in autumn and the first to shed its brilliant scarlet leaves. Ruffed grouse and wild turkeys enjoy its bluish black berries.

The forest deepens as the trail passes between young Atlantic white cedar, pin oak, and sweet gum. Pin oak and sweet gum (with its easily identified star-shaped leaves) were introduced to Whitesbog as ornamentals.

At post 13 the trail passes through the Old Bog, an original cranberry bog from the 1850s. Forest succession has filled in the bog with trees. This change only hints at the metamorphosis undergone by this land over the past 300 years. What began in precolonial days as a lowland cloaked in pitch pine and Atlantic white cedar was logged over by the 1790s. Whitesbog was then dredged for bog iron, which nearby Hanover Furnace turned into War of 1812 cannonballs. Only in the mid-1800s was the much-disturbed earth with its high water table recognized as the perfect spot for water-loving cranberries.

The Nature Trail ends as it exits the woods onto a sand road at 0.4 mile. Turn right and follow the unblazed sand road past Elizabeth White's home, Suningive. This little house was once surrounded not by a conventional flower garden, but by Ms. White's arboretum of acid-loving Pine Barrens plants, including rare orchids and insectivorous sundews. Plans are in the works to restore the garden.

Make a right turn off the main sand road onto a second major sand road at 0.6 mile, out into the open bogs. A variety of possible routes are now available as you move along the unblazed sand roads and dikes marking the edges of roughly rectangular bogs and ponds. I suggest that you complete your loop walk by ignoring the next two lefts (at 0.9 mile and 1.1 miles). Take a third left at 1.4 miles. Then at 1.5 miles turn left again, following the main sand road back into Whitesbog village, reaching the general store and the end of your walk at 2.5 miles.

The abandoned and cultivated bogs, reservoir ponds, and swamps, plus the pitch pine, oak, and Atlantic white cedar woods you see surrounding you, feature land use relatively compatible with wildlife needs. For every acre of active cranberry and blueberry bog, 10 acres of upland watershed are needed to provide clean water for the bogs. That means that the Pine Barrens' 11,000 active acres of bog require the preservation of 100,000 acres of forested upland.

We found fox scat and white-tailed deer and raccoon tracks. Four hundred tundra swans (also called whistling swans) winter at Whitesbog. In fact, the swans so love the tubers of a cranberry bog weed called redroot that active bogs must be armed with propane cannons to spook the birds. We heard the thunderous boom of these guns as we walked here in November. Fortunately the whistling swans find plenty to eat in nearby abandoned bogs.

This is an ideal haven for wading birds and waterfowl. Blue herons, green herons, and great egrets fish the bog reservoirs. Green-winged teal, wood ducks, black ducks, and northern pintails migrate through. Most unusual are flocks of gull-billed terns arriving in late summer. This shorebird normally feeds in salt marshes, but feasts on Whitesbog insects, tadpoles, and frogs. More than 200 bird species have been observed here. As you walk these life-giving bogs, it becomes clear that the Pine Barrens is far from barren.

For More Information

The sand roads are open to hikers dawn to dusk. While all the company town buildings have been stabilized, most are not open to the public. Tours are available when the general store is open: Saturday and Sunday 10 A.M. to 4 P.M., April through October.

Brendan Byrne State Forest, P.O. Box 215, New Lisbon, NJ 08064; 609-726-1191

Whitesbog Preservation Trust, 120–13 Whitesbog Road, Browns Mills, NJ 08015; 609-893-4646; www.whitesbog.org/

All About Berries

While neither cranberry nor blueberry plants seem to resemble each other, botanists tell us that their flower anatomies are closely related. These heath family plants also sometimes share the same wetland habitat, though cranberries require a more acidic environment.

Nourishing cranberries are food for ring-necked pheasant, ruffed grouse, and mourning doves. Among humans, the tart autumn-harvested fruit only graced Thanksgiving and Christmas dinner tables until the cranberry juice craze put "cranberry cocktail" in American refrigerators year-round.

While Elizabeth White's plump commercial blueberries in their cellophane-covered berry boxes are known to every shopper, hikers who are willing to brave bog and swamp know that the taste of the commercial fruit pales by comparison with wild varieties. The Chippewa tribe may have developed the strangest use for the plant. They burned its flowers and inhaled the smoke to calm and cure the crazy. For those of us who relish the peace and solitude of berry picking, the belief rings true.

Dot and Brooks Evert Memorial Nature Trail

New Jersey Conservation Foundation

Trail: **Dot and Brooks Evert Memorial Nature Trail (loop)**
Distance: **1.5 miles**
Length: **1 hour**
Difficulty: **Easy; no elevation gain**

A secluded walk amid a profusion of spring warblers

Getting There

From US 206 in Vincentown, take County Route 530 east to Pemberton. Turn right onto Magnolia Road, then right onto Ongs Hat Road. The Dot and Brooks Evert Memorial Trail is on the right, before reaching Stockton's Bridge Road. Other nearby walks are available on the north end of the Batona Trail at Ongs Hat, and at the New Jersey Conservation Foundation 4-Mile Springs Preserve (call 980-234-1225 for trail info).

Special Features

- Terrific birding in springtime
- Plant and animal diversity
- Tannin-stained Pine Barrens stream
- Very wet in winter and spring; wear high boots

John McPhee, in his classic 1967 Pine Barrens profile, describes how he was lucky enough to go walking with Dot and Brooks Evert. He relates how Brooks reverently scooped up an insectivorous sundew in a handful of soggy sand, showed it to McPhee, then gently returned it to the spongy ground. Dot Evert intoned, "As a rule we take nothing, and we leave nothing."

The Everts, gone from the earth now, did leave something significant behind. When McPhee walked with them, the future of nature in the Pine Barrens was gravely in doubt. A 32,500-acre jetport and 250,000-person "city of the future" had been proposed by the Pinelands Regional Planning Committee. The airport, covering 51 square miles, was to be four times larger than Kennedy, Newark, and LaGuardia Airports combined. A would-be developer told McPhee, "This area of the pinelands simply begins to jump out at you if you're going to go for urbanization. It's magnificent."

But Dot and Brooks Evert saw a different kind of magnificence in the pines. They found splendor in a tiny sundew; in the bog asphodel and corn snake. It was their vision that gained ascendance. Today preservation of much of the Pine Barrens for future generations looks assured (see the sidebar).

The Everts left behind a second legacy: their reverence for the region's botanical and biological diversity. The New Jersey Conservation Foundation, a statewide, private nonprofit land trust of which they were both active members, has created a preserve and 1.5-mile nature trail in their honor.

This little 170-acre preserve straddles the border between the Inner and Outer Coastal Plains and is cloaked in a mature red maple, sweet gum, and holly swamp forest. It is split by Stop-the-Jade Run, a small stream meandering westward out of the Pine Barrens. Its waters eventually blend with Rancocas

Dot and Brooks Evert Memorial Nature Trail

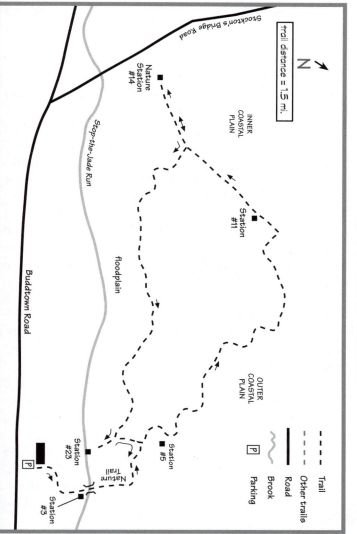

trail distance = 1.5 mi.

N

Stockton's Bridge Road

INNER COASTAL PLAIN

Nature Station #14

Station #11

Stop-the-Jade Run

floodplain

Buddtown Road

OUTER COASTAL PLAIN

Station #23

Station #5

Nature Trail

Station #3

P

Trail
Other trails
Brook
Parking

Creek (see Trip 33), the Lower Delaware River, and the Atlantic Ocean.

The ecology of the Dot and Brooks Evert Memorial Nature Trail has been described in wonderful detail in a nature guide written by Emile DeVito of the New Jersey Conservation Foundation. Be sure to pick up one of these fine Pine Barrens primers at the trailhead.

From the parking area, follow the 1.5-mile loop Nature Trail into the woods. The solitude immediately impresses. Sweet gum, black tupelo (sour gum), willow oak, red maple, and sassafras form a loose canopy overhead. In the 1980s the invasive gypsy moth caterpillar caused extensive damage to these woods and to much Pine Barrens acreage. Stripped of foliage, trees died, opening the forest floor to sunlight and inviting a riot of shrubby growth. Here a viny tangle of Virginia creeper entwines tree trunks in a struggle to rise above an impenetrable jungle of greenbrier and sweet pepperbush.

Nature Trail station 3 (at 0.1 mile) puts you on a small bridge over Stop-the-Jade Run. This sluggish stream is copper colored with iron absorbed from the soil and with mildly acidic tannins found in leaves and tree bark. This pure "cedar water" is common to Pine Barren streams.

The natural diversity of the preserve is enhanced by two factors. The forested stream corridor is wet, providing plentiful moisture to the floodplain species that flourish here (much of the trail is elevated on boardwalk). The preserve is also located within an ecotone, a transition zone between two habitats, fostering species richness. It straddles the older, richer soils of the Inner Coastal Plain and Delaware River Basin, plus the younger, acidic soils of the Outer Coastal Plain and Pine Barrens.

Luxuriant growths of cinnamon fern.

Walk here in springtime and you stand a good chance of sampling ecotone diversity firsthand. The New Jersey Audubon Society believes that there may be a greater diversity of breeding songbird species in these woods than in all the rest of South Jersey.

The Nature Trail brochure asks walkers to listen for the *sweet-sweet-sweet-sweet* song of the prothonotary warbler or the *weetee-weetee-wee-tee-o* of the hooded warbler. It suggests that you may be the first to hear a Kentucky warbler in the preserve. This is no longer the case; this rarely detected warbler was recently discovered along the trail, as was the worm-eating warbler. These migratory species more common to the Delaware River Basin than the Pinelands, are joined by many Pine Barrens birds. Prairie warblers, pine warblers, and yellow-billed cuckoos nest here.

Just beyond the footbridge the trail splits (0.2 mile into the walk). Take the right fork. Near station 5, holly and sweet bay magnolia trees mix with the sweet gums, black tupelos, and red maples. The undergrowth is still dense here, encouraging a large population of small mammals (mice, shrews, and voles) and nonpoisonous snakes (northern black racers and black rat snakes), which feed on the rodents. What you're unlikely to find are red-shouldered hawks or barred owls, which are less able to hunt the hidden mammals in the dense thickets.

As the land rises slightly, becoming drier, chest-high mountain laurel fills in the understory. One of the most versatile plants in the state, this acidic-soil-loving heath thrives from the Highlands to the Pine Barrens. It is a favorite nesting place of worm-eating and hooded warblers.

Beyond station 8, an observation tower allows walkers to get 15 feet above the impenetrable shrub layer, a perfect vantage point for bird spotting.

As you reach station 9 (0.5 mile), notice that pitch pine and a diversity of oaks (southern red, blackjack, willow, white, northern red, swamp white, and scrub oak) become prominent and that the canopy is less dense. Pitch pine needs much light to survive. It relies on regular forest fires to prevent the closure of the canopy by dense deciduous foliage.

At station 11 you cross from the acidic sterile soils of the Outer Coastal Plain into the nutrient-rich soils of the Inner Coastal Plain. Notice how tall the American holly, sassafras, willow oaks, and red maples are here. Persimmons grow too, bearing a sweet fruit tasting much like dates and used to flavor puddings, cakes, and beverages and consumed by birds, opossums, skunks, and raccoons. Just after station 13, a short trail branches right for 0.1 mile to station 14, your deepest penetration into the Inner Coastal Plain.

Backtrack from station 14 and turn right to reach station 15 (1.0 mile). Water along this trail section can get shin deep from November through April. If you would rather stay dry, return the way you came. The last 0.5 mile is through a climax red maple hardwood forest dotted with large holly trees. A short trail spur leads right at station 23 for a view of Stop-the-Jade Run. The main path closes the loop. Just past station 24, turn right and return to the parking lot.

For More Information

The trail is open dawn to dusk.

New Jersey Conservation Foundation, Bamboo Brook, 170 Longview Road, Far Hills, NJ 07931; 908-234-1225; www.njconservation.org

Pine Barrens Preservation

The outrageous jetport and "city of the future" proposal that would have paved much of the Pine Barrens may have spared it. This attempted land grab spurred South Jersey residents like Dot and Brooks Evert to organize and act. A vigorous grassroots coalition was led by the Pine Barrens Conservationists, Citizen's Committee to Preserve State Lands, New Jersey Conservation Foundation, New Jersey Audubon Society, and The Nature Conservancy.

A proposal for a Pine Barrens National Monument failed, but the Pine Barrens Coalition (an umbrella of environmental organizations) championed the creation of the federal Pinelands National Reserve in 1978. Today the Pinelands Commission, a state agency, is charged with managing, preserving, and protecting 935,000 wild acres at the heart of the region. In 1983 the United Nations recognized the uniqueness of the Pine Barrens, designating it an International Biosphere Reserve.

A 1995 attempt by conservative politicians and developers to abolish the national reserve fell on deaf ears. While the reserve seriously controls development, many local people heartily defend it, seeing the protection of species like the bog asphodel as a means for maintaining their own quality of life.

The New Jersey Conservation Foundation, born in 1960, continues to play an active role in keeping New Jersey green. The group has helped preserve well over 100,000 acres of woodland, wetland, and farmland statewide.

From 1995 to 1998 the foundation preserved 4,230 acres in the Forked River Wilderness, while The Nature Conservancy protected another 3,578 acres. This Pine Barrens locale lies at the heart of the proposed 1960s megadevelopment. Instead, these wildlands will continue to ensure the survival of the endangered Pine Barrens gentian, curly grass fern, and globally rare Kniesekern's beaked rush.

Rancocas Nature Center of the New Jersey Audubon Society

Rancocas State Park

Trail: **Nature Trail (loop)**
Distance: **1.5 miles**
Length: **1 hour**
Difficulty: **Easy; very minor elevation gain**

Hike from field to forest to river floodplain

Getting There

From I-295, use Exit 45A for Rancocas Road. In 1.7 miles turn right into the Rancocas Nature Center.

Special Features

- Observe field succession
- Woodland birds and wildflowers
- South Jersey floodplain forest
- Rancocas River waterfowl

In colonial times the marshes of the Inner Coastal Plain along the Lower Delaware River and its tributaries such as Rancocas Creek supported waterfowl by the hundreds of thousands. "I have nowhere seen so many ducks together," declared Jasper Daenckaerts in 1679. "When they flew up there was a rushing and vibration of the air like a great storm coming through the trees and even like the rumbling of distant thunder."

Over the next three centuries the thundering wings were silenced. Sportsmen launched flat-bottomed skiffs, laid out decoys, and gunned for the "reedbirds," slaughtering uncounted flocks. Blackbirds were also massacred in cattail marshes. Muskrats were relentlessly trapped, and catfish netted.

New Jersey's Inner Coastal Plain also had the misfortune of perfectly co-aligning with the vital transportation corridor connecting Washington, Baltimore, Philadelphia, and New York. By the late twentieth century most forest and marsh had vanished beneath the New Jersey Turnpike; NJ 130 and I-295; or condominiums, subdivisions, factories, malls, gas stations, and golf courses.

State parks are spread thin along the overdeveloped Inner Coastal Plain. But one struggling park, Rancocas, has allied itself with the nonprofit New Jersey Audubon Society. When budget cuts in the 1970s forced the 1,100-acre park to close, the New Jersey Audubon Society stepped in. It established a fine nature center in an old farmhouse and built a Nature Trail exploring a portion of the park's fields, lowland deciduous forest, freshwater streams, and marshes. The New Jersey Audubon Society is a privately supported group that has preserved thousands of acres statewide within thirty nature sanctuaries, all open to the public.

Begin your 1.5-mile loop walk at Rancocas State Park with a look at the Rancocas Nature Center exhibits housed within

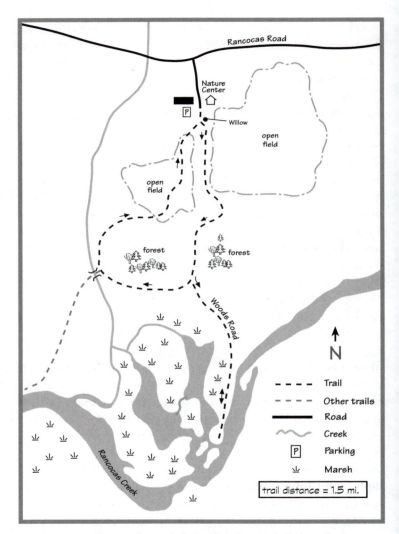

Rancocas Nature Center of the New Jersey Audubon Society

the hundred-year-old farmhouse. The informed volunteer interpreters will tell you about their terrarium-housed northern pine snake, corn snake, and spotted turtle. The endangered corn snake is a constrictor feeding on mice and rats. Be sure to pick up a copy of the excellent numbered interpretive Nature Trail guide before starting your walk.

The Nature Trail begins behind the farmhouse at the end of the driveway. A large graceful willow oak rises to the left of the trailhead. With its slim, lance-shaped leaves, it may look like no oak you've ever seen before. The tree does bear acorns, however—one of the defining characteristic of the oak (*Quercus*) genus. Willow oaks are to the southern United States what American elms once were to the North, a top choice for a handsome shade tree with which to line city streets.

The first 100 yards of the Nature Trail provide a vivid lesson in field succession. As you move past the numbered posts, pause and imagine that the forest is slowly growing toward you: it is! Eventually the surrounding woods will completely overgrow this abandoned farm field.

The field dotted with red cedar to the left (last cultivated more than twenty years ago) supports at least a hundred different plants. Some have names perfectly describing their appearance. In late summer, nodding foxtail grass sprouts a bushy green top resembling a fox's drooping tail, goldenrod possesses an erect stalk encircled by bright yellow blossoms, and Queen Anne's lace (originally from Europe) is topped by an ornate creamy white crown of florets resembling an old-fashioned doily. Saint-John's-wort also flourishes. This plant, with showy five-petaled yellow flowers blooming in July, was used in old England to ward off evil spirits and is currently in vogue as a treatment for depression.

Rancocas Creek, the only major Pine Barrens river to flow to the Delaware.

Light-loving plants edge the field. Black cherry, red maple, black locust, and arrowwood trees serve as scaffolding for viny tendrils of frost grape, multiflora rose, and Asiatic bittersweet. Shrubby arrowwood has arrowhead-shaped leaves, but it was named for its strong straight stems, fashioned by Native Americans into arrows. Its juicy blue-black berries are a fall favorite of birds.

At Nature Trail post 5 you walk into the future of the abandoned farm field: the forest closes in around you. Vines and red cedars, starved for light, are dying out. These young woods are composed of red maple, black locust, and tulip tree, all reaching for the sun and competing for light.

At post 7 you enter a planted pine plantation of native white pine, Austrian pine (easily confused with American red pine), and Norway spruce. These trees have been growing here since 1957. Note the absence of the lush plant understory usually found beneath deciduous trees. Conifers lay down a dense bed of acidic pine needles, which prevents the seeds of competing broad-leaf plants from taking hold. Only acid-tolerant ferns and grasses grow well in this gloomy blue shade.

Just before post 11, look for a river birch. This easily identified tree appears to have a fatal case of acne: its bark is broken into peeling salmon-pink and reddish brown patches. Common in the Mid-Atlantic states, the river birch, as its name implies, thrives on wet sites, making it useful in erosion control.

Just beyond post 11 (0.3 mile into the walk), turn left and descend a woods road to the north branch of Rancocas Creek. The way down into the stream floodplain is lined by red maple, holly, sweet gum, and umbrella magnolia. The magnolia, with its glossy 2-foot-long leaves, is easy to spot. This is a southern tree, common in the Great Smoky Mountains of North Carolina. Its white flowers, blooming in spring, are as ostentatious as its leaves, forming beautiful (but disagreeably smelling) 6- to 10-inch-wide cups.

A dense growth of sweet pepperbush, spicebush, and winterberry hides the banks of the creek from view. At about 0.6 mile into your walk, the woods road ends at Rancocas Creek on a muddy streambank imprinted with the tracks of white-tailed deer, mice, and shrews. Look for wading great blue herons standing on stiltlike legs amid the cattails, arrow arum, and pickerelweed.

Rancocas Creek forms the second largest watershed in the Pine Barrens and is the only major Pine Barrens stream to flow west into the Delaware River Basin. All other major South Jersey streams flow to the Atlantic.

The edge of the wide, amber-colored creek is lined with head-high aquatic sunflowers in autumn. The stream's wild rice marsh attracts migratory waterfowl, including wood ducks, northern pintails, and green-winged and blue-winged teals. The green-winged teal is one of the fastest-flying ducks, making it a favored and challenging target for duck hunters. While it's easy to condemn sportsmen as villains who diminish species, the survival of waterfowl and their habitat in the United States has been significantly enhanced by the advocacy of hunting organizations such as Ducks Unlimited.

Return the way you came from the shore of Rancocas Creek to the Nature Trail and turn left, picking up where you left off at post 12.

The trail now loops through a dark forest dominated by hard-to-miss sweet gum. This tree's distinctive five-pointed-star-shaped leaves and its green fruit resembling a spiked medieval mace make it a perfect candidate for Tree Identification 101. Sweet gum is a valuable southern timber tree, used in furniture making and as plywood and pulpwood. The tree was named for a medicinal chewing gum early settlers produced from it.

The trail loops back toward the Nature Center through a mature forest of sweet gum, black oak, tulip tree, beech, and red maple. In April and May more than twenty species of migrant warblers pass through these woods. The yellow-billed cuckoo, Carolina wren, scarlet tanager, and barred owl nest here. The yellow-billed cuckoo's taste for hairy and spiny caterpillar species (which other birds avoid) makes it a valuable natural control for pests like the tent caterpillar and gypsy moth caterpillar. The cuckoo has evolved a mechanism for eliminating indigestible caterpillar parts. Spiny caterpillar hairs mat in the bird's stomach, then the stomach lining is shed and the cuckoo merely grows a new one.

The Nature Trail circles back to the forest-field edge at post 23, where vines of frost grapes hang like frayed ropes from black cherry and sassafras saplings. In 100 feet the trail pops into the open back at the Nature Center parking lot (1.5 miles).

For More Information

The Rancocas Nature Center is open Tuesday through Saturday from 9 A.M. to 5 P.M. and on Sunday noon to 5 P.M.; it's closed Monday and holidays. Admission is free. Dogs and bicycles are not permitted on the trail.

Rancocas Nature Center, 794 Rancocas Road, Mount Holly, NJ 08060; 609-261-2495

New Jersey Audubon Society, P.O. Box 126, Bernardsville, NJ 07924; 908-204-8998; www.njaudubon.org/

Apple Pie Hill Fire Tower
Wharton State Forest

Trip 34

Trail: Batona Trail (out-and-back)
Distance: 8.0 miles
Length: 5 1/2 hours
Difficulty: Challenging, due to length; some gentle ups and downs

A vista stretching from Philadelphia to the Atlantic Ocean

Getting There

From US 70, take US 206 south and turn left (east) at the sign that directs you to the town of Tabernacle and the Carranza Monument. In 2.3 miles cross County Route 532 in Tabernacle. The Carranza Memorial parking area is 7.0 miles farther straight ahead on the right.

Special Features

- Hike deep into the Pinelands' interior
- Atlantic white cedar swamp
- Upland pine and oak forest
- 205-foot-high Apple Pie Hill

Walking in the Pine Barrens is like hiking along an ancient ocean bottom. The Outer Coastal Plain disappeared beneath ocean waves many times in the past 135 million years, and the sea laid down a gently sloping and nearly featureless terrain of permeable sand, silt, and clay more than 0.5 mile thick.

Hiking here is also like walking atop a great desert oasis. While the Pine Barrens receive more than 40 inches of rain annually, that water drains quickly away, allowing only the hardiest of trees and heathlike shrubs to survive in bone-dry soils. But just below ground, plentiful life-giving waters flow. A staggering 17 trillion gallons are cached in the Cohansey Formation, New Jersey's largest aquifer. This crystal-pure water feeds 200,000 acres of Pine Barrens bog and swamp, plus its many sleepy miles of winding river.

The value of this aquifer was not lost on Pennsylvania financier Joseph Wharton, who began buying up the Pine Barrens in 1876. Wharton hoped to build canals and aqueducts with which to bring its sweet waters to the lips of millions of thirsty Philadelphians. The New Jersey legislature blocked Wharton's plan, and his 97,000 wooded acres became Wharton State Forest in 1955. Recognition of the value of the Pinelands aquifer has since thwarted other plans to cover the Outer Coastal Plain with model cities and a jetport (see Trip 32).

There are no natural vistas from which to overlook the vast pine and oak wildlands overlaying the Cohansey Formation aquifer. But 205-foot-high Apple Pie Hill with its fire tower offers a stunning human-made view of this, the most extensive primitive tract remaining along the mid-Atlantic seaboard.

This 8.0-mile out-and-back hike along the Batona Trail is one of the longest walks featured in this book, but, with an altitude gain of just a few hundred feet, it's not overly challenging.

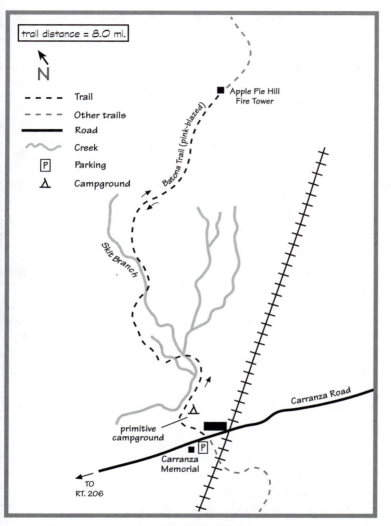

trail distance = 8.0 mi.

N

- - - - Trail
- - - - Other trails
─── Road
∼∼∼ Creek
P Parking
⛢ Campground

Batona Trail (pink-blazed)

Apple Pie Hill
Fire Tower

Skit Branch

Carranza Road

primitive
campground

Carranza
Memorial

TO
RT. 206

Apple Pie Hill Fire Tower

Highlights include a cedar swamp, upland pine and oak forest, and the extraordinary view from Apple Pie Hill.

The walk begins in the parking area of the Carranza Memorial. This obelisk with its faded inscription marks the ill-fated end to a goodwill flight made by aviator Emilio Carranza. "Mexico's Lone Eagle" successfully flew a Ryan monoplane of the type used by Charles Lindbergh from Mexico City to Washington, D.C., and New York City in 1928. A Pine Barrens thunderstorm brought down the twenty-three-year-old pilot on his flight home.

Walk across the road from the Carranza Memorial and turn right. In a few hundred feet turn left and follow the pink blazes of the Batona Trail as they lead into the woods. The 50-mile-long Batona Trail was built by the Batona Hiking Club of Philadelphia between 1961 and 1967. You'll be following the pink blazes for the entire hike.

Look closely. Beside the trail we found earthstars sprinkled in the sand. This tiny fungus is perfectly adapted to Pine Barrens desert-dry soil conditions. Only about 2 inches across, these tiny gray rootless puffballs are surrounded by four to eight dark, starlike rays. The puffball (with a small hole in its top) is the fruiting body of the earthstar, and when sent skittering along by wind it spills forth its spores. Possessing no chlorophyll, the earthstar doesn't directly use the sun as a food source but derives its nutrients from organic matter found in the soil.

About 0.3 mile into your walk, you arrive at Batona Primitive Camp (a camping permit is required from Wharton State Forest). The camp has tentsites, a water pump, and outhouses. Follow the pink blazes through the campground.

The trail penetrates a forest of pitch pine, short-leaf pine, blackjack oak, and post oak, the predominant trees seen on most of this walk. All four species thrive in nutrient-poor, acidic Pine Barrens soils. Pitch pines once were tapped for their thick, sticky sap, called oleoresin, which was distilled into turpentine. Cut trees were also burned to boil off the tar and pitch used to waterproof ship bottoms. Short-leaf pine is valued as lumber and pulpwood. In the 1800s blackjack oak was primarily used as firewood and for charcoal. Post oak was more valuable, with its wood serving as mine timbers, posts, and railroad ties.

The Carranza Monument commemorates the ill-fated goodwill flight of "Mexico's Lone Eagle," who crashed his plane here in 1928.

Just beyond the campground the trail repeatedly intersects with a sand road (watch blazes closely). Beneath the pines and oaks, a scrubby understory of blueberries, sheep laurel, golden-heather (Pine Barrens heather), and reindeer lichen thrives.

The pink-blazed Batona Trail intersects the sand road one last time, turns left, and crosses the Skit Branch of the Batsto River on a major bridge at about 1.0 mile.

Like all Pine Barrens streams, this one is the color of steeped tea. This "cedar water" is rich in tannin found in tree bark and leaves. Don't let its dark appearance fool you. Sailors once prized Pine Barrens cedar water because it stayed fresh and potable longer (even so, never drink unfiltered water in the wild).

While cedar waters are very acidic, with a 5.0 pH, they also support significant plant life. Along Skit Branch's peaty shores flourish insectivorous sundews and golden club, an aquatic herb with long-stalked leaves. Golden club blooms with a compact spike of yellow flowers in April and May. Fragrant water lilies with pinkish white flowers blossom here from June to October.

After crossing the stream, the trail immediately turns right as it leaves the sand road for the last time. The path now straddles the boundary between upland and wetland. To the left, the drier pitch pine and oak forest continues unabated, with its mountain laurel, inkberry, and sand myrtle understory. To the right, the dark reaches of a cedar swamp beckon. Bordering the still waters are highbush blueberry, dangleberry, and leatherleaf shrubs. Farther in, stately Atlantic white cedars rise from sphagnum moss hummocks. The tree trunks glisten eerily with bluish green santee lichen. Woodpeckers have worked over the silver skeletons of dead cedars.

The trail crosses three small walking bridges before leaving the swamp behind at about 2.0 miles, and begins to climb into a dry pine and oak upland. Here we saw ants at work. They brought dark clay particles up from underground, building a chocolate-brown mound atop white surface sand. Their excavations demonstrate the complex soil substrata displayed in the Pine Barrens. Thirteen major soil varieties top the Cohansey Formation.

The trail crosses two small unnamed hills (rising to just 139 feet and 104 feet) before ascending to Apple Pie Hill (205 feet), the highest elevation in the Pine Barrens.

The view from the tower sweeps in an unbroken plain from horizon to horizon. It overlooks what John McPhee calls "a bewildering green country," 2,250 square miles, 1.4 million acres of flat, sandy, acidic, and sterile soils, blanketed by pitch pine and oak forests and cedar bogs. Here, within the major transportation corridor connecting New York City, Philadelphia, and Atlantic City, there are few people or paved roads and no factories. On a clear day the skyscrapers of Philadelphia can be spotted, as can the silvery water towers marking New Jersey's many Atlantic Ocean barrier island towns. Mount Holly, a mere bump, climbs 183 feet above sea level to the west.

Apple Pie Hill is composed of Beacon Hill Formation gravels and is slightly more erosion resistant than surrounding sands and clays. It may have been deposited by ancient rivers that once drained the Pine Barrens. The fire tower surveys a vast country and in dry times offers a first defense against wildfire, which can burn through leaf litter, dry underbrush, and resinous pines at the speed of a runaway freight train.

Amazingly, as we stared down from the tower top we saw a tree on the ground beneath us with huge, floppy tropical leaves. How this single invasive royal paulownia tree found its way here we could only guess. Perhaps it arrived as a seed carried in a bird's intestine, or maybe it was planted by a fire warden in need of its cheery, fragrant violet spring blooms. This native of China has become a New Jersey pest, popping up everywhere from the Palisades to the Piedmont and Pine Barrens. One botanist has estimated that a single royal paulownia annually produces 21 million seeds. He also figured that if all those seeds grew, the offspring of that single tree would, by the third generation, produce enough royal paulownias to cover 20,442 worlds the size of our earth!

When you've finished marveling at the sprawling Pine Barren wilderness surrounding this lone fire tower and royal paulownia tree, return the way you came to the Carranza Memorial parking area.

For More Information

The Batona Trail is open daily year-round and allows camping with a permit at designated sites. The Batona Trail Club is always seeking volunteers.

Wharton State Forest, Batsto, R.D. 9, Hammonton, NJ 08037; 609-561-0024; www.state.nj.us/dep/forestry/parks/wharton.htm

Batona Trail Club: 215-657-1058; http://members.aol.com/batona

Parvin State Park

Trail: **Parvin Lake Trail, Long Trail, Thundergust Lake Trail (loop)**
Distance: **4.6 miles**
Length: **3½ hours**
Difficulty: **Moderate; sometimes wet; very minor elevation gain**

Huge biological diversity in a tiny state park

Getting There

Take NJ 55 south of Glassboro to Exit 45. Drive south on County Route 553 for about 8.0 miles to Centerton. Turn left onto County Route 540 for about 2.0 miles. Parvin Park is on the right.

Special Features
• Observe plentiful species in an ecotone
• American holly forest
• Great blue herons, green herons, and red-bellied turtles
• Springtime warblers, vireos, and scarlet tanagers

Parvin State Park

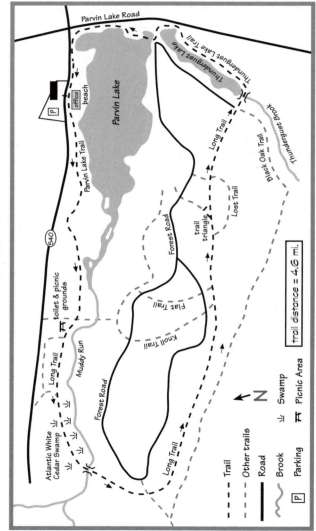

Parvin Lake Road

Parvin Lake

Thundergust Lake Trail

Thundergust Lake

beach

office

P

Parvin Lake Trail

540

toilet & picnic grounds

Long Trail

Muddy Run

Atlantic White Cedar Swamp

Long Trail

Forest Road

Forest Road

Knoll Trail

Flat Trail

trail triangle

Lost Trail

Long Trail

Black Oak Trail

Thundergust Brook

N

trail distance = 4.6 mi.

- - - Trail
- - - Other trails
——— Road
〰〰 Brook
P Parking
⊻ Swamp
⛱ Picnic Area

Where habitats collide, botanical and biological diversity rules. In Parvin State Park northern and southern ecosystems meet in a preserve that lies just below the Mason-Dixon line. Here oak pine upland, swamp hardwood forest, stream floodplain, and Atlantic white cedar bog habitats weave together into a rich woodland tapestry.

Parvin State Park is known as a hidden gem of the New Jersey park system. This tiny preserve, at a mere 1,135 acres, explodes with life. It boasts 40 tree types, 61 woody shrubs, 17 ferns and club mosses, plus 200 herbaceous flowering plants. Migrant and nesting birds number at more than 135 species. White-tailed deer, river otters, raccoons, skunks, turtles, salamanders, and nonpoisonous snakes thrive amid dense foliage.

The explanation for so much variety packed into such a tight space is a concept biologists call the ecotone. An ecotone marks the boundary between two or more ecosystems or habitats. In an ecotone the species of one habitat freely mix, interact, and compete with those of another for soil moisture and nutrients, light, space, and food. Species variety in these transition zones tends to be rich. This 4.6-mile loop walk uses the Parvin Lake Trail, Long Trail, and Thundergust Lake Trail to sample this wealth of life.

Begin by walking from the parking lot toward the park office and beach (you can get an excellent detailed trail map at the park office). Turn sharply right just before reaching the building. The green-blazed Parvin Lake Trail leads immediately into the woods.

Forest diversity is instantly apparent. Parvin is a jumble of northern and southern, upland and wetland plant species, all jostling for dominance. In the first few hundred yards of this hike we identified six oak species (white, scarlet, chestnut, northern red, southern red, and post oak), three pines (white, short-leaf, and pitch pine), two hickories (bitternut and shagbark), plus sassafras, sweet gum, black cherry, red maple, flowering dogwood, and holly trees.

The forest floor was equally luxurious. Chaotic jungles of shrubs (arrowwood, mountain laurel, winterberry, greenbrier, and sweet pepperbush) and vines (wild grape, Virginia creeper, and poison ivy) compete for light and space. Waist-high cinnamon fern, partridgeberry, and wintergreen spread out over the leaf litter.

Experienced birders spy assorted warblers, vireos, and scarlet tanagers in these wet woods during spring migration. Regular nesting birds at Parvin Park include Acadian flycatchers, yellow-billed cuckoos, barred owls, and Kentucky warblers. For best birding, walk here in late April and early May before lush leaf growth obscures the action. This is a hike where the tree, wildflower, and bird books are a must.

The first 0.9 mile of this walk feels like Christmas: festive American holly trees with prickly, glistening evergreen leaves and red berries in autumn flourish in damp soils. American holly's beauty was nearly its undoing in parts of the United States. Over-pruning for Yuletide decoration killed many of these slow-growing trees. Holly is spread primarily by berry-eating birds and mammals. Robins overwinter in South Jersey hardwood swamps and rely on the sugar-rich berries for survival.

Warbler watchers are rewarded at the bridge over Muddy Run.

Another common tree along this trail section is the southern red oak, or Spanish oak. This tree has distinctive leaves with a long narrow central lobe, plus one to three shorter lobes on either side of a bell-shaped base. A large, graceful tree, the Spanish oak is valued as an ornamental but not for its lumber, which is inferior to that of its relative, the northern red oak.

At 0.9 mile the green-blazed Parvin Lake Trail turns abruptly left. Continue straight ahead on the red-blazed Long Trail. There are picnic grounds and a toilet to the right. At 1.0 mile the white-blazed Nature Trail goes off to the right and reconnects with the Long Trail at 1.2 miles. Stay on the Long Trail.

Muddy Run, a branch of the Maurice River, now parallels the path on the left. The trail descends into an Atlantic white cedar swamp, passing among black tupelos, sweet bay magnolias, sensitive fern, royal fern, and, in drier spots, eastern burning bush (also known as the wahoo tree). In fall, burning bush is hard to miss, with bright red-orange fruit capsules and hot-pink leaves. The Native American term for the plant was *wahoo*. Could this, we wondered, have something to do with the purgative effect of its powdered bark?

Arrow arum, an aquatic relative of skunk cabbage, jack-in-the-pulpit, and wild calla, is abundant in the stream floodplain. It has foot-long glossy arrow-shaped leaves. It flowers in June, and wears green berries in autumn.

The Long Trail crosses Muddy Run on a bridge at 1.6 miles. Willows and red maples rise over the creek. Willow bark was long used by Native Americans as a pain reliever. Modern science caught up with aboriginal peoples in 1829 when glucoside salicin, a basic aspirin ingredient, was isolated and marketed.

Muddy Run rewards patient warbler watchers in spring. Prothonotary warblers have been sighted nesting in tree cavities near this bridge in past years. This golden bird, common to southern cypress swamps and bayous, is at the northern extreme of its breeding range in South Jersey.

The name *Muddy Run* seems to be a misnomer. When we walked here the stream ran crystal clear over a gravel bottom. Absent was the tannin-rich tea-colored "cedar water" found in the Pine Barrens.

The Long Trail climbs slightly away from Muddy Run and at 1.7 miles intersects a short side trail to the left, which meets Forest Road. Continue straight ahead on the Long Trail, crossing an unnamed trail at 1.9 miles.

The path now curves slowly left, passing through much drier terrain. An upland forest of oak and pine takes over. White oaks, red oaks, hickories, and varied pines rise above sweet pepperbush, greenbrier, mountain laurel, scrub oak, and blueberry bushes.

At roughly 2.7 miles the Long Trail passes the Knoll Trail and the Flat Trail (which both turn to the left). Continue straight ahead. Ignore a right turn onto the Lost Trail. At 3.0 miles you arrive at a triangular trail junction. Stay to the right, following the Long Trail. At 3.1 miles the Long Trail intersects the Lost Trail again. Continue straight ahead. The Long Trail intersects the Black Oak Trail at a paved dead end. Continue straight ahead.

The Long Trail intersects with the yellow-blazed Thundergust Lake Trail at a stream bridge at 3.5 miles. Walk straight ahead, then curve to the left through the picnic area. The pretty shore of Thundergust Lake is on the left. The lakeshore is overhung with black tupelo and holly and lined with sweet pepperbush and ferns. We saw great blue herons and green herons wading amid the duckweed, and red-bellied turtles sunning on snags in October.

At 4.0 miles you reach the far end of Thundergust Lake. Swerve left, cross a major park road, and follow the Parvin Lake Trail (the shore of Parvin Lake will be on the left). From here you can see the point at which you started, the park office and beach across the lake.

The trail passes over a horseshoe-shaped concrete spillway, a reminder that there are few natural lakes in South Jersey. Lamuel Parvin bought this land in 1796 with the intention of damming Muddy Run to turn a sawmill waterwheel. The property became a state park in 1930 at the start of the Great Depression. While Hitler solved Germany's unemployment problems by arming his nation's youth with guns, Franklin Roosevelt armed America's financially strapped young men with shovels. The Civilian Conservation Corps built Parvin's roads, trails, cabins, and beach.

Follow the trail as it curves left around Parvin Lake and returns you to the park office at 4.6 miles.

For More Information

The trails of Parvin State Park are open dawn to dusk year-round. From September 30 to May 1, office hours are 8 A.M. to 3:30 P.M. weekdays (closed on weekends). From May 1 to September 30 the office is open seven days a week.

Parvin State Park, R.D. 1, Box 374, Elmer, NJ 08318; 856-358-8616; ww.state.nj.us/dep/forestry/parks/parvin.htm

Sandy Hook, Old Dune Trail
Gateway National Recreation Area

Trip 36

Trail: **Old Dune Trail**
Distance: **1.0 mile (plus optional 1.1-mile loop, or 9.6 miles out-and-back)**
Length: **1 or 2 hours; 7 hours for the longer trip**
Difficulty: **Easy; no elevation gain**

Witness the diversity of coastal life

Getting There

Take Exit 117 off the Garden State Parkway to NJ 36 east. Follow signs for the Atlantic Highlands and Sandy Hook, Gateway National Recreation Area. After crossing the bridge onto Sandy Hook, follow signs to the park entrance. The visitor center is 2.0 miles ahead on the right.

Special Features

- 350 coastal bird species
- Cold War Nike missile emplacements
- Diverse coastal forest
- Beach walk, shell collecting, and views of New York City

Gateway National Recreation Area, including the 6.5-mile-long sand spit known as Sandy Hook, is a study in diversity. Fresh water from the Hudson and Raritan River watersheds mingles with the saline waters of Long Island Sound. This creates an estuary ecosystem unlike that of open ocean or inland river, yet combining elements of both. Sandy Hook itself supports four types of plant communities (beach/dune, shrub thicket, mixed forest, and holly forest) and stands as a buffer between open ocean to the east and sheltered salt marsh to the west.

Located on the edge of one of the most populated areas of this continent, Gateway has played diverse roles in the protection (and, ironically, possible self-destruction) of human inhabitants of the area. On Sandy Hook a lighthouse built in 1764 still operates today, the Coast Guard patrols the coast, and Fort Hancock—decommissioned by the military in 1972—serves as a museum and environmental research facility. Abandoned Nike missile sites attest to Cold War bunker mentality. Fortunately the better angels of our nature prevailed; in October 1972 Congress proclaimed Gateway and San Francisco's Golden Gate Park the first urban National Recreation Areas.

Thus Sandy Hook affords a rare sight indeed: a stretch of Jersey Shore undeveloped. Endangered piping plovers nest here every summer. Holly trees, some more than one hundred years old, canopy a variety of plants that would be considered unique anywhere.

A pre–Memorial Day or post–Labor Day visit to Sandy Hook offers a chance to explore the dunes—via trails only—without summer crowds of beachgoers. A winter walk may reward you with a glimpse of a snowy owl, a visitor from the far north. Even the off-season sun on these dunes can be unrelenting. No matter

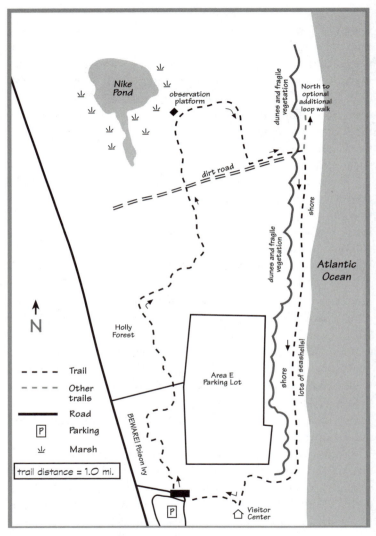

Sandy Hook, Old Dune Trail

Nike Pond

observation platform

dunes and fragile vegetation

North to optional additional loop walk

dirt road

shore

Atlantic Ocean

dunes and fragile vegetation

Holly Forest

Area E Parking Lot

shore

lots of seashells

BEWARE! Poison Ivy

P

Visitor Center

N

- - - Trail
- - - Other trails
—— Road
P Parking
↓ Marsh

trail distance = 1.0 mi.

what time of year you walk here, don't let the short distance lull you into thinking you need not carry water or wear a hat.

Begin at the visitor center, itself a former lifesaving station of historic interest. Inside, displays alert you to some of the creatures you might see (kids of all ages will enjoy learning the names of shells they'll likely find on the beach). Pick up a brochure for the self-guiding nature trail.

Leave the visitor center, heading back toward the main road. Almost immediately turn right onto the Old Dune Trail.

Note at once that this is a natural laboratory for the close study of poison ivy, which attains the size of small shrubs here. You definitely do not want to stray off the trail or even casually brush against the foliage. Shiny green in spring, dull green in summer, and flaming red in autumn, think of poison ivy for what it is: a successful member of this ecosystem and a provider of food for the glorious avian life of this coastal habitat.

Wildflowers such as beach goldenrod and pokeweed, and grasses like switchgrass, line the trail. Tolerance is the key to life on the dunes: shrubs such as bayberry (with its pale blue fruit clusters in autumn, used to scent candles) and groundsel (with small white summer flowers and silky white autumn tufts) tolerate dry, nutrient-poor sand, salty breezes, and occasional inundation by salt surf during storm-driven high tides.

The prize for tolerance, however, must go to the prickly pear cactus, a reminder that life in dry sand, accumulated salt residue, and incessant wind resembles life in a desert. The prickly pear cactus stores fresh water in its padlike stalks, and its needles are actually modified leaves (less surface area means less water loss from transpiration).

Sandy Hook is a veritable paradise for birds. About 350 species either nest here or find temporary sustenance and shelter

Beach grasses act as a skeleton for the dunes, withstanding the power of wind and wave.

during spring and fall migrations. The native trees you see along the trail (red cedar, black cherry, holly) and the shrubs (winged sumac, beach plum, beach rose, and the garden escapee multi-flora rose) all provide succulent fruits and well-protected nesting sites for songbirds. The bark of some of the taller trees shows the work of woodpeckers. Small mammals such as mice, shrews, and rabbits attract raptors.

The trail crosses a road and then immediately enters the dunelands again. Take a moment to look around at the remarkable density of plant life. Without the sand-stabilizing effects of this root network, the dunes would eventually be carried away by wind and wave, and Sandy Hook would cease to exist. Within 0.2 mile, you'll be amazed to find yourself in a forest. Years of vegetative recycling have laid down a layer of richer soil above the sand. Holly trees, which grow only an inch or so each year, tower overhead; their thick evergreen leaves retain moisture.

Keep going straight (paralleling the road to the left and the beach to the right) as the trail crosses an old dirt road. You are in the vicinity of an abandoned Nike missile site, an eerie reminder of the Cold War.

Just as the path makes a right turn, an observation platform offers a vista out over a small freshwater pond. Take a moment to observe the abundant bird life or look for raccoon footprints around the base of the platform.

Smaller plants dominate the landscape again as you near the beach. Golden-heather, seaside goldenrod, and tall wormwood line the way to the front dune.

Once out on the beach, you can see north to New York City. You'll want to head south (right) to complete this loop walk. (Options: Explore the beach northward, entering the dunes again at parking area F; at the visitor center, a trail map is available for a 1.1-mile loop walk around the South Beach Dune Trail. Or ask for the "Sandy Hook Hiking Trail" map that offers an all-day 9.6-mile hike to the Fort Hancock Coastal Defense Batteries and back to the visitor center.)

Seashells abound, washed up on shore by the tides (see the sidebar). Follow the beach south for about 0.3 mile; watch for power lines and the visitor center tower on the right. This is the end of the walk, if you can pull yourself away from the allure of sand and surf.

For More Information

The visitor center is open daily 10 A.M. to 5 P.M. Parking fees are collected from Memorial Day through Labor Day.

Sandy Hook Unit, Gateway National Recreation Area, P.O. Box 530, Fort Hancock, NJ 07732; 732-872-0115; www.nps.gov/gate

—Jean LeBlanc

See Some Seashells

Translucent amber jingle shells. Ridged and furrowed oysters. Scallops in hues of blue and gray. Blue mussels like the sky at twilight. These are just a few of the bivalves (two-shelled mollusks) you'll find along the beach at Sandy Hook. Snail shells (univalves) also abound. The pleasing shapes and subtle colors of slipper shells, channeled whelks, knobbed whelks, and northern moon snails are here too.

The "dead" shells you find along the beach once housed living animals. The shell offered protection from predators and from exposure to air (shell-less slugs produce slime instead). Calcium carbonate, concentrated in the animal's blood, is secreted by an organ called the mantle to form the shell. As the snail or clam grows, it adds more calcium carbonate to the edge of the existing shell. Pigmentation cells in the mantle produce colors and patterns.

A shell is not foolproof protection. Some snails bore through the shells of living bivalves to eat the soft animal within, while seagulls regularly drop live mollusks (as well as crabs) from on high, smashing the shells on rocks.

Mollusks first evolved about 600 million years ago, making them one of the oldest life-forms on Earth. Today the phylum Mollusca is the second largest group of animals, with more than 50,000 species (only the phylum Arthropoda—insects, spiders, crabs, and their kin—has more species). Snails and clams also live in freshwater habitats, and snails live on land and even in trees in the tropics. Octopus, squid, nautiloids, nudibranchs (shell-less marine mollusks resembling ornate slugs), chitons (armadillo-looking mollusks with eight-sectioned shells), and the slugs in your garden are all members of the phylum Mollusca.

—Jean LeBlanc

Cattus Island

Ocean County Park

Trail: **Unpaved road and Blue Trail (loop)**
Distance: **3.2 miles**
Length: **2 hours**
Difficulty: **Easy; flat**

Visit a salt marsh, home to the osprey and diamondback terrapin

Getting There

From the Garden State Parkway, take Exit 82, follow NJ 37 east for about 4.4 miles, then use a right-hand jug handle to make a left turn onto Fischer Boulevard (Spur Route 549). In about 2.0 miles turn right on Cattus Island Boulevard. The park entrance is 100 yards ahead on the left and leads to the Cooper Environmental Center in about 1.0 mile.

Special Features
- Exceptional birding
- Salt hay and cordgrass marsh
- Ospreys and diamond terrapins
- Cooper Environmental Center

When the last glacial age subsided 15,000 years ago, meltwater from mile-thick layers of ice swelled the world's oceans, causing them to rise and drown lowland coasts. As the climate warmed, two salt-tolerant marsh grasses took hold in shallow sheltered bays and estuaries along the Atlantic seaboard.

Salt hay (*Spartina patens*), a fine, slender grass, colonized near the shore and above the high-tide level. Cordgrass (*Spartina alterniflora*), a taller, coarser, extremely salt-tolerant plant, took hold farther from shore at midtide level.

These two grasses form the basis for an ecosystem that is among the most bountiful found on Earth. Salt marshes are the lifeblood of our oceans, adding nutrients and oxygen to coastal waters while removing pollutants. They provide vital nurseries to many commercially valuable fish. Tuna, clams, shrimp, oysters, and other shellfish are dependent on tidal wetlands for survival. Thousands of migratory shorebirds and waterfowl also rely on salt marshes for food and resting and nesting places.

From colonial times down to the mid–twentieth century, most Americans failed to recognize the ecological value of these wetlands. Salt marshes were seen only as resources to be exploited. Salt hay was harvested to feed cattle. Tidal wetlands were diked, drained, and built upon. They were ditched and sprayed with DDT and other pesticides to kill mosquitoes. Oil spills, industrial pollution, urban sewage, and garbage choked the marshes.

Today half of the 12,500 square miles of salt marsh that once lined the Atlantic coast is gone. New Jersey has lost more than a million acres, and what remains is not nearly as healthy as it once was. But in recent years the tide has begun to turn as the public has come to understand the worth of these wetlands.

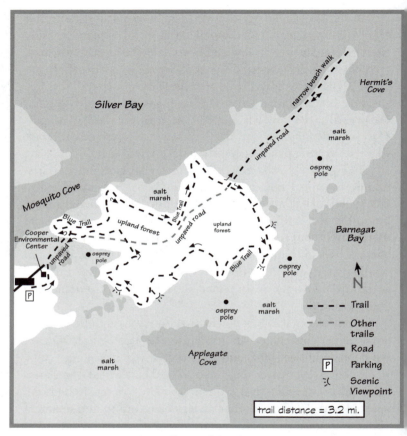

Silver Bay

Hermit's Cove

salt marsh

osprey pole

Mosquito Cove

salt marsh

Blue Trail

Blue Trail

unpaved road

upland forest

upland forest

Cooper Environmental Center

unpaved road

Barnegat Bay

osprey pole

osprey pole

Blue Trail

osprey pole

salt marsh

Applegate Cove

salt marsh

N

- - - Trail

- - - Other trails

——— Road

P Parking

Scenic Viewpoint

trail distance = 3.2 mi.

Cattus Island

Cattus Island County Park and its Cooper Environmental Center naturalists have contributed to this public appreciation. This 500-acre Ocean County park protects a salt marsh at the heart of Barnegat Bay. Surrounded on all sides by beach development and pleasure-boat docks, this fine preserve boasts breeding ospreys, migrating warblers, and diamondback terrapins.

Begin this 3.2-mile loop hike with a tour of the environmental center. Be sure to ask plenty of questions; the naturalists are particularly friendly and knowledgeable.

From the back of the building follow the unpaved road leading out onto the marsh causeway raised above the bay. Cattus Island is not truly an island but rather a very wet peninsula. It consists of an upland completely encircled by an expansive salt marsh.

As you walk out onto the causeway, notice the salt hay (closest to shore) and the cordgrass (farther out in the marsh). Salt typically sucks water out of living cells, destroying them. But salt-marsh grasses have developed an ingenious adaptation that allows them to convert salt water into fresh: a root membrane filters out most of the salt. Any remaining brine is excreted by glands in the plant's leaves.

From the causeway the waters of Applegate Cove lie to the right, while those of Mosquito Cove lie to the left. The much-cursed mosquito (jokingly called New Jersey's state bird) is prolific in coastal salt marshes. While a pest to humans, this insect is a boon to hungry birds and fish.

A scattering of red cedar and groundsel trees and bayberry bushes dots the causeway. The bayberry is easily recognized when its waxy green berries darken to blue gray by late summer. Often lasting through the winter, they offer meals to such songbirds as the yellow-rumped warbler, to shorebirds, and to red foxes. Bayberry takes the edict "be fruitful and multiply" seriously. Its tiny but numerous seeds (55,000 to a pound!), diffused in animal droppings, ensure that the plant is widespread.

At the end of the causeway (about 0.2 mile into the walk), leave the unpaved road by turning left onto the Blue Trail. This path follows the edge between upland and marsh habitat. As you walk on dry land amid pitch pine, holly, southern red oak, blackjack oak, sweet bay magnolia, and greenbrier, you can repeatedly look left out into the open salt marsh.

The adjacency of marsh and upland enriches species diversity. The uplands, for example, provide shelter to nesting eastern phoebes and other songbirds, while the marsh provides insects as food.

The wooded upland through which you are walking was once the port of call for Revolutionary War privateer Timothy Page. Privateers were licensed pirates invited by the Continental Congress to raid British shipping. Later the island was the site for a sawmill, and by the 1890s it had become a weekend retreat. Sold to developers in the 1960s, it narrowly escaped being built upon when New Jersey enacted tough wetland-protection laws. Cattus Island opened as an Ocean County park in 1976.

Continue following the marsh edge on the Blue Trail until it intersects with the wide unpaved road again at about 1.0 mile, turn left onto the unpaved road, and follow it out onto a causeway that extends through the marsh into the bay. Look for the hoofprints of white-tailed deer in the soft sand.

As you walk the causeway, scout the marsh to the right for ospreys sitting atop poles. These towers were placed by the park to encourage nesting raptors. One pair of ospreys have nested actively here for more than a decade. The pair arrive at Cattus Island to breed in late March and are gone by September, though migrating ospreys continue passing through until late fall. These large, majestic birds, also known as fish hawks, were nearly eliminated by eggshell-thinning DDT in the 1950s and 1960s but are enjoying a promising recovery. They fly and hover above the surface of the bay, then dive steeply and snatch fish with their talons.

Continue following the unpaved road to where it dead-ends at a sandy point on the shore of Hermit's Cove (about 1.5 miles into the hike). A sweeping view of Barnegat Bay surrounds you. Backtrack along the unpaved road over the causeway, and upon returning to the forested upland turn left onto the Blue Trail.

Cattus Island is a haven for birds in an otherwise suburbanized coastal area. In springtime, thirty species of warblers, including common yellowthroats, black-throated blues, and Cerulean warblers, may be spotted. In summer, great blue herons and great and snowy egrets frequent the marsh. In spring and fall, migrating raptors such as red-tailed hawks, northern harriers, merlins, and rare peregrine falcons stop to rest. Goldfinches, house finches, Carolina chickadees, and tufted titmice overwinter in the thickets of the island uplands.

The fact that the diamondback terrapin makes its home in the Cattus Island salt marsh attests to the cleanness of Barnegat Bay. This little turtle can't tolerate polluted waters. Just 5 to 8 inches long, the diamondback terrapin was considered such a gourmet delicacy in the early 1900s that it brought $7 per inch, which soon made it scarce. Less sought after as a soup ingredient these days, the little turtle has made something of a comeback. It lays its eggs in the sand at the edge of the Cattus Island marsh. Skunks and raccoons frequently prey on the eggs before they can hatch.

Continue following the edge between forest and marsh. When the Blue Trail intersects the unpaved road, turn left and return over the causeway to the Cooper Environmental Center at 3.2 miles.

For More Information

Cattus Island trails are open daily 8 A.M. to dusk. Cooper Environmental Center is open in winter 10 A.M. to 4 P.M., and in summer from 9 A.M. to 5 P.M. Admission is free.

Cattus Island Park, Cooper Environmental Center, 1170 Cattus Island Boulevard, Toms River, NJ 08753; 732-270-6960; www.co.ocean.nj.us/parks/cattus.html

Island Beach State Park

Trail: Aeolium Nature Trail, Bird Blind Trail, and beach walk (out-and-back)
Distance: 4.1 miles
Length: 3 hours
Difficulty: Easy; no elevation gain

Explore dynamic coastal habitats shaped by a tumult of tide, wind, and storm

Getting There

Take the Garden State Parkway to Exit 82. Follow NJ 37 east over the Barnegat Bay bridge, turning right onto NJ 35 south and driving 2.5 miles. After paying at the park gate, look for the Aeolium Nature Center 1.5 miles ahead on the left. Parking lot A-23 is about 6.5 miles farther south. Note that the park is crowded, and parking can be hard to find on summer weekends.

Special Features
- Bird-blind views of Barnegat Bay
- Stroll the wild surf
- Views of Barnegat Light
- Coolest and least crowded in spring or fall

New Jersey's barrier islands, stretching from Sandy Hook to Cape May, are utterly ephemeral. Just 15,000 years ago they didn't exist. At that time much of the world's water lay locked within mile-thick glaciers. Earth's oceans were shallower, and the Atlantic coast lay 80 miles east of its present location.

When a global warming trend melted away the continental ice sheet, torrential rivers flooded outward from the glaciers. In New Jersey these streams hurled tons of sand and gravel—flecks of quartz, garnet, and magnetite, the remains of ancient mountains—from the Highlands toward the sea.

Glacial melting also caused the world's oceans to rise, inundating the leading edge of the Coastal Plain. Violent tides swept sand up from the sea floor and heaped it in narrow islands lining the coast. These barrier islands with their beaches, dunes, marshes, lagoons, and back bays were constantly reshaped by the flux of stream and tidal deposition and by rising ocean levels.

These radical alterations took place within the memory of the human race. New Jersey archaeologists surmise that the 12,000-year-old coastal campsites of Paleolithic hunter-gatherers are lost to us, submerged beneath the sea covering the continental shelf. Likewise, change continues: nineteenth-century farm fields are salt marsh today, and will be brackish lagoons tomorrow.

Human-influenced global warming is quickening the pace of change. The sea now rises 1 inch every six years along the Jersey coast, driving barrier beaches westward about 2 feet annually. Storms speed this movement. Hurricanes and nor'easters alter the face of the coast within hours: melting away beaches, closing or opening inlets, extending or contracting islands.

Island Beach State Park (10 miles long but just a few hundred yards wide) protects one of the best unspoiled barrier island ecosystems on the North Atlantic. Unburdened by

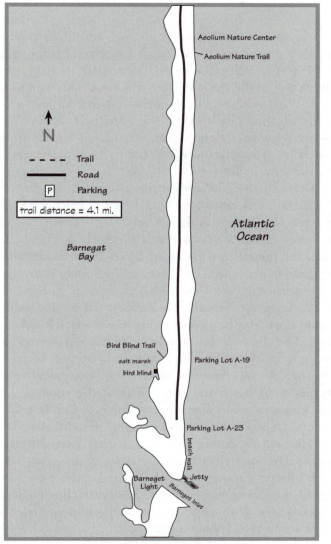

N

- - - Trail
——— Road
P Parking

trail distance = 4.1 mi.

Aeolium Nature Center

Aeolium Nature Trail

Atlantic
Ocean

Barnegat
Bay

Bird Blind Trail

salt marsh

bird blind

Parking Lot A-19

Parking Lot A-23

beach walk

Barneget
Light

Jetty

Barneget Inlet

Island Beach State Park

boardwalks and beach houses, life here continues to adapt to turbulent coastal conditions begun less than 15,000 years ago.

This 4.1-mile walk explores three park locales. It begins with a tour of the Aeolium Nature Center and stroll along its 0.1-mile self-guiding trail. It continues with a 0.5-mile out-and-back walk from beach to back bay, and ends with a 3.5-mile out-and-back hike along ocean beach to the south tip of the park, where a jetty juts seaward, offering views of Barnegat Inlet and Barnegat Light.

Enjoy hands-on exhibits at the state park's Aeolium Nature Center (a Greek word for "wind")—a fun place for kids. We were perplexed at first by the difference between bottled samples of coarse-grained beach sand from Sandy Hook 35 miles to the north and fine-grained sand from Island Beach State Park. The explanation is simple. The heavily silted Raritan River deposits the weightiest, coarsest suspended particles at its Sandy Hook mouth. Lighter, finer sands are then carried steadily southward toward Cape May by waves striking barrier island beaches at an angle. This effect, called littoral drift, makes and unmakes inlets, sand spits, points and hooks, islands and peninsulas.

The 0.1-mile Aeolium Nature Trail loop offers an introduction to barrier island flora. Begin at the butterfly garden; here we saw autumn monarchs sipping nectar from wild bergamot and butterfly bush before winging on to Mexico.

The trail penetrates an old dune area covered in a dense thicket community. The foliage and roots of red cedar, sassafras, black cherry, shining sumac, holly, and pitch pine serve as windbreaks and anchors, reducing erosion and holding together tenuous sands. Without plant roots acting as internal skeletons, dunes would quickly blow away.

Low-lying plants provide dune-stabilizing anchorages too. Sheep laurel, greenbrier, bayberry, Virginia creeper, and blueberry form an impenetrable understory where cedar waxwings and other birds find cover and plentiful fruit. Beach plum is a showy dune species with masses of white spring flowers and plump autumn plums enjoyed by birds and red foxes.

The trail passes among other plants ideally suited to arid, sun-scorched dune life. Prickly pear, a native eastern cactus, blossoms with yellow flowers in July. Its thickened stems possess tremendous water-storage capacity, while its spines are modified leaves, minimized in size to reduce water loss. The plant can also withstand internal temperatures of up to 145 degrees Fahrenheit. Woolly Hudsonia or beachheather spreads in a 3-inch-tall yellow carpet around Memorial Day. Its tiny needle-like leaves minimize evaporation. Seaside goldenrod offers a fine flowering display after Labor Day. It too has succulent stems to store extra water, an adaptation not needed by inland goldenrods. These dune plants are very vulnerable to trampling, so always stay on trails.

Now that you've familiarized yourself with barrier island habitats, drive south along the park road to parking lot A-19. Take a short 100-yard jaunt east, crossing from primary dunes to beach. Watch for plumes of seaside goldenrod, clumps of beach wormwood (commonly known as dusty

Barrier islands are dynamic, always in motion, as these lengths of snow fence drowned in sand attest.

miller, a beneficial dune-building exotic plant from Asia), and tufts of beachgrass.

Return to the parking lot and walk a short distance south along the road. Turn right onto the 0.25-mile Bird Blind Trail. This secluded sand road offers a 0.5-mile round-trip walk to the back bay. It traverses red cedar woodland. Holly, cedar, black cherry, and shadbush rise ever taller as you walk farther from the harsh habitat near the beach. Rugosa rose, bayberry, shining sumac, poison ivy, and bearberry fill in a dense understory.

In 0.25 mile the trail passes among a few groundsel trees, then bursts into the open at the quiet bay. The enclosed Spizzle Creek Bird Blind overlooks an expansive salt marsh. New Jersey's sheltered bays provide refuge to migratory waterfowl and shorebirds.

Return the way you came to your car and drive south to where the road ends at parking lot A-23. This parking area once marked the southern tip of the park, but in the past ninety years littoral drift has piled up more than 1.5 miles of new southward-extending dune.

From the parking lot walk out to the beach where Atlantic surf rolls up on the shore. Turn right and head south toward Barnegat Light, built in 1858. Stay off fragile dunes that provide nesting spots for shorebirds and wintering grounds for an occasional snowy owl. This beach walk is not quite as solitary as you might hope. Four-wheel-drive vehicles and gleaming campers are parked like immense metal shells along the beach. Anglers, like hermit crabs, depend on their "hard-shell" habitats for protection from the elements.

The beach is littered with tide-tossed debris. Look for moon jellies (3-inch-diameter translucent lenses), bay scallop shells (made familiar by the Shell Oil Company logo), Atlantic surf clams, and northern quahog shells (offered by countless beachcombing children to vacationing parents as ashtrays). Starfish also wash ashore. This invertebrate is no fish. *Sea star* is a more apt name for this five-armed fierce predator, which feeds on oysters by applying the powerful suction of its tubular feet to open shells. Anyone who has ever tried to pry open a live oyster by hand will appreciate the sea star's strength.

Oysters, a commonly found New Jersey shellfish, prove a survival-by-the-numbers law of the sea. At various stages of its life cycle this mollusk provides food to sea stars, flatworms, oyster drills, flounder and other fish, birds such as the scoter and oystercatcher, and of course humans. Each female oyster lays 50 million eggs per spawning season to assure species survival, also inadvertently aiding in the survival of its many predators.

At the south tip of Island Beach State Park a stone jetty extends into the ocean and is intended to halt the littoral drift of sands into Barnegat Inlet. A steady flow of pleasure boats roars through the inlet. On the far shore the picturesque silhouette of Barnegat Light stands in profile against the sky. If weather is good and waves are low, a rock-hopping walk over the jetty is fun.

Return the way you came up the beach. At 3.5 miles keep your eyes open for a first gap in the dune fence, marking the way back to parking lot A-23.

For More Information

Island Beach State Park is open from 8 A.M. to 8 P.M. in summer, and from 8 A.M. to dusk in winter. The Aeolium Nature Center is usually open from 9 A.M. to 4:30 P.M. Park fees are $6 on weekdays, $7 on weekends Memorial Day through Labor Day, and $4 the rest of the year.

Island Beach State Park, Seaside Park, NJ 08752; 732-793-0506; www.state.nj.us/dep/forestry/parks/island.htm

Holgate

Edwin B. Forsythe National Wildlife Refuge

Trip 39

Trail: Follow the beach (out-and-back)
Distance: 5.5 miles
Length: 4 hours
Difficulty: Moderate; flat, but walking in soft sand can be tiring

Investigate the domain of piping plovers, least terns, and black skimmers

Getting There

From the Garden State Parkway, take Exit 63 for Manahawkin. Follow NJ 72 east for 7.0 miles onto Long Beach Island. At the third traffic light, turn right onto Bay Avenue (Long Beach Boulevard). Continue straight for 9.0 miles to the parking area at the end of the road.

Special Features

• Barrier island beach walk
• Great shorebird watching
• Best in September (closed April through August for nesting season)

Holgate at first glance appears to be a hike for minimalists who thrive on overlapping plains of beige, brown, gray, and blue, where sandy shore and grassy dune merge with a horizon line of sea and sky.

But this initial minimalist image is all illusion. Holgate is an ecosystem in motion. It is one of the last New Jersey barrier islands unrestricted by jetty, seawall, and condominium, or dredged for sand to perpetuate public swimming. It is a dynamic place, an unspoiled sand beach, low dune, mud flat, and salt marsh shaped and reshaped by the Herculean powers of surf and storm. Any creature that thrives here must adapt to the relentless flux.

Naturally enough, birds with their gliding and soaring mobility are the most visible rulers of this shifting landscape. Least terns, piping plovers, and black skimmers—all on New Jersey's list of endangered species—nest, incubate their eggs, and raise their fledglings on Holgate's exposed beaches. Back from the shoreline amid the older dunes, egrets, herons, and ibises breed among tangled stands of bayberry and marsh elder.

This 5.5-mile out-and-back barrier island walk extends 2.75 miles into the ocean and bay, ending on a low, hook-shaped sand spit battered by whitecapped waves. The hike directions are the simplest of any in this book: head south from the parking area along the hard-packed beach. Stay out of the fragile posted dunes. Continue walking until you run out of land.

Civilization—cottages and motels—abruptly vanishes just beyond the Holgate parking area. A few plants have taken tenuous hold in sheltered spots. Seaside goldenrod blooms in yellow spikes in autumn, and a few scattered bayberry bushes rise above snatches of dune grass. Within a few yards a sign announces your entrance into the wilderness area of the Holgate Unit of the

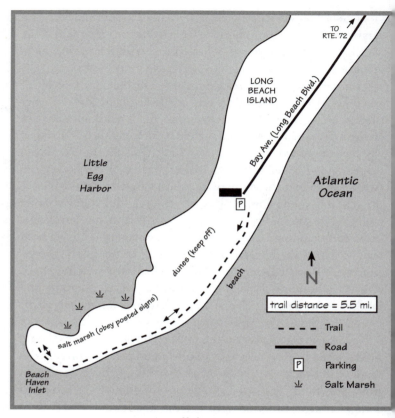

Holgate

Edwin B. Forsythe National Wildlife Refuge. Cats, dogs, and kites, all harmful to wildlife, are prohibited.

Ahead, a sand spit sweeps away in a seemingly infinite brown arc. On the left, the ocean breaks and crashes onto a gently rising expanse of beach that stops abruptly at the low, grass-covered dunes. To the far right, Little Egg Harbor separates Holgate from the mainland.

This is a federal refuge for endangered birds. A refuge differs from a park in that wildlife needs come first. People are forbidden entry during the critical nesting season between April 1 and August 31. The birders' loss is the birds' gain. Skittish black skimmers, for example, which can find no safe haven at New Jersey's other beaches, flourish here (see the sidebar).

From September 1 to March 31 you'll share this beach with other walkers and four-wheel-drive vehicles. We were pleased to find on our visit that the motorists were well-mannered, slow-driving anglers. The same can't be said for two hot-dogging Jet Skiers, spewing noise and gas fumes while disturbing birds and walkers. These leaf blowers of the sea reminded us just how easily the serenity of this fragile ecosystem can be disrupted. Conservationists are working to have Jet Skis banned from the refuge.

The beach at Holgate at first glance seems to be a wasteland, a desert landscape speckled by debris and dried grasses. A closer look reveals the intricate cycle of life.

The sea feeds the shore. Look for curving black swash marks made on the beach by the leading edge of waves. Each swash left by the flood is a litter of seaweed, algae, plankton, tiny crabs, and dead fish, which is scavenged by beach creatures. The algae are consumed by sand worms and the plankton siphoned away by clams underground. Surf-edge feeders, such as piping plovers, feast upon the crabs and clams. Nothing goes to waste: dung and feathers dropped by birds decompose to provide phosphates for nutrient-poor sand, nurturing such plants as seaside goldenrod and sea-rocket.

A smorgasbord of edible tidbits isn't the only thing provided by the sea. Shifting tides deposit flotsam: driftwood, pebbles, and broken shells, which serve as camouflage for nesting terns. Black skimmers build their nests atop wracks of dried seaweed (called eelgrass) in summer.

A walk along the beach at Holgate in autumn reveals a continuous play of tide, sand, and sun. Low sandbars are overwashed by each incoming wave. Little bays fill up with a rush of shallow water, and tiny stranded minnows are scooped up by pouncing birds. Sanderlings skitter and race along the bars just ahead of your own shadow and feed on tiny mollusks and crustaceans.

Birds at Holgate ebb and flow with the seasons. Endangered plovers, terns, and skimmers nest here in summer, a time when walkers aren't allowed. But you can still see these birds loafing and feeding through September. The fall migration season is also the time to observe black-bellied plovers, godwits, willets, sanderlings, and sandpipers. Thousands of migrating barn swallows stop here in early September to feast on insects.

Winter rewards with more than beach solitude. Snowy owls, which migrate here from Canada, hunt over the bayside salt marsh. A few seals even show up at Holgate in March. The first Arctic seals appeared on New Jersey beaches in winter 1988. These migrating harp and hooded seals are usually young animals, probably unable to compete with adults in commercially overfished Arctic waters.

In autumn it's fun to stop and watch anglers surf cast for striped bass and bluefish. Like the shorebirds, bluefish are migrators. They annually travel along the continental shelf from Nova Scotia to Uruguay in schools of like-sized individuals (preventing them from practicing their propensity for species cannibalism!). The Jersey coast serves as a spawning ground and its estuaries as important nurseries for young bluefish.

As you approach the end of the island at 2.75 miles, the landscape becomes nearly featureless, as the dunes diminish in size and the beach tapers away into a graveyard of shells and a few straggling stems of beach grass. The mile-wide Beach Haven Inlet stretches before you into nothingness. Just offshore to the south is the last sandy vestige of Tucker Island. Fifty years ago the island boasted a village and lifeguard station, but both fell victim to the tides. At this seemingly remote spot, the skyline of Atlantic City with its gambling tables is visible to the southwest. From the end of the sand spit, either return the way you came or explore a little farther along the bay side of the refuge, obeying posted regulations. Holgate in autumn offers a deeply meditative walk, a place to contemplate the realm of surf, silence, and shorebirds.

For More Information

Holgate is open dawn to dusk from September 1 to March 31. It is closed during nesting season, April through August.

Edwin B. Forsythe National Wildlife Refuge, Great Creek Road, P.O. Box 72, Oceanville, NJ 08231-0072; 609-652-1665; http://forsythe.fws.gov/index.htm

A Look at Black Skimmers

The black skimmer is a beach nester, and that has nearly doomed it in New Jersey. Unlike the unflappable gull, the black skimmer flees its nest at the sight of a human being and stays away until the threat has passed. The bird is victim to habitat loss and to domestic animals such as cats, which eat its eggs.

The black skimmer is a distinctive-looking bird: black on top, snowy white beneath, with red legs. Its long lower bill protrudes well beyond its upper one, allowing it to eat on the wing. A precision night flier, the skimmer usually feeds after dark, plowing along at water level, slicing the water's surface and scooping up small fish. It forages by touch: the bill snaps closed when the bird feels a fish. The skimmer is easily identified when not feeding. It sometimes relaxes its lower bill and flies along with its mouth dangling open, appearing less than streamlined.

In summer black skimmers breed among the least terns on secluded New Jersey beaches. They make simple nests atop dried eelgrass wracks or by squatting and spinning their bodies into the soft sand.

While you won't see black skimmers nesting at Holgate, since the beach and dunes are off-limits during their breeding season, you may see young birds making practice flights and honing their skimming skills in September. By the end of the month the birds leave their New Jersey colonies for winter quarters as far away as the tropics.

Cape May Point State Park

Trail: Red, Yellow, and Blue Trails (loop)
Distance: 2.0 miles
Length: 1 hour
Difficulty: Easy; no elevation gain

Experience the wonder of the Atlantic flyway in autumn

Getting There

Take the Garden State Parkway south to its end, where it joins Lafayette Street (County Route 633) into the city of Cape May. Bear right onto West Perry Street, which will turn into Sunset Boulevard. Go west on Sunset Boulevard (County Route 606) and turn left onto Lighthouse Avenue. The park entrance is on the left in 0.7 mile. Park in the main lot.

Special Features

- Autumn raptor, songbird, and shorebird migrations
- Autumn monarch butterfly and dragonfly migrations
- Cape May Lighthouse
- Woods, pond, marsh, dune, and beach habitat

A late-summer cold front blasts out of the northwest, and in the dark of night all across the northern United States and Canada, birds take flight. By September up to 12 million per evening appear on airport radar screens. They pour south on powerful tailwinds in an ancient migration that still intrigues ornithologists. One great focus for the continent's southward migration is Cape May, New Jersey.

Cape May peninsula is to migrating raptors, songbirds, and butterflies what a rest stop is to tired motorists on the Garden State Parkway: a place to reconnoiter, refuel, and restore. It is the last land a southward flier encounters before making the challenging 13-mile open-water crossing of Delaware Bay. Cape May Point is a wedge-shaped attracter, a narrowing funnel of land that concentrates birds and butterflies within its revitalizing marshes and the plenty of its forests and fields.

The migration opens in August when a few ospreys and bald eagles appear over the point. It peaks in autumn when trees sometimes virtually drip with birds. More than 80,000 raptors—sharp-shinned and broad-winged hawks, harriers, kestrels, merlins, and peregrine falcons—glide through in a single season. More than 200 species of songbirds also make the passage. Flycatchers, thrushes, vireos, and warblers wing toward the tropics. Migrating waterfowl and shorebirds add raucous cries and calls to the Cape May cacophony. Amid this tumult the monarch butterfly passes voicelessly. Fluttering south on orange wings, this feather-light flier follows an instinctual map on a 2,000-mile journey to an ancestral wintering ground to which it has never traveled before. Dragonflies too migrate through Cape May, some swarming as far south as Mexico's Yucatán Peninsula.

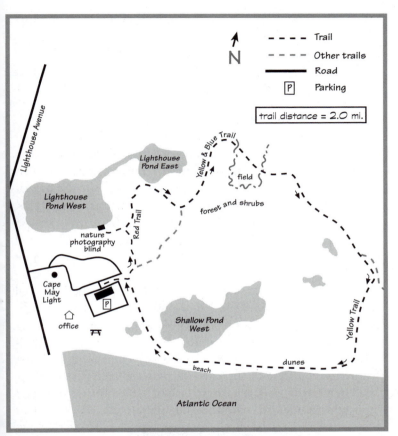

Cape May Point State Park

Cape May Point State Park, once a military base that protected Delaware Bay with gun emplacements and concrete bunkers, is now a boon to birders. In fall, its 300 acres and 5 miles of trail can be as thick with binocular-wielding naturalists as with the bird species they come to observe.

This 2.0-mile loop walk samples the Red, Yellow, and Blue Trails and explores woods, thicket, pond, marsh, dune, and beach habitat. While a fall hike rewards with the migratory spectacle, the preserve is worth a visit anytime.

Check out the visitor center exhibits, then cross the parking lot to the trailhead. All three trails (Red, Yellow, and Blue) begin on a boardwalk at the same spot. Just to the right of the trailhead is the Hawk Watch Platform. Crowded in autumn, this is a prime place to gaze at the migration. Cape May holds seasonal migration records for many of the fifteen species of raptors, including sharp-shinned hawk (61,800 sightings), kestrel (30,268), broad-winged hawk (14,000), osprey (5,400), and peregrine (702). Ornithologists still marvel at the means for the migration, studying how birds find their way (see the sidebar).

In a short distance turn sharply left, following the Red Trail (also called the Nature Trail). Phragmites (reed grass) immediately surrounds you. This plant thrives where humans have disturbed wetlands. While phragmites has little nutritional worth, it does have value: least bitterns and marsh wrens roost and nest within its protecting cover; it also keeps marshlands from eroding.

On a spring walk the sunny face of yellow thistle stared up at us from beside the boardwalk. Edging salt marshes, this plant blossoms with a rounded yellow flower hung amid radiating rays of spiny leaves. While celebrated for its birds, Cape May Point boasts more than 240 wildflower species. Showiest along the trail are multiflora rose (blooming white from May to June), trumpet creeper (reddish orange flowers from July to September), and seaside goldenrod (blossoming on dunes from August to November).

More than 385 bird species and 104 butterfly species have been spotted in Cape May County. The area's vital location along the Atlantic flyway promotes this diversity, but so does the richness of edible flora. The county is an ecotone, a transition zone where the plants of North and South merge. Nature Trail marker 2 is bayberry, a northern species, while marker 4 is wax myrtle, its southern counterpart. Both shrubs thrive in the Cape May transition zone.

Walking along the boardwalk, note that phragmites has colonized wet ground to the left and that red cedars have taken hold in drier, higher ground to the right. The blue-gray berries produced by the red cedar are not really berries but modified cones, a food for robins and cedar waxwings.

At Nature Trail marker 7, a side trail branches left to a dead end at a nature photography blind overlooking Lighthouse Pond West. Stop for impressive views of Cape May Light, built in 1859. Marsh birds, painted turtles, bullfrogs, muskrats, and red foxes rely on freshwater ponds like this one.

The Red Trail passes through woody thickets of cedar, pitch pine, and poison ivy, a valuable plant with white berries that feeds thirty-five bird and mammal

Cape May Lighthouse, built in 1859, overlooks the spectacular fall migration of raptors, songbirds, and monarch butterflies.

species. Some deciduous trees are dying out here due to the intrusion of salt water. The Atlantic Ocean is rising along this coast by 1 inch every six years, a trend starting at the end of the last ice age that is accelerating significantly due to human-caused global warming. The Cape May Lighthouse is the third light station at this location; the other two became victims of the encroaching sea.

At marker 12 the Red Trail reaches Lighthouse Pond East, where we watched mute swans, egrets, pied-billed grebes, and coots sharing open water in May. The sociable coot, a dark gray ducklike bird with a white bill, would rather dive when frightened than fly away. It is an adept swimmer, making brief forays underwater to eat vegetation. We also spotted swooping barn swallows. From late August to early October massed numbers of tree swallows, in the tens of thousands, descend on Cape May, lining its telephone wires.

After passing marker 15, leave the Red Trail, turning left onto the combined Yellow and Blue Trails. This path alternates between boardwalk and dry ground, passing among sassafras and dying cedars that support climbing tangles of multiflora rose. Sun-dappled patches of wild geranium pepper the forest floor. The sweet scent of red cedar and roar of nearby surf fill the air.

When the Blue Trail proceeds straight ahead, turn right onto the Yellow Trail, passing among dense vegetation. More than 200 species of migrating songbirds forage for seeds, fruits, and insects within this shoreside jungle. Countless common migrants such as the catbird, with its squeaky-gate call; yellow warbler; and red-eyed vireo may be joined occasionally by regionally rare birds like the western tanager.

Just beyond the dunes the Yellow Trail turns right, offering a short walk along the Atlantic shore. Look for waterfowl and shorebirds in Shallow Pond West. Saltwater ponds harbor such endangered New Jersey birds as the black skimmer, least tern, and piping plover. The beach walk returns you to the parking lot.

For More Information

The park is open dawn to dusk year-round. The environmental center is open seven days a week April to October (8 A.M. to 6 P.M.), and Wednesday to Sunday (9 A.M. to 4 P.M.) in winter. Admission is free. For birding information, contact the New Jersey Audubon Society.

Cape May Point State Park, P.O. Box 107, Cape May Point, NJ 08212; 609-884-2159; www.state.nj.us/dep/forestry/parks/capemay.htm

New Jersey Audubon Society, Cape May Bird Observatory, Northwood Center; 609-884-2736; www.njaudubon.org

Mysterious Migrations

Linnaeus, the eighteenth-century Swede who gave us our modern system of plant and animal classification, dismissed the then newfangled theory that small songbirds flew thousands of miles to escape northern winters. He, like the ancients, theorized that swallows dived deep beneath the surface of lakes and rivers, buried themselves in mud, and hibernated away the cold months.

The truth is far more fantastic. The mass migration of birds is on a scale that stirs the imagination. It seems unfathomable that birds such as the Arctic tern, the champion long-distance flier, can repeatedly make a 22,000-mile round trip from Arctic to Antarctica and back with pinpoint accuracy.

Why migrate? The seasonal commute offers the best of both worlds: bountiful food supply and avoidance of stressful winter conditions. Many migrating birds breed in summer within the plenty of northern deciduous forests or the insect-rich Arctic, while waiting out winter months in tropical climes.

The "how" of migration has proven harder to decipher. Ongoing investigation reveals that birds utilize visual cues and internal clocks. They know the position of sun, moon, and stars at particular times of day and follow coastlines and mountain ranges. They even seem to recognize particular groves of trees. They may have an innate directional sense, possibly using Earth's magnetic field, sound, faint smells, or even gravity to find their way.

Appendix A
Useful Names and Addresses

General
American Hiking Society
1422 Fenwick Lane
Silver Spring, MD 20910
www.americanhiking.org
301-565-6704

Appalachian Mountain Club
5 Joy Street
Boston, MA 02108
www.outdoors.org
617-523-0655

Appalachian Mountain Club
New York–North Jersey Chapter
5 Tudor City Place
New York, NY 10017
www.amc-ny.org
212-986-1430

Appalachian Trail Conference
P.O. Box 807
Harpers Ferry, WV 25425
304-535-6331

The Canal Society of New Jersey
P.O. Box 737
Morristown, NJ 07963
www.canalsocietynj.org
908-722-9556

Garden State EnviroNet
(Conservation and parks info online)
www.gsenet.org
mailbox@gsenet.org
voice mail: 973-394-1313

New Jersey Audubon Society
P.O. Box 126
Bernardsville, NJ 07924
www.njaudubon.org
908-204-8998

New Jersey Conservation Foundation
Bamboo Brook
170 Longview Road
Far Hills, NJ 07931
www.njconservation.org
908-234-1225

New York–New Jersey Trail Conference
156 Ramapo Valley Road
Mahwah, NJ 07430-1149
www.nynjtc.org
201-512-9348

The Nature Conservancy
Kay Environmental Center
200 Pottersville Road
Chester, NJ 07930
http://nature.org/wherewework/northamerica/states/newjersey/
908-879-7262

State Government
New Jersey Department of Environmental Protection
401 East State Street
P.O. Box 402
Trenton, NJ 08625-0402
www.state.nj.us/dep/
609-777-DEP3

New Jersey Division of Parks and Forestry
P.O. Box 404
501 East State Street
Trenton, NJ 08625
www.state.nj.us/dep/forestry/parknj/divhome.htm
609-984-0370

Appendix B
Recommended Reading

Boyd, Howard P. *A Field Guide to the Pine Barrens of New Jersey: Its Flora, Fauna, Ecology and Historic Sites*. Medford, NJ: Plexus Publishing, 1991. 423 pp.

Collins, Beryl Robichard, and Karl H. Anderson. *Plant Communities of New Jersey: A Study in Landscape Diversity*. New Brunswick, NJ: Rutgers University Press, 1994. 287 pp.

Eastman, John. *The Book of Forest and Thicket*. Mechanicsburg, PA: Stackpole Books, 1992. 212 pp.

————. *The Book of Swamp and Bog*. Mechanicsburg, PA: Stackpole Books, 1995. 237 pp.

Little, Elbert L. *National Audubon Society Field Guide to North American Trees: Eastern Region*. New York: Alfred A. Knopf, 1980. 714 pp.

McPhee, John. *The Pine Barrens*. New York: Farrar, Straus and Giroux, 1968. 157 pp.

Neiring, William A., and Nancy C. Olmstead. *National Audubon Society Field Guide to North American Wildflowers: Eastern Region*. New York: Alfred A. Knopf, 1979. 887 pp.

Newcomb, Lawrence. *Wildflower Guide*. Boston: Little, Brown, 1977. 490 pp.

Perry, Bill. *A Sierra Club Naturalist's Guide: The Middle Atlantic Coast, Cape Hatteras to Cape Cod*. San Francisco: Sierra Club Books, 1985. 470 pp.

Peterson, Roger Tory. *Peterson Field Guide: Eastern Birds*. Boston: Houghton Mifflin, 1980. 384 pp.

Rezendes, Paul. *Tracking & the Art of Seeing: How to Read Animal Tracks & Sign*. Charlotte, VT: Camden House Publishing, 1992. 320 pp.

Roberts, David C. *Peterson Field Guide: Geology of Eastern North America*. Boston: Houghton Mifflin, 1996. 402 pp.

Whitaker, John O., Jr. *National Audubon Society Field Guide to North American Mammals*. New York: Alfred A. Knopf, 1996. 937 pp.

Alphabetical Listing of Walks

About the Author

GLENN SCHERER is a native of New Jersey, an environmental writer, and a naturalist. He is author of *America's National Trails*, and coauthor of *Exploring the Appalachian Trail (Mid-Atlantic States)* and *Exploring the Appalachian Trail (Northern New England)*. He is a contributing editor for *Appalachian Trailway News* and has published work in *Backpacker* magazine, *Outside*, AMC *Outdoors*, *American Hiker*, *General Store*, and *New Jersey Country Roads*.

Contributor JEAN LEBLANC grew up in Massachusetts and inherited her love of the outdoors from her parents. She is a nationally published essayist, poet, and reviewer. Her column on the flora of the Appalachian Trail titled "Growing Wild" appeared regularly in *Appalachian Trailway News*.

About the AMC

 Since 1876, the Appalachian Mountain Club and its members have worked to promote the protection, enjoyment, and wise use of the mountains, rivers, and trails of the Northeast. We encourage people to enjoy and appreciate the natural world because we believe that successful conservation depends on this experience.

Join us!

Hiking, paddling, biking, skiing—from backyard nature walks to weeklong wilderness explorations, the AMC offers activities for all kinds of outdoor adventurers. Join the AMC and connect with new people, learn new skills, and feel good knowing you're helping to protect the natural world you love. In addition to hundreds of activities offered every month through your local AMC chapter, you can also enjoy discounts on AMC workshops, lodging, and books.

Outdoor Adventures and Workshops

Develop your outdoor skills and knowledge through the AMC programs! From beginner backpacking and family canoeing to guided backcountry trips, you'll find something for any age or interest.

Lodging

AMC's huts, lodges, camps, and campsites—located throughout the Northeast—offer unique outdoor adventures. Perfect for every kind of mountain traveler.

Books and Maps

AMC's hiking, biking, and paddling guides lead you to the most spectacular destinations in the Northeast. We're also your definitive source for how-to guides, trail maps, and adventure tales.

For more information about the Appalachian Mountain Club, call 617-523-0636 or visit us online at www.outdoors.org.

Appalachian Mountain Club
5 Joy Street ◆ Boston, MA 02108
www.outdoors.org

Leave No Trace

The Appalachian Mountain Club (AMC) is a national educational partner of Leave No Trace, Inc. a nonprofit organization dedicated to promoting and inspiring responsible outdoor recreation through education, research, and partnerships. The Leave No Trace program seeks to develop wildland ethics—ways in which you can act in the outdoors to minimize your impact on the areas you visit and to protect our natural resources for future enjoyment.

By practicing and passing along these seven principles, you can help protect the special places you love:

- Plan ahead and prepare
- Travel and camp on durable surfaces
- Dispose of waste properly
- Leave what you find
- Minimize campfire impacts
- Respect wildlife
- Be considerate of other visitors

If you would like to learn more about how you can help promote these simple principles, consider the Leave No Trace Master Educator Course. This five-day course is designed especially for outdoor professionals and land managers. The AMC has joined the National Outdoor Leadership School (NOLS) as the sole providers of the Leave No Trace Master Educator course through 2004. The AMC offers this course at locations throughout the Northeast.

For more information or to join Leave No Trace, please contact:

Leave No Trace, Inc.
P.O. Box 997 ◆ Boulder, CO 80306
800-332-4100
www.LNT.org

APPALACHIAN MOUNTAIN CLUB BOOKS

EXPLORE THE POSSIBILITIES

on foot...

Nature Walks in Connecticut
Order #1-878239-69-4 $14.95

Nature Walks near Philadelphia
Order #1-878239-52-X $12.95

Catskill Mountain Guide
Order #1-929173-16-4 $19.95

or by canoe and kayak...

Sea Kayaking along the Mid-Atlantic Coast
Order #1-878239-31-7 $14.95

Quiet Water New Jersey: Canoe and Kayak Guide
Order #1-929173-04-0 $14.95

Classic Northeastern Whitewater Guide
Order #1-878239-63-5 $19.95

Sales of AMC Books support our mission of protecting the Northeast outdoors.

AMC Books · 5 Joy Street Boston, MA 02108 · 800-262-4455
SHOP ONLINE: WWW.OUTDOORS.ORG